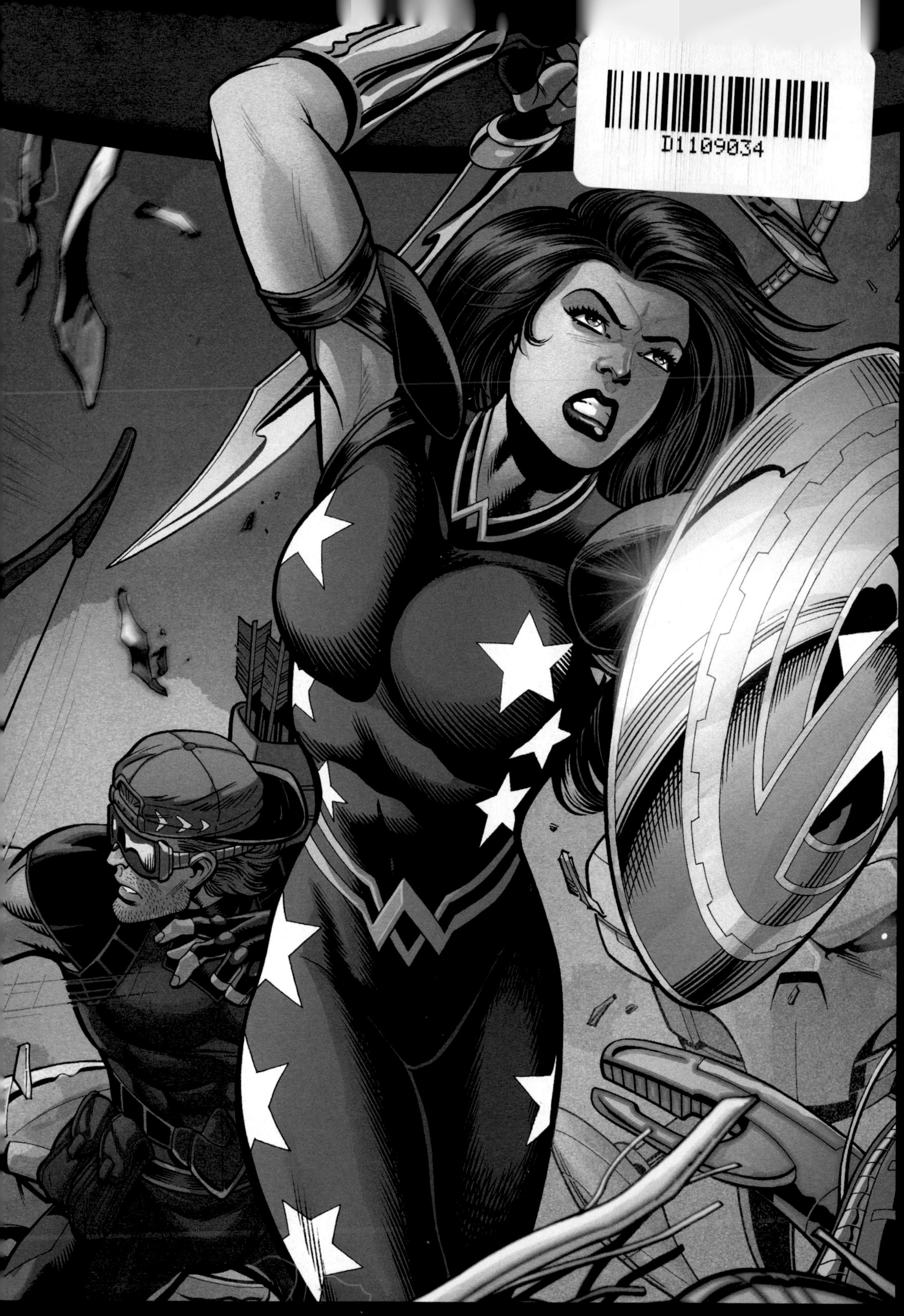

TITANS

VOL.4 TITANS APART

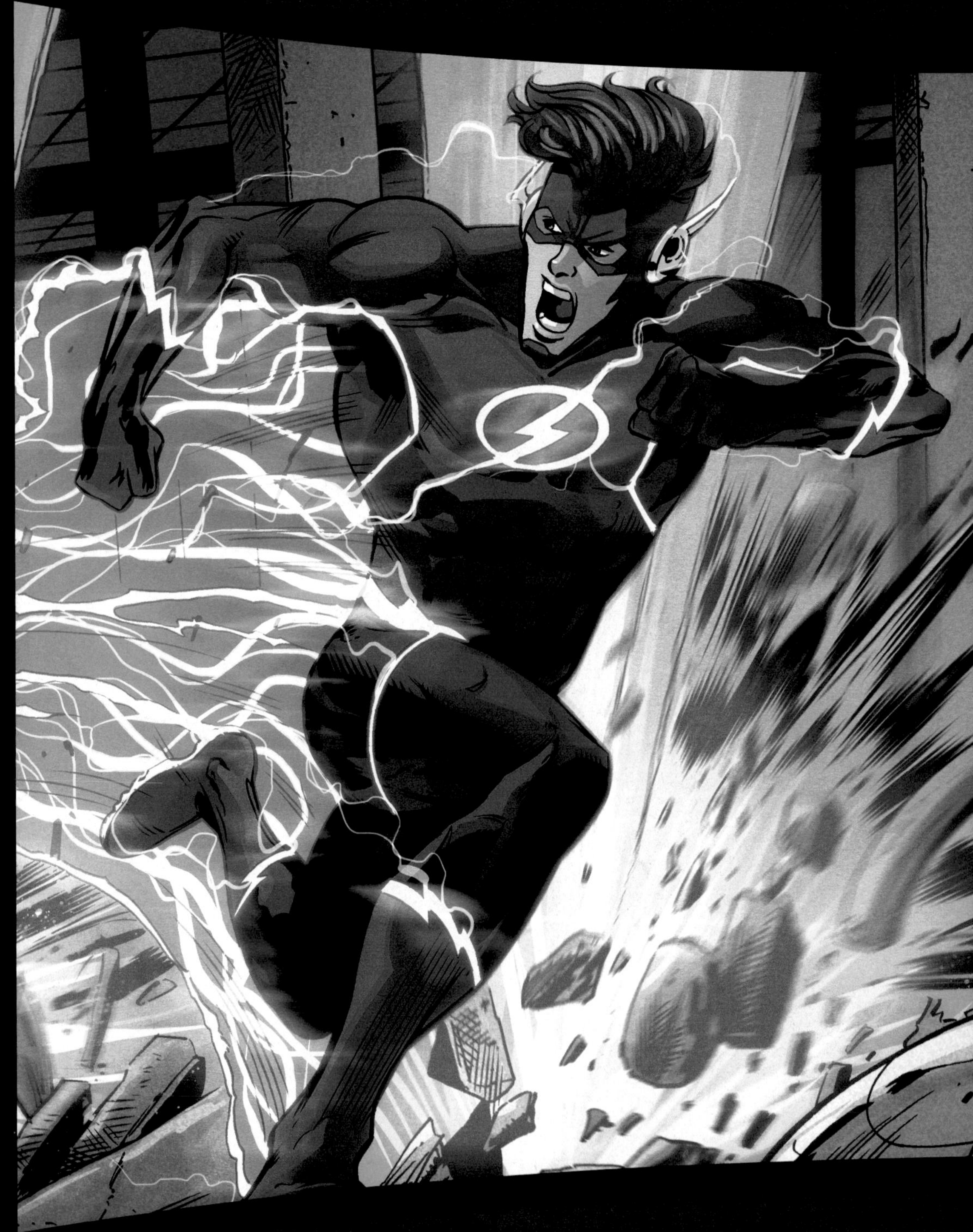

TITANS
VOL.4 TITANS APART

DAN ABNETT
writer

PAUL PELLETIER
TOM GRUMMETT * TOM DERENICK
pencillers

ANDREW HENNESSY
CAM SMITH * MICK GRAY * TREVOR SCOTT
inkers

ADRIANO LUCAS
colorist

JOSH REED * **CARLOS M. MANGUAL** * **TRAVIS LANHAM**
letterers

PAUL PELLETIER, ANDREW HENNESSY & ADRIANO LUCAS
collection cover artists

SUPERMAN created by **JERRY SIEGEL** and **JOE SHUSTER**
By special arrangement with the Jerry Siegel family

DONNA TROY created by **BOB HANEY**

ALEX ANTONE BRIAN CUNNINGHAM Editors - Original Series * **DAVE WIELGOSZ** Assistant Editor - Original Series
JEB WOODARD Group Editor - Collected Editions * **TYLER-MARIE EVANS** Editor - Collected Edition
STEVE COOK Design Director - Books * **MEGEN BELLERSEN** Publication Design

BOB HARRAS Senior VP - Editor-in-Chief, DC Comics
PAT McCALLUM Executive Editor, DC Comics

DAN DiDIO Publisher * **JIM LEE** Publisher & Chief Creative Officer
AMIT DESAI Executive VP - Business & Marketing Strategy, Direct to Consumer & Global Franchise Management
BOBBIE CHASE VP & Executive Editor, Young Reader & Talent Development * **MARK CHIARELLO** Senior VP - Art, Design & Collected Editions
JOHN CUNNINGHAM Senior VP - Sales & Trade Marketing * **BRIAR DARDEN** VP - Business Affairs
ANNE DePIES Senior VP - Business Strategy, Finance & Administration * **DON FALLETTI** VP - Manufacturing Operations
LAWRENCE GANEM VP - Editorial Administration & Talent Relations * **ALISON GILL** Senior VP - Manufacturing & Operations
JASON GREENBERG VP - Business Strategy & Finance * **HANK KANALZ** Senior VP - Editorial Strategy & Administration * **JAY KOGAN** Senior VP - Legal Affairs
NICK J. NAPOLITANO VP - Manufacturing Administration * **LISETTE OSTERLOH** VP - Digital Marketing & Events * **EDDIE SCANNELL** VP - Consumer Marketing
COURTNEY SIMMONS Senior VP - Publicity & Communications * **JIM (SKI) SOKOLOWSKI** VP - Comic Book Specialty Sales & Trade Marketing
NANCY SPEARS VP - Mass, Book, Digital Sales & Trade Marketing * **MICHELE R. WELLS** VP - Content Strategy

TITANS VOL. 4: TITANS APART

DC Comics, 2900 West Alameda Ave., Burbank, CA 91505
Printed by LSC Communications, Kendallville, IN, USA. 8/24/18. First Printing.
ISBN: 978-1-4012-8448-0

Library of Congress Cataloging-in-Publication Data is available.

PEFC Certified

Printed on paper from
sustainably managed
forests, controlled
sources

PEFC/29-31-337   www.pefc.org

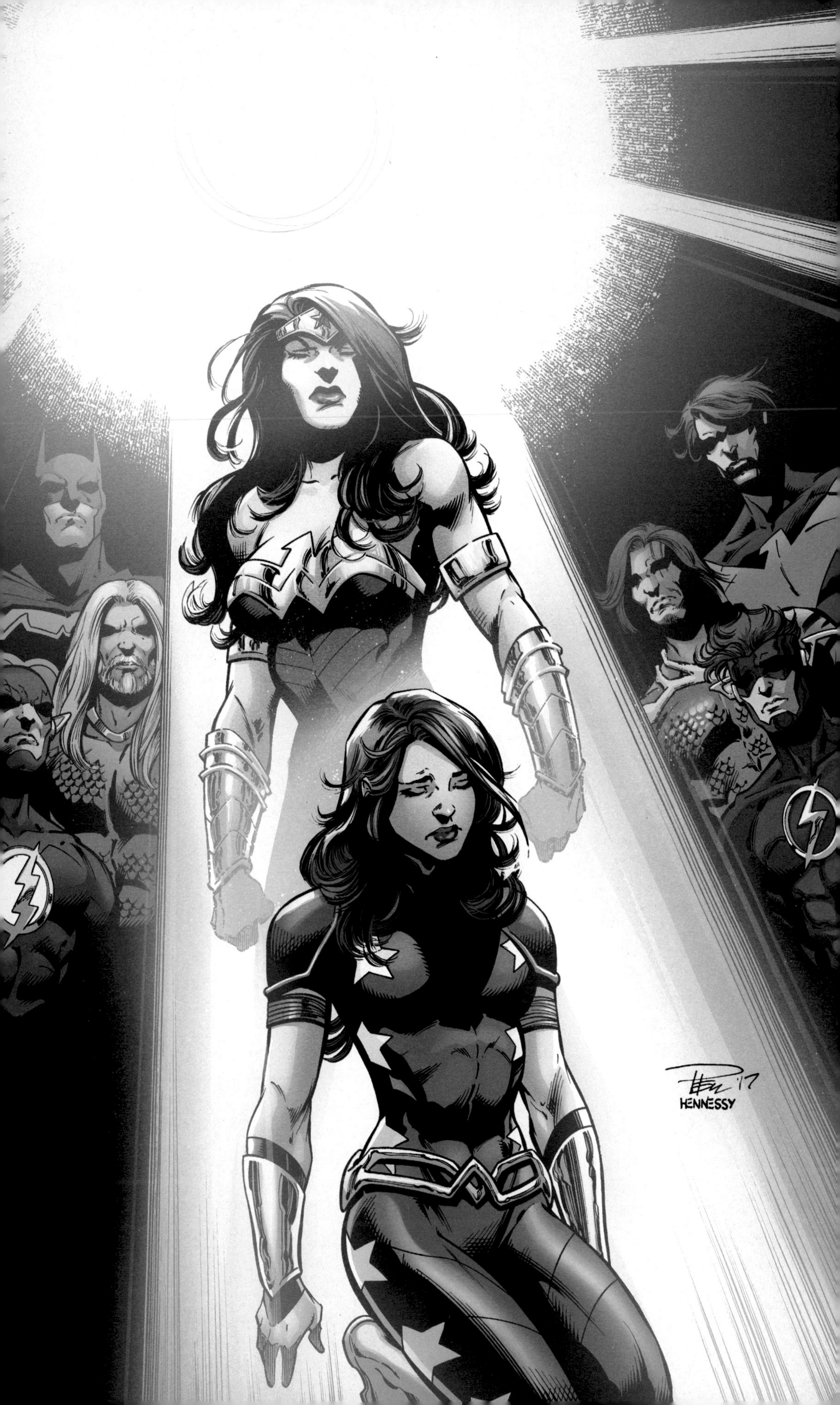
'17
HENNESSY

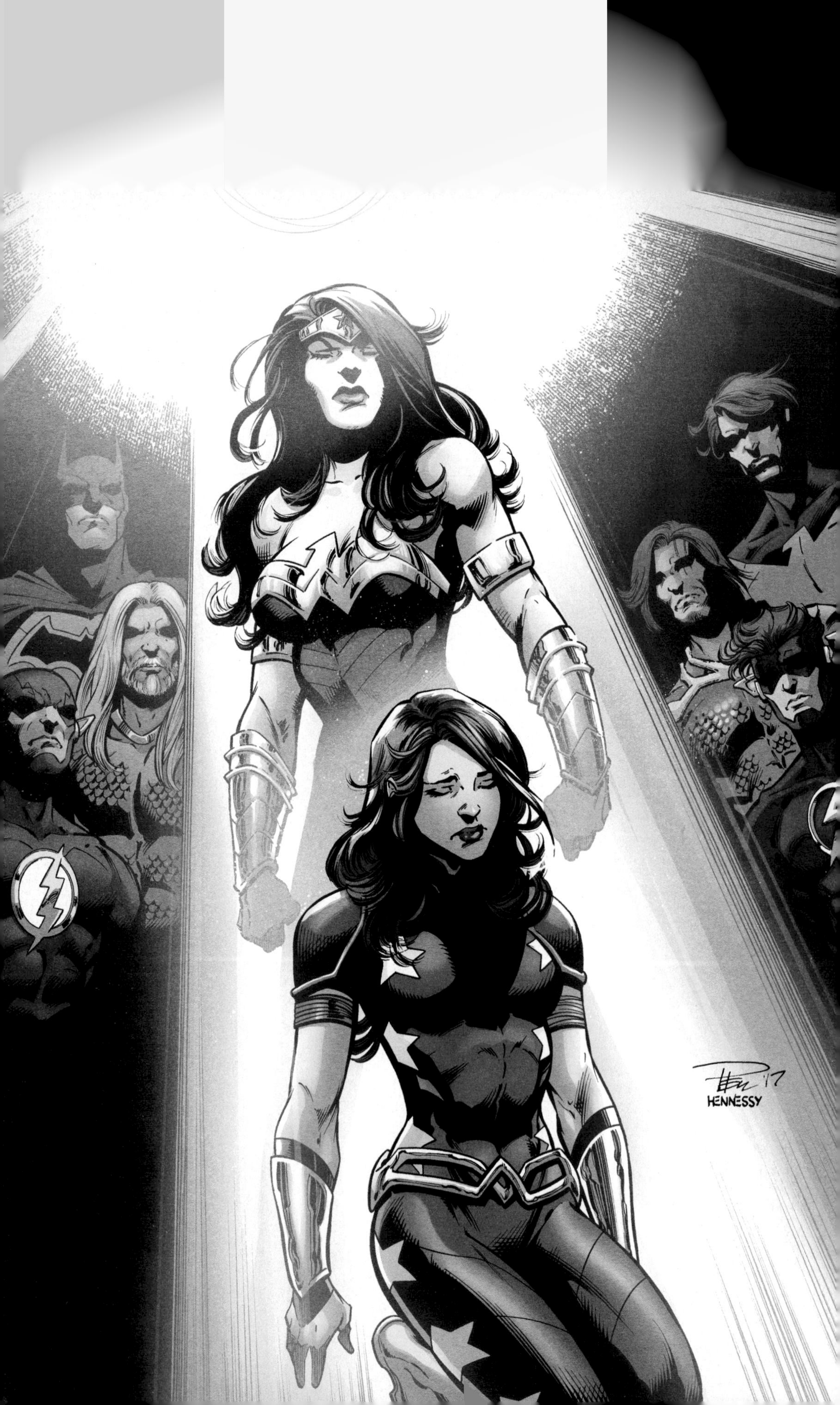
HENNESSY

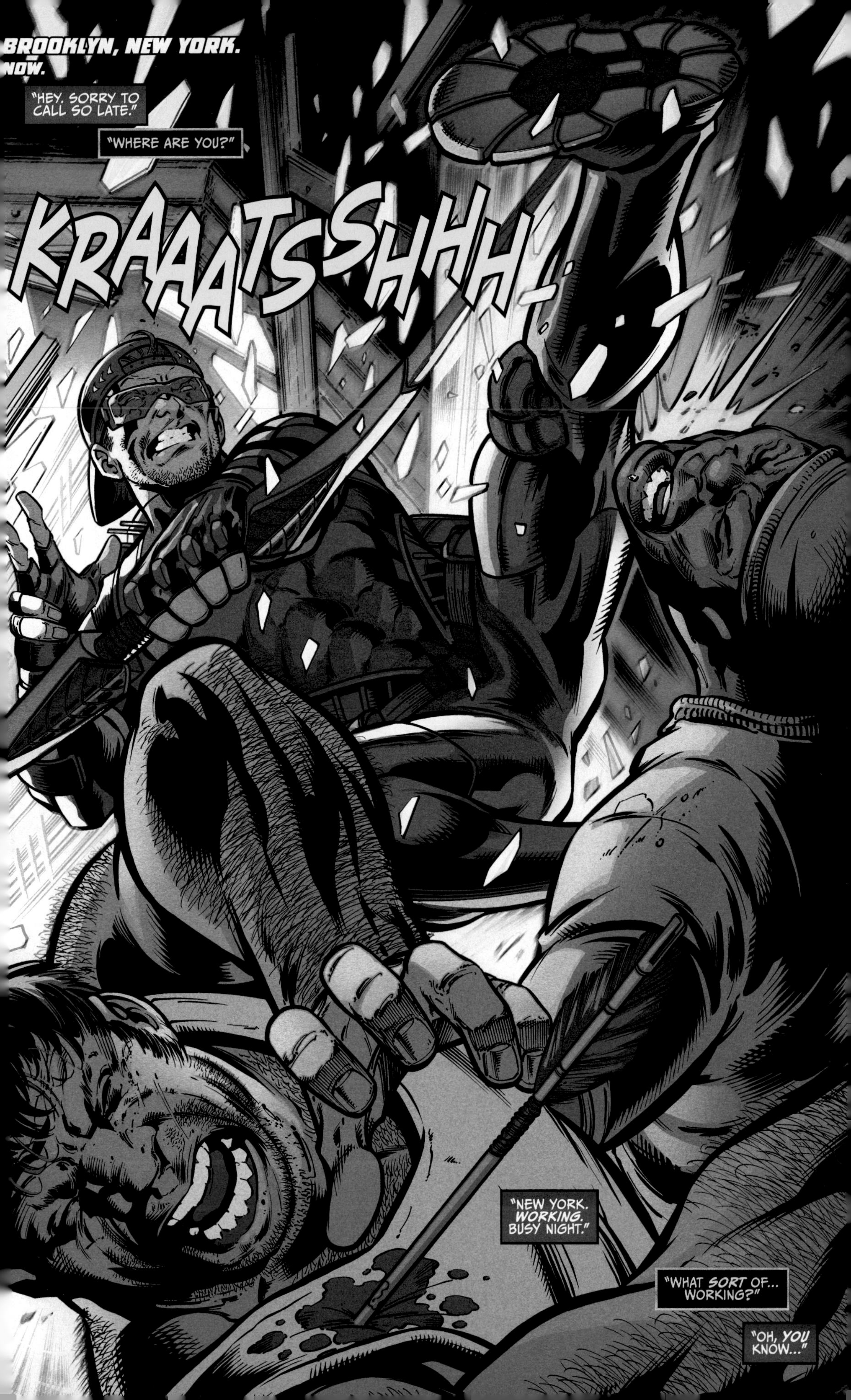
BROOKLYN, NEW YORK.
NOW.
"HEY. SORRY TO CALL SO LATE."
"WHERE ARE YOU?"
KRAAATSSHHH
"NEW YORK. *WORKING.* BUSY NIGHT."
"WHAT *SORT* OF... WORKING?"
"OH, *YOU* KNOW..."

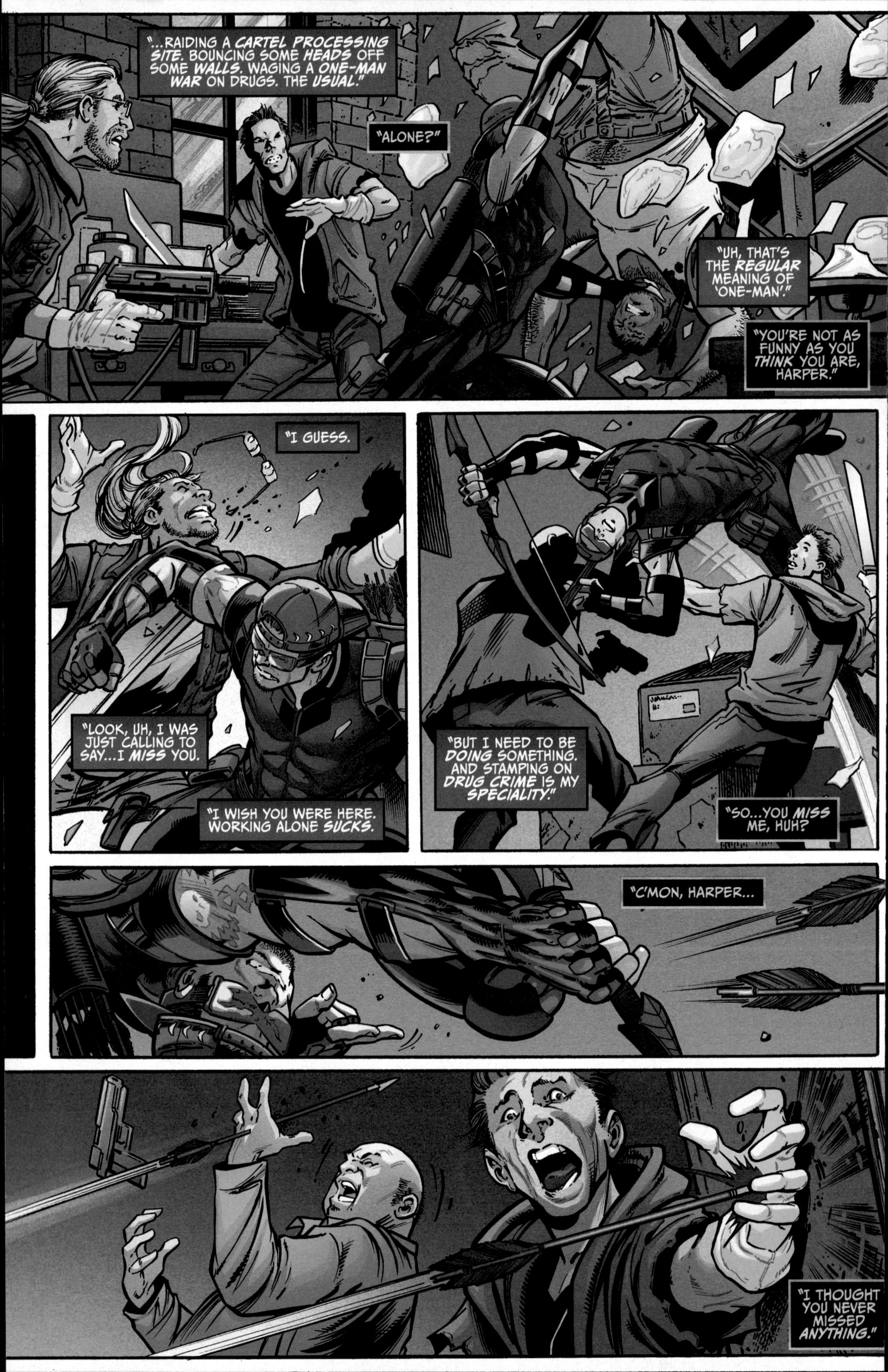
"...RAIDING A CARTEL PROCESSING SITE. BOUNCING SOME HEADS OFF SOME WALLS. WAGING A ONE-MAN WAR ON DRUGS. THE USUAL."
"ALONE?"
"UH, THAT'S THE REGULAR MEANING OF 'ONE-MAN'."
"YOU'RE NOT AS FUNNY AS YOU THINK YOU ARE, HARPER."
"I GUESS.
"LOOK, UH, I WAS JUST CALLING TO SAY...I MISS YOU.
"I WISH YOU WERE HERE. WORKING ALONE SUCKS.
"BUT I NEED TO BE DOING SOMETHING. AND STAMPING ON DRUG CRIME IS MY SPECIALITY."
"SO...YOU MISS ME, HUH?
"C'MON, HARPER...
"I THOUGHT YOU NEVER MISSED ANYTHING."

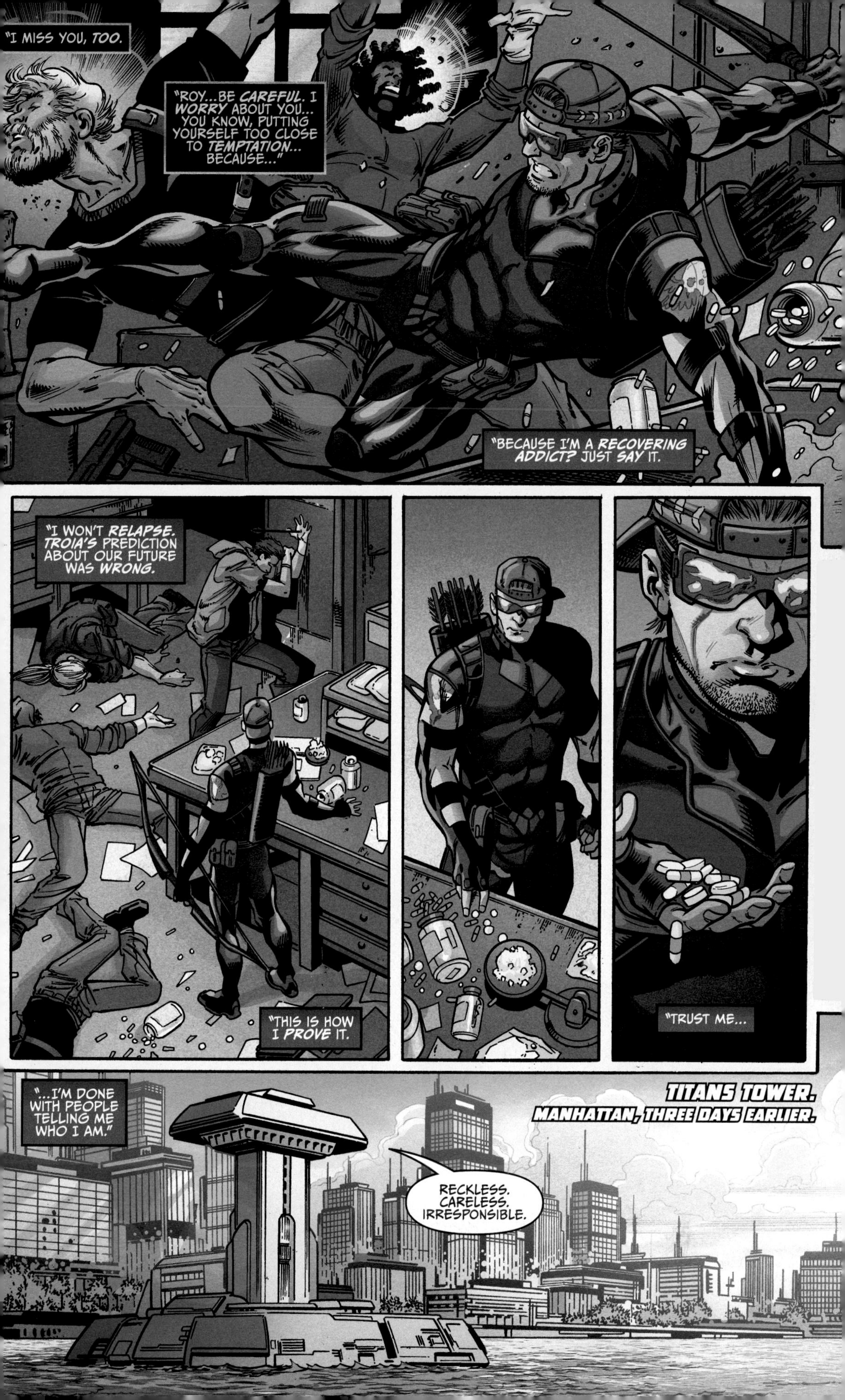
"I MISS YOU, TOO.
"ROY...BE CAREFUL. I WORRY ABOUT YOU... YOU KNOW, PUTTING YOURSELF TOO CLOSE TO TEMPTATION... BECAUSE..."
"BECAUSE I'M A RECOVERING ADDICT? JUST SAY IT.
"I WON'T RELAPSE. TROIA'S PREDICTION ABOUT OUR FUTURE WAS WRONG.
"THIS IS HOW I PROVE IT.
"TRUST ME...
"...I'M DONE WITH PEOPLE TELLING ME WHO I AM."
TITANS TOWER.
MANHATTAN, THREE DAYS EARLIER.
RECKLESS. CARELESS. IRRESPONSIBLE.

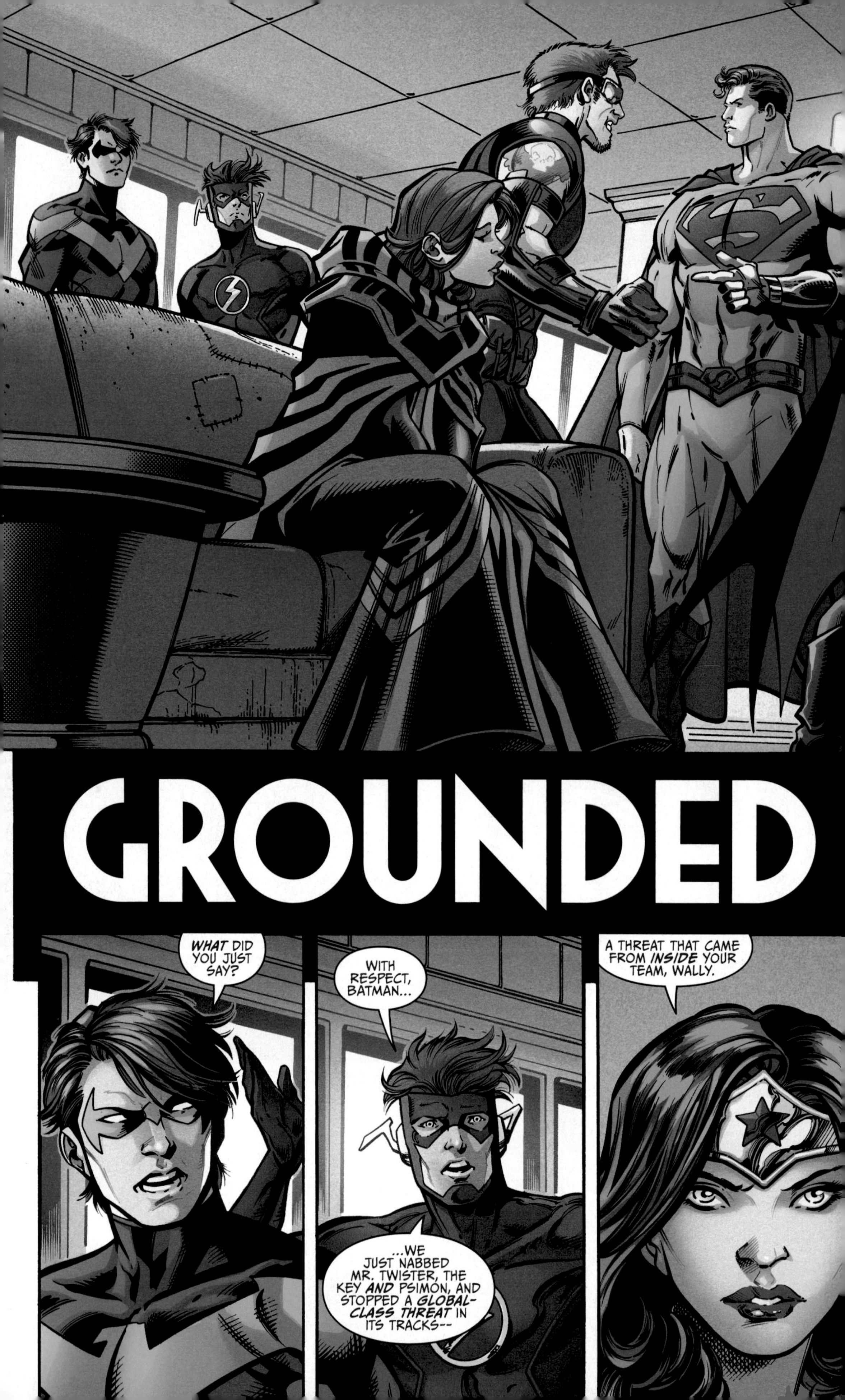
GROUNDED
WHAT DID YOU JUST SAY?
WITH RESPECT, BATMAN...
...WE JUST NABBED MR. TWISTER, THE KEY AND PSIMON, AND STOPPED A GLOBAL-CLASS THREAT IN ITS TRACKS--
A THREAT THAT CAME FROM INSIDE YOUR TEAM, WALLY.

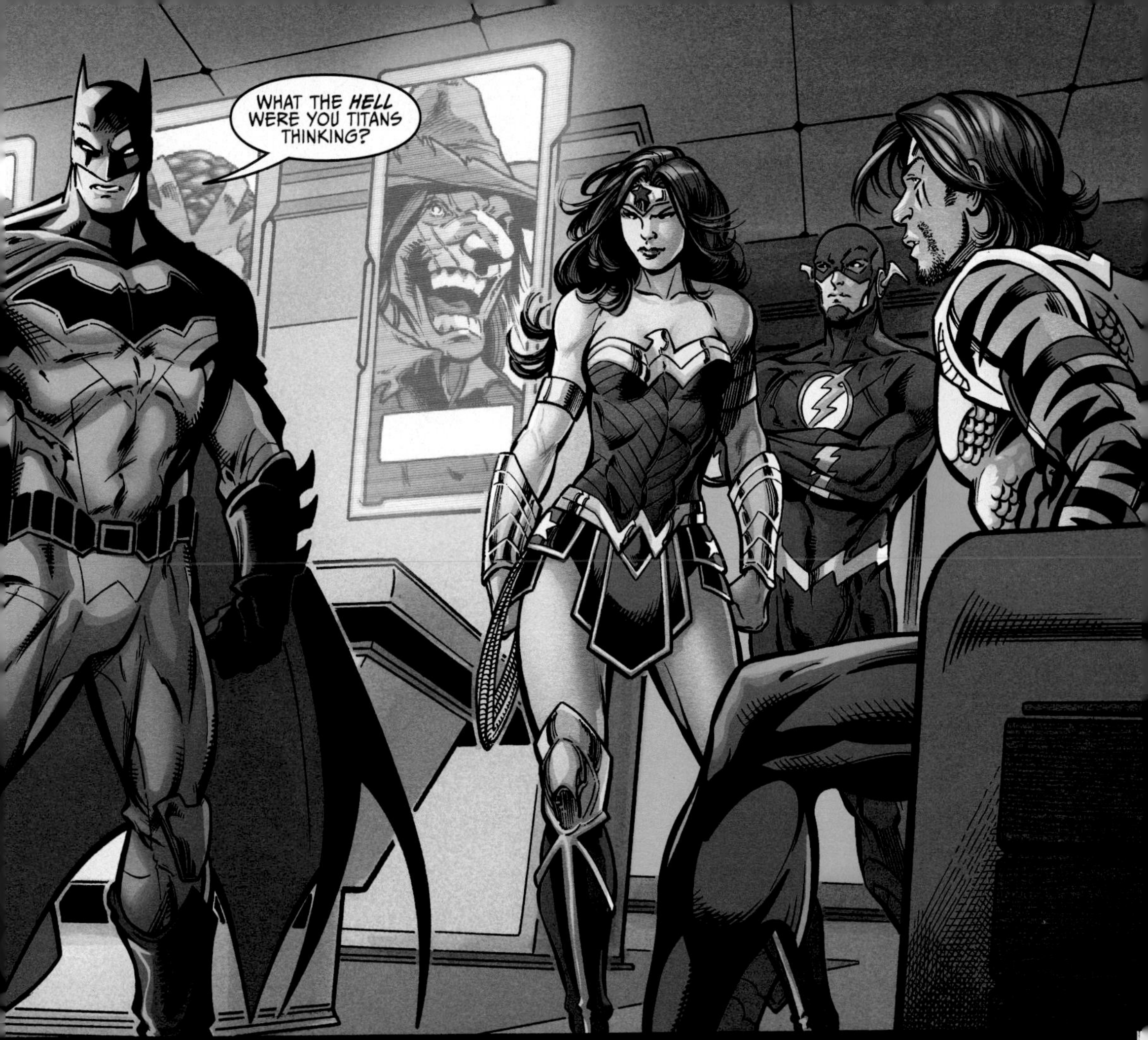
WHAT THE HELL WERE YOU TITANS THINKING?

DAN ABNETT WRITER • **PAUL PELLETIER** PENCILS
ANDREW HENNESSY INKS • **ADRIANO LUCAS** COLORS • **JOSH REED** LETTERS
PELLETIER, HENNESSY & LUCAS COVER • **DAN MORA** VARIANT COVER
DAVE WIELGOSZ ASST. EDITOR • **ALEX ANTONE** EDITOR • **BRIAN CUNNINGHAM** GROUP EDITOR

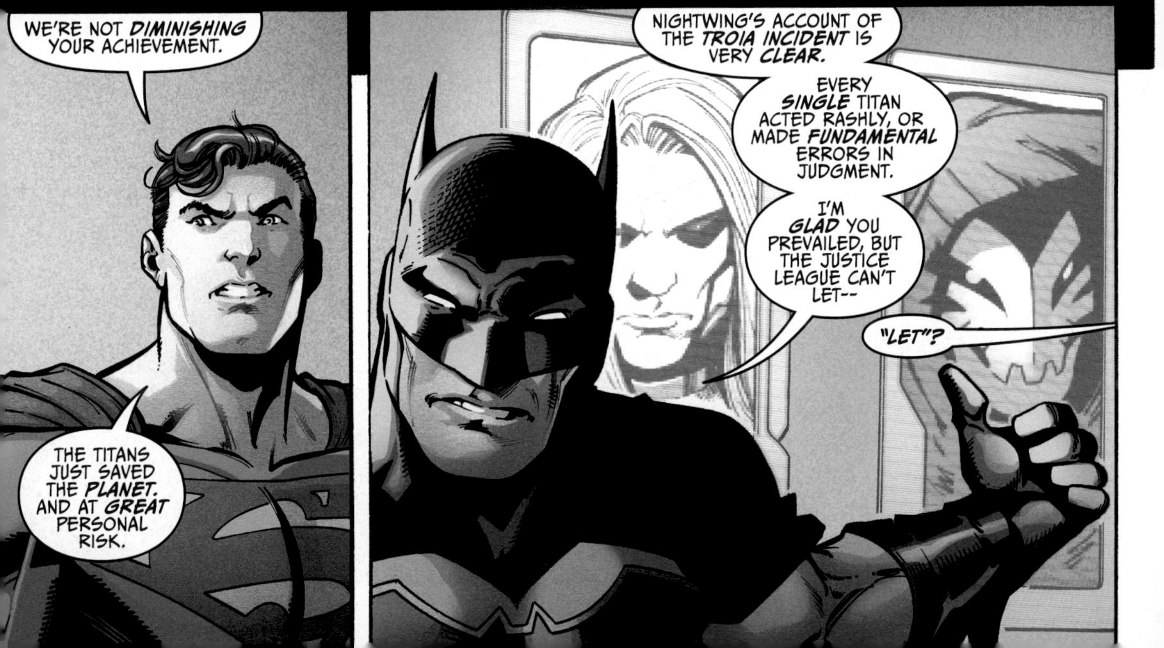
WE'RE NOT DIMINISHING YOUR ACHIEVEMENT.
THE TITANS JUST SAVED THE PLANET. AND AT GREAT PERSONAL RISK.
NIGHTWING'S ACCOUNT OF THE TROIA INCIDENT IS VERY CLEAR.
EVERY SINGLE TITAN ACTED RASHLY, OR MADE FUNDAMENTAL ERRORS IN JUDGMENT.
I'M GLAD YOU PREVAILED, BUT THE JUSTICE LEAGUE CAN'T LET--
"LET"?

HE'S JOKING, RIGHT?

ROY...

WHAT, DICK? DADDY'S HOME, AND HE WANTS A WORD ABOUT OUR REPORT CARD?

WE'RE NOT YOUR SIDEKICKS ANYMORE--

YOU ARE MOST CERTAINLY NOT, ARSENAL.

YOU'RE ADULTS WHO'VE CHOSEN TO PROTECT THE HUMAN RACE.

AND IT ALMOST WENT HORRIBLY WRONG.

BY YOUR OWN ADMISSION, YOU EXHIBITED ZERO LEVELS OF CAUTION OR PROFESSIONALISM--

THAT'S NOT FAIR. THERE WERE COMPLEX ISSUES INVOLVED--

THEN ASK FOR HELP FROM PEOPLE WHO'VE BEEN DOING THIS AWHILE.

BARRY? COME ON, HOW MANY TIMES HAVE YOU GUYS--

WELL, KINDA--

WALLY, YOU DIED, FOR GOD'S SAKE!

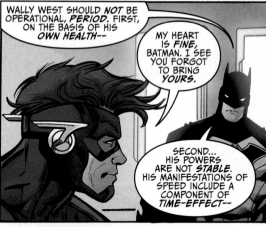

WALLY WEST SHOULD NOT BE OPERATIONAL, PERIOD. FIRST, ON THE BASIS OF HIS OWN HEALTH--

MY HEART IS FINE, BATMAN. I SEE YOU FORGOT TO BRING YOURS.

SECOND... HIS POWERS ARE NOT STABLE. HIS MANIFESTATIONS OF SPEED INCLUDE A COMPONENT OF TIME-EFFECT--

I WAS ADRIFT IN THE TIME STREAM! I'M STILL FIGURING OUT HOW THAT'S AFFECTED MY SPEED--

SPEEDSTERS POSSESS ONE OF THE MOST POTENTIALLY DANGEROUS POWER SETS OF ANY METAHUMAN.

THAT INCLUDES LANTERNS AND KRYPTONIANS.

YOU COULD REWRITE THE WORLD IN THE BLINK OF AN EYE WITHOUT MEANING TO.

AND YOU HAVE NO IDEA WHAT YOUR POWER LIMITS ARE, OR HOW TO CONTROL THEM.

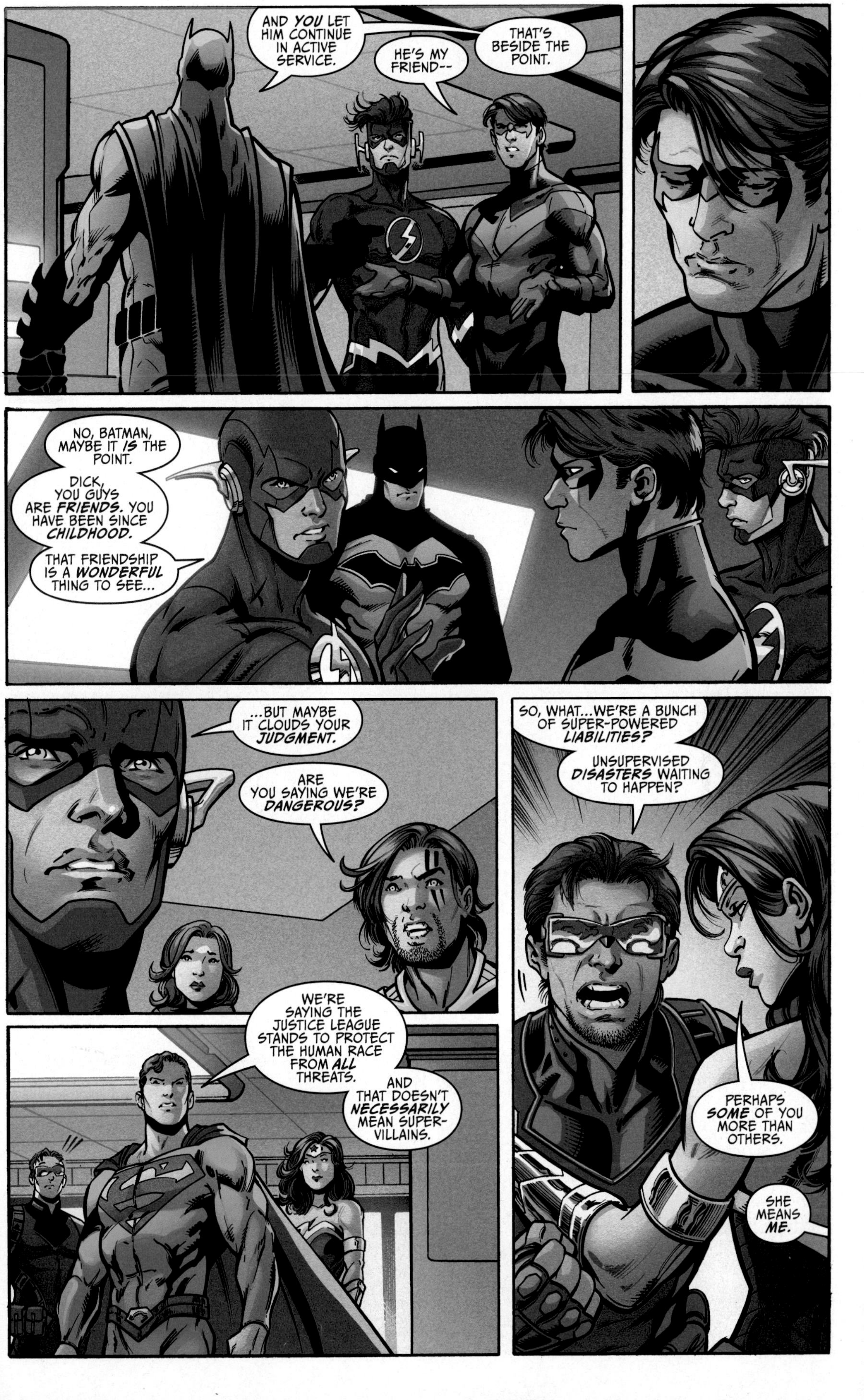
AND YOU LET HIM CONTINUE IN ACTIVE SERVICE.
HE'S MY FRIEND--
THAT'S BESIDE THE POINT.
NO, BATMAN, MAYBE IT IS THE POINT.
DICK, YOU GUYS ARE FRIENDS. YOU HAVE BEEN SINCE CHILDHOOD.
THAT FRIENDSHIP IS A WONDERFUL THING TO SEE...
...BUT MAYBE IT CLOUDS YOUR JUDGMENT.
ARE YOU SAYING WE'RE DANGEROUS?
WE'RE SAYING THE JUSTICE LEAGUE STANDS TO PROTECT THE HUMAN RACE FROM ALL THREATS.
AND THAT DOESN'T NECESSARILY MEAN SUPER-VILLAINS.
SO, WHAT...WE'RE A BUNCH OF SUPER-POWERED LIABILITIES?
UNSUPERVISED DISASTERS WAITING TO HAPPEN?
PERHAPS SOME OF YOU MORE THAN OTHERS.
SHE MEANS ME.

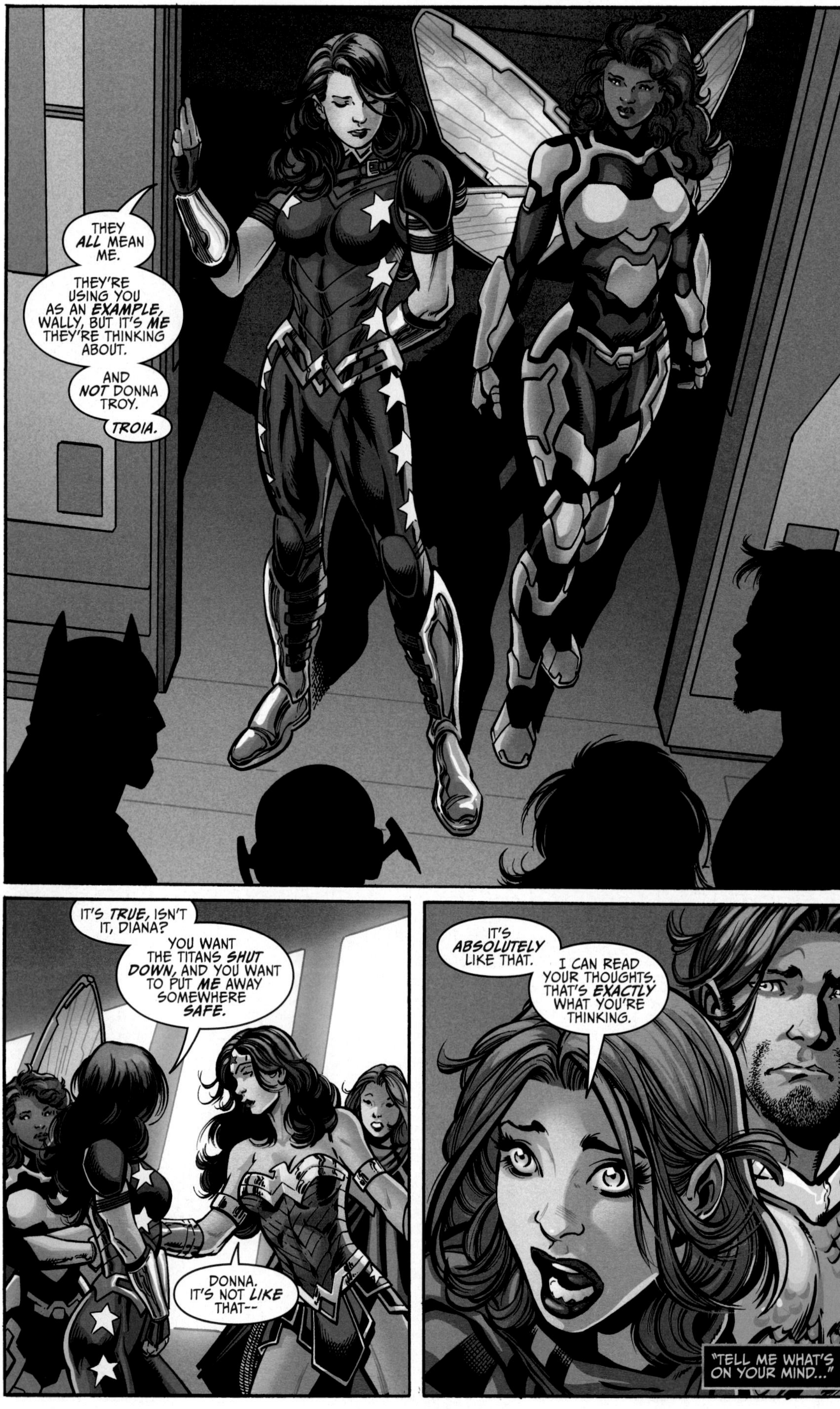
THEY ALL MEAN ME.
THEY'RE USING YOU AS AN EXAMPLE, WALLY, BUT IT'S ME THEY'RE THINKING ABOUT.
AND NOT DONNA TROY.
TROIA.
IT'S TRUE, ISN'T IT, DIANA?
YOU WANT THE TITANS SHUT DOWN, AND YOU WANT TO PUT ME AWAY SOMEWHERE SAFE.
DONNA. IT'S NOT LIKE THAT--
IT'S ABSOLUTELY LIKE THAT.
I CAN READ YOUR THOUGHTS. THAT'S EXACTLY WHAT YOU'RE THINKING.
"TELL ME WHAT'S ON YOUR MIND..."

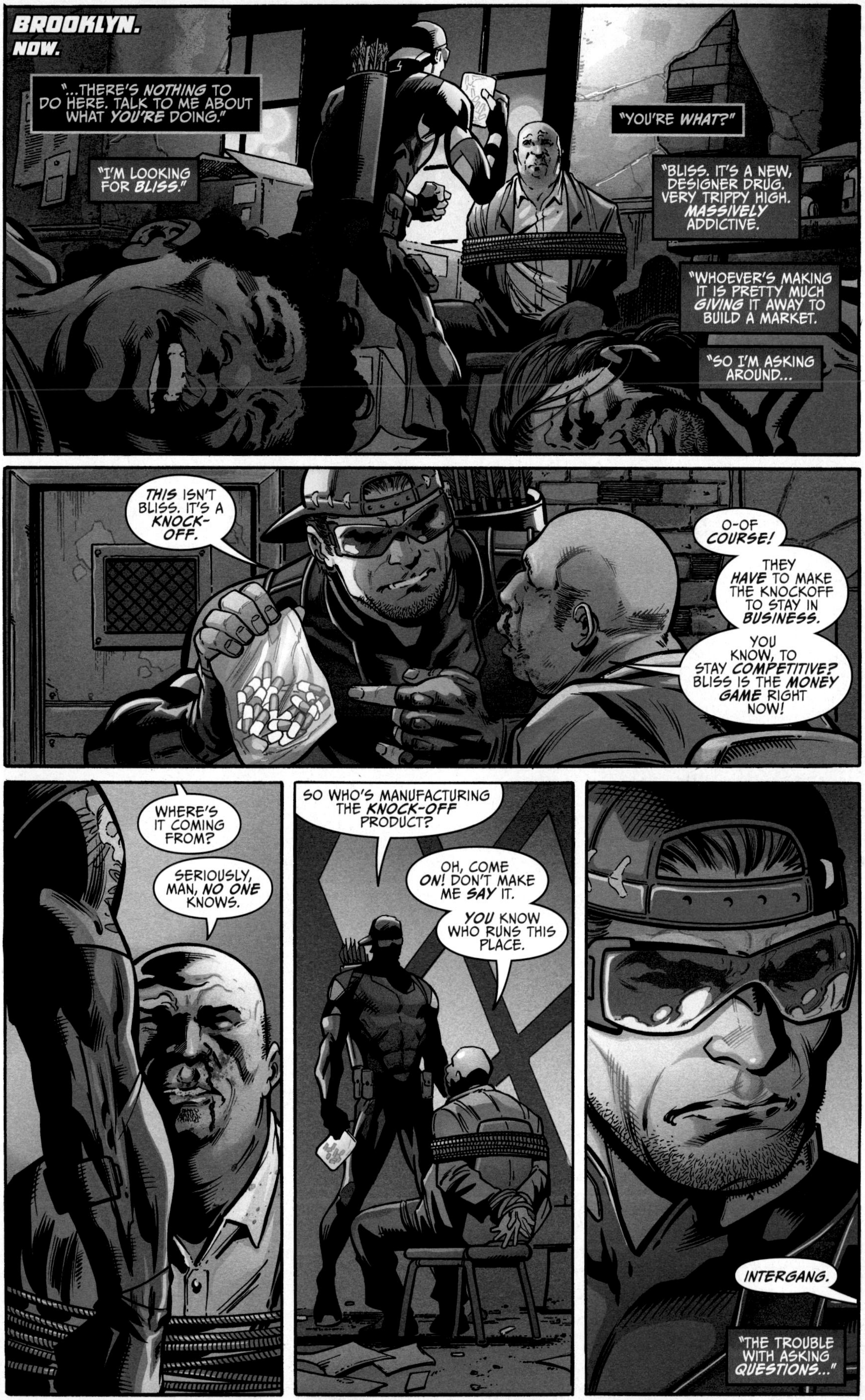
BROOKLYN.
NOW.
"...THERE'S NOTHING TO DO HERE. TALK TO ME ABOUT WHAT YOU'RE DOING."
"I'M LOOKING FOR BLISS."
"YOU'RE WHAT?"
"BLISS. IT'S A NEW, DESIGNER DRUG. VERY TRIPPY HIGH. MASSIVELY ADDICTIVE.
"WHOEVER'S MAKING IT IS PRETTY MUCH GIVING IT AWAY TO BUILD A MARKET.
"SO I'M ASKING AROUND...
THIS ISN'T BLISS. IT'S A KNOCK-OFF.
O-OF COURSE!
THEY HAVE TO MAKE THE KNOCKOFF TO STAY IN BUSINESS.
YOU KNOW, TO STAY COMPETITIVE? BLISS IS THE MONEY GAME RIGHT NOW!
WHERE'S IT COMING FROM?
SERIOUSLY, MAN, NO ONE KNOWS.
SO WHO'S MANUFACTURING THE KNOCK-OFF PRODUCT?
OH, COME ON! DON'T MAKE ME SAY IT.
YOU KNOW WHO RUNS THIS PLACE.
INTERGANG.
"THE TROUBLE WITH ASKING QUESTIONS..."

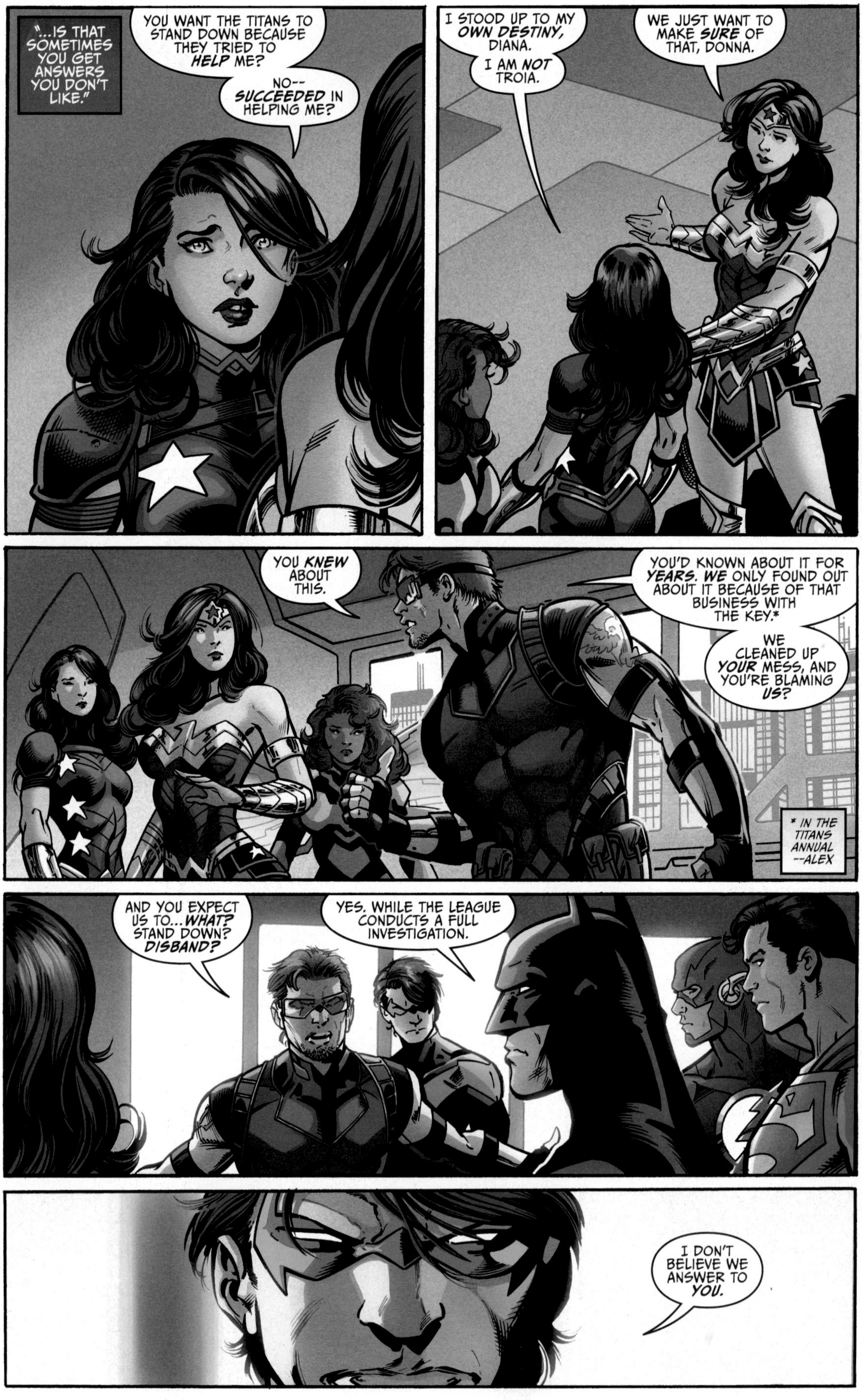
"...IS THAT SOMETIMES YOU GET ANSWERS YOU DON'T LIKE."
YOU WANT THE TITANS TO STAND DOWN BECAUSE THEY TRIED TO *HELP* ME?
NO-- *SUCCEEDED* IN HELPING ME?
I STOOD UP TO MY *OWN DESTINY,* DIANA.
I AM *NOT* TROIA.
WE JUST WANT TO MAKE *SURE* OF THAT, DONNA.
YOU *KNEW* ABOUT THIS.
YOU'D KNOWN ABOUT IT FOR *YEARS. WE* ONLY FOUND OUT ABOUT IT BECAUSE OF THAT BUSINESS WITH THE KEY.*
WE CLEANED UP *YOUR* MESS, AND YOU'RE BLAMING *US?*
* IN THE TITANS ANNUAL --ALEX
AND YOU EXPECT US TO...*WHAT?* STAND DOWN? *DISBAND?*
YES. WHILE THE LEAGUE CONDUCTS A FULL INVESTIGATION.
I DON'T BELIEVE WE ANSWER TO *YOU.*

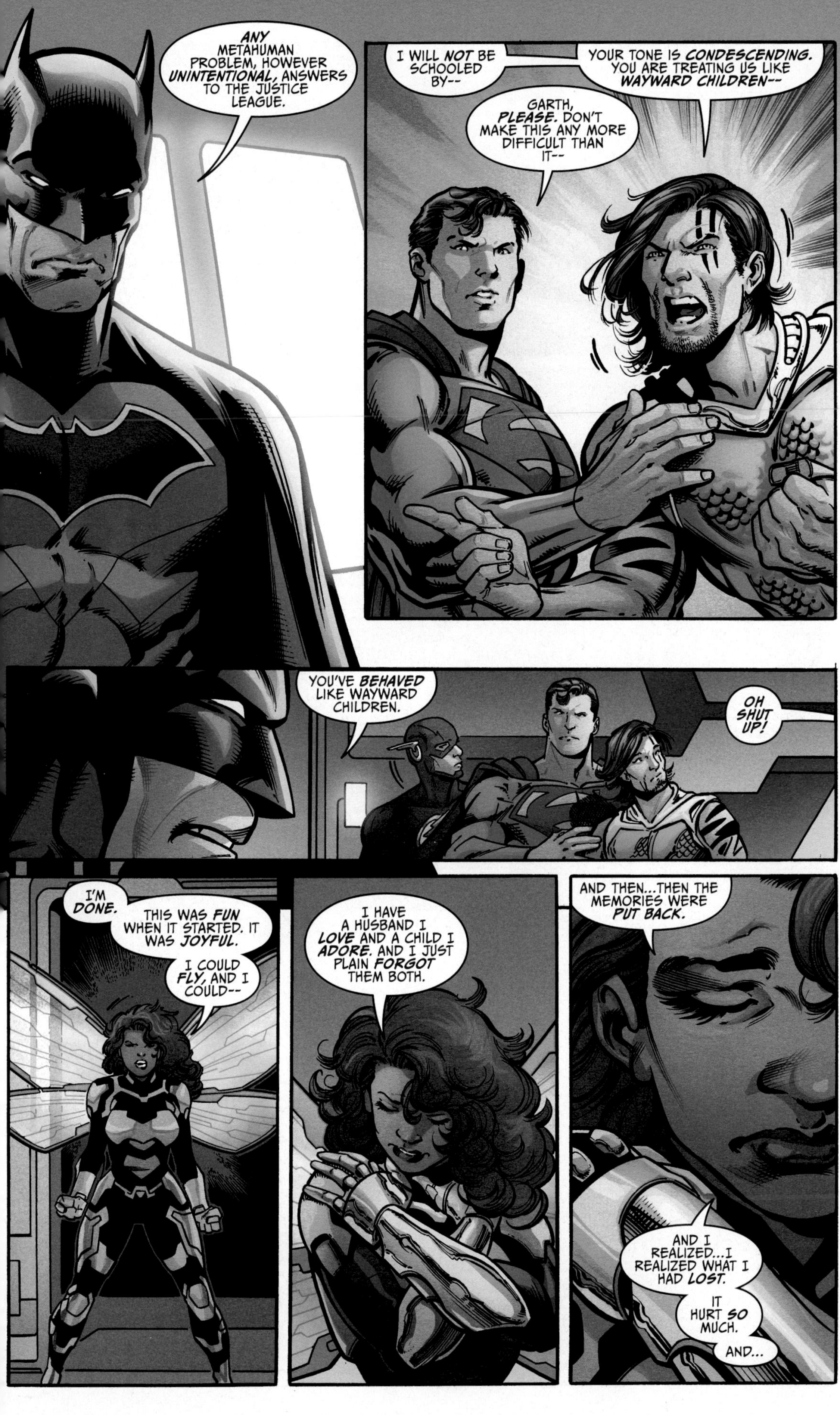
ANY METAHUMAN PROBLEM, HOWEVER UNINTENTIONAL, ANSWERS TO THE JUSTICE LEAGUE.
I WILL NOT BE SCHOOLED BY--
YOUR TONE IS CONDESCENDING. YOU ARE TREATING US LIKE WAYWARD CHILDREN--
GARTH, PLEASE. DON'T MAKE THIS ANY MORE DIFFICULT THAN IT--
YOU'VE BEHAVED LIKE WAYWARD CHILDREN.
OH SHUT UP!
I'M DONE.
THIS WAS FUN WHEN IT STARTED. IT WAS JOYFUL.
I COULD FLY, AND I COULD--
I HAVE A HUSBAND I LOVE AND A CHILD I ADORE. AND I JUST PLAIN FORGOT THEM BOTH.
AND THEN...THEN THE MEMORIES WERE PUT BACK.
AND I REALIZED...I REALIZED WHAT I HAD LOST.
IT HURT SO MUCH.
AND...

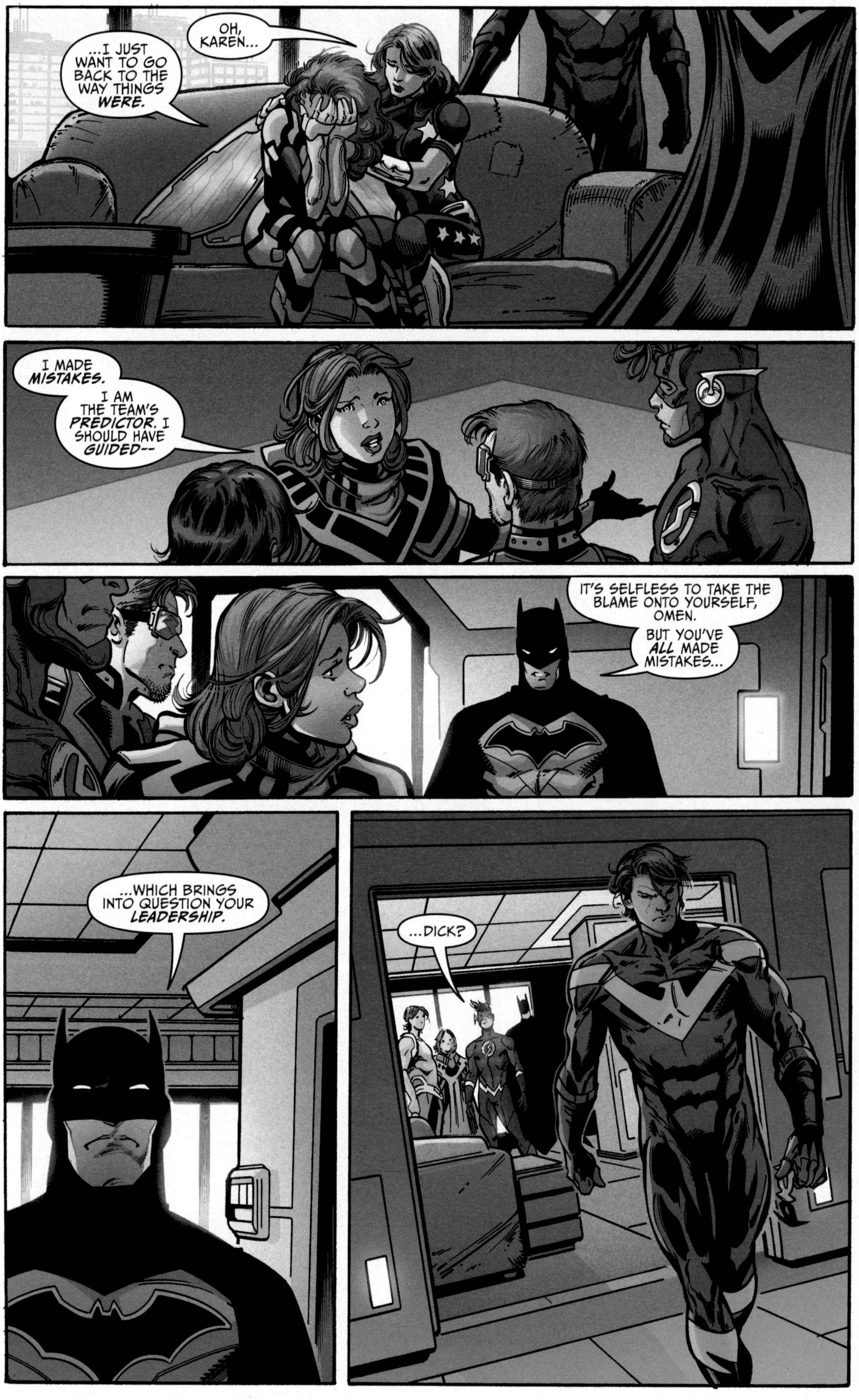
...I JUST WANT TO GO BACK TO THE WAY THINGS *WERE.*
OH, KAREN...
I MADE *MISTAKES.*
I AM THE TEAM'S *PREDICTOR.* I SHOULD HAVE *GUIDED--*
IT'S SELFLESS TO TAKE THE BLAME ONTO YOURSELF, OMEN.
BUT YOU'VE *ALL* MADE MISTAKES...
...WHICH BRINGS INTO QUESTION YOUR *LEADERSHIP.*
...DICK?

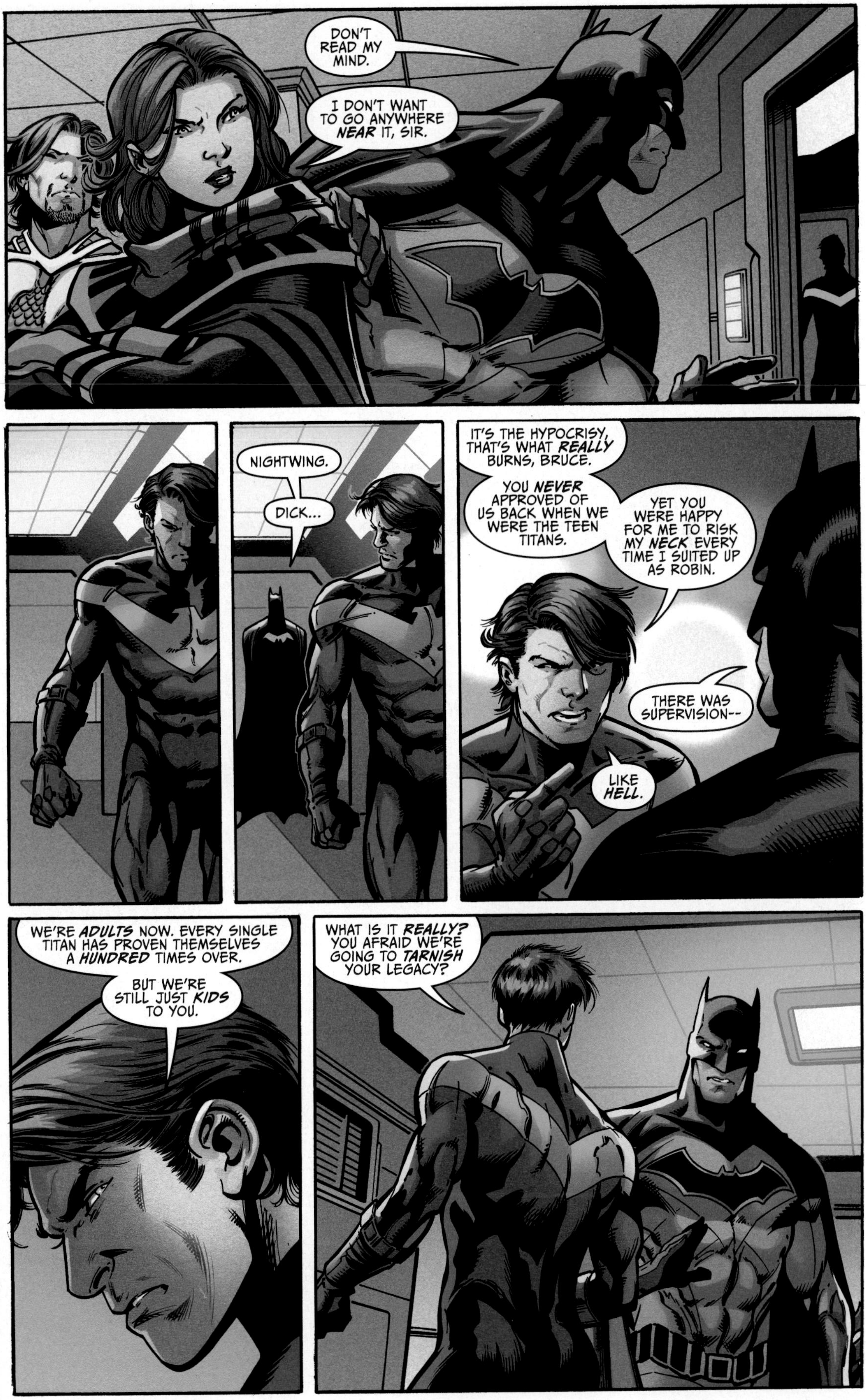

DON'T READ MY MIND.
I DON'T WANT TO GO ANYWHERE NEAR IT, SIR.
NIGHTWING.
DICK...
IT'S THE HYPOCRISY, THAT'S WHAT REALLY BURNS, BRUCE.
YOU NEVER APPROVED OF US BACK WHEN WE WERE THE TEEN TITANS.
YET YOU WERE HAPPY FOR ME TO RISK MY NECK EVERY TIME I SUITED UP AS ROBIN.
THERE WAS SUPERVISION--
LIKE HELL.
WE'RE ADULTS NOW. EVERY SINGLE TITAN HAS PROVEN THEMSELVES A HUNDRED TIMES OVER.
BUT WE'RE STILL JUST KIDS TO YOU.
WHAT IS IT REALLY? YOU AFRAID WE'RE GOING TO TARNISH YOUR LEGACY?

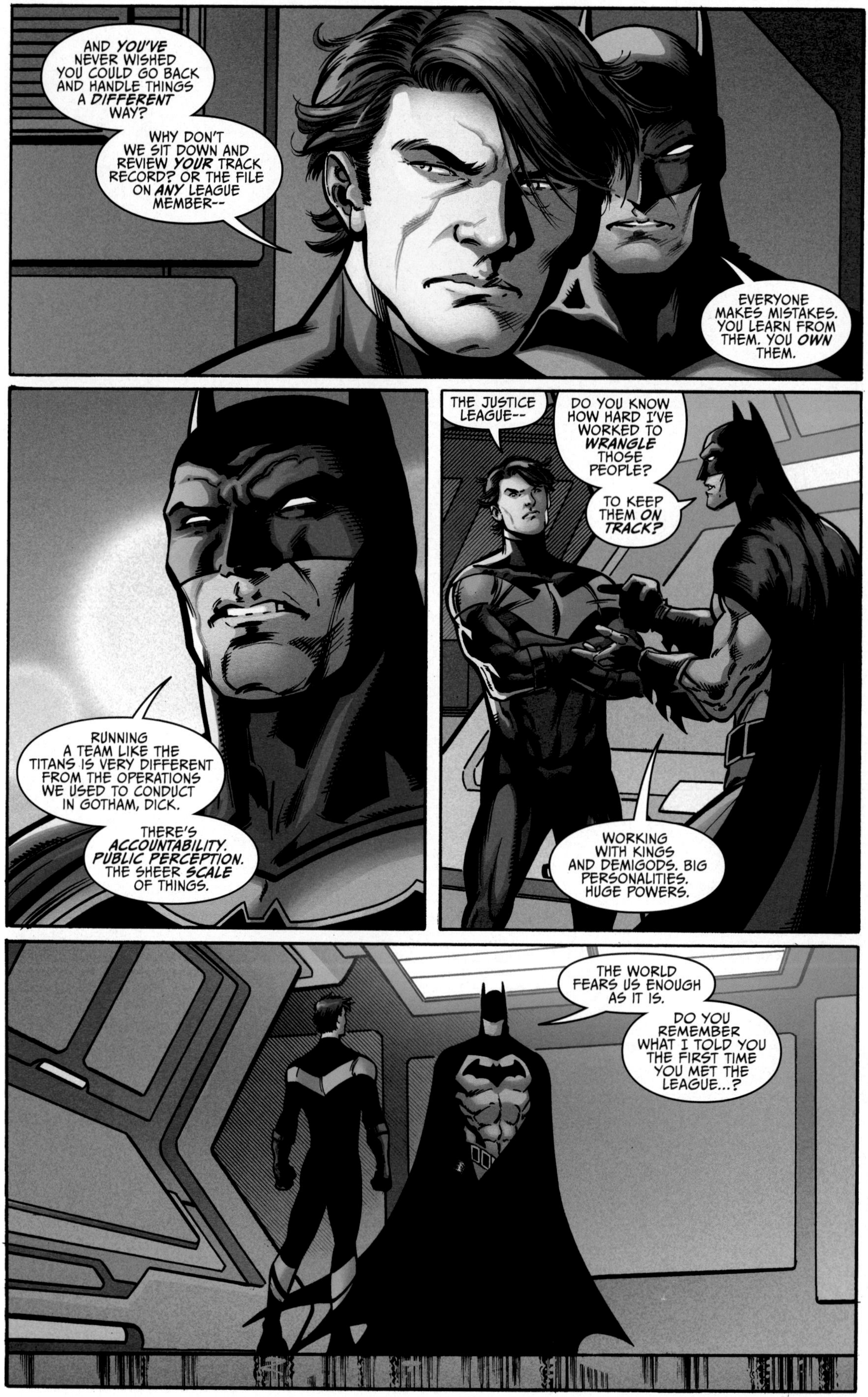
AND YOU'VE NEVER WISHED YOU COULD GO BACK AND HANDLE THINGS A DIFFERENT WAY?
WHY DON'T WE SIT DOWN AND REVIEW YOUR TRACK RECORD? OR THE FILE ON ANY LEAGUE MEMBER--
EVERYONE MAKES MISTAKES. YOU LEARN FROM THEM. YOU OWN THEM.
RUNNING A TEAM LIKE THE TITANS IS VERY DIFFERENT FROM THE OPERATIONS WE USED TO CONDUCT IN GOTHAM, DICK.
THERE'S ACCOUNTABILITY. PUBLIC PERCEPTION. THE SHEER SCALE OF THINGS.
THE JUSTICE LEAGUE--
DO YOU KNOW HOW HARD I'VE WORKED TO WRANGLE THOSE PEOPLE?
TO KEEP THEM ON TRACK?
WORKING WITH KINGS AND DEMIGODS. BIG PERSONALITIES. HUGE POWERS.
THE WORLD FEARS US ENOUGH AS IT IS.
DO YOU REMEMBER WHAT I TOLD YOU THE FIRST TIME YOU MET THE LEAGUE...?

IF I CAN BE A VIABLE MEMBER OF THIS TEAM, *WITHOUT* META-CLASS POWERS LIKE THE OTHERS, SO CAN *YOU*.

I...I'M GOING TO BE A MEMBER OF THE *JUSTICE LEAGUE* ONE DAY?

NO.

YOU'RE GOING TO *LEAD* IT.

HAVE I DISAPPOINTED YOU?

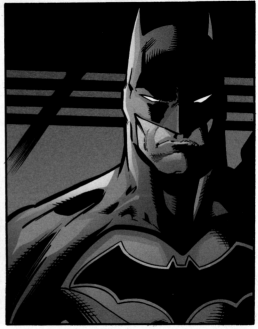

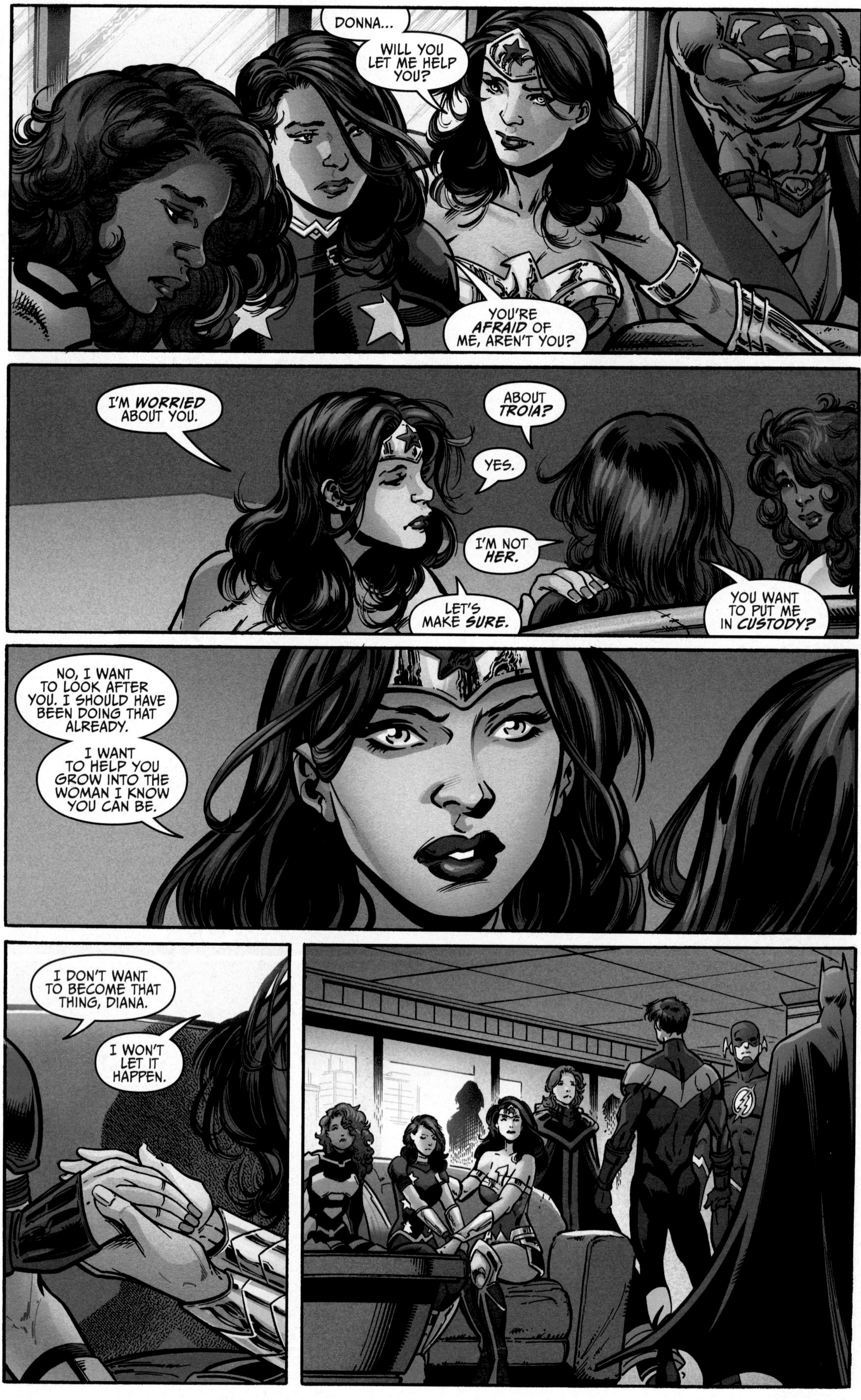
DONNA...
WILL YOU LET ME HELP YOU?
YOU'RE AFRAID OF ME, AREN'T YOU?
I'M WORRIED ABOUT YOU.
ABOUT TROIA?
YES.
I'M NOT HER.
LET'S MAKE SURE.
YOU WANT TO PUT ME IN CUSTODY?
NO, I WANT TO LOOK AFTER YOU. I SHOULD HAVE BEEN DOING THAT ALREADY.
I WANT TO HELP YOU GROW INTO THE WOMAN I KNOW YOU CAN BE.
I DON'T WANT TO BECOME THAT THING, DIANA.
I WON'T LET IT HAPPEN.

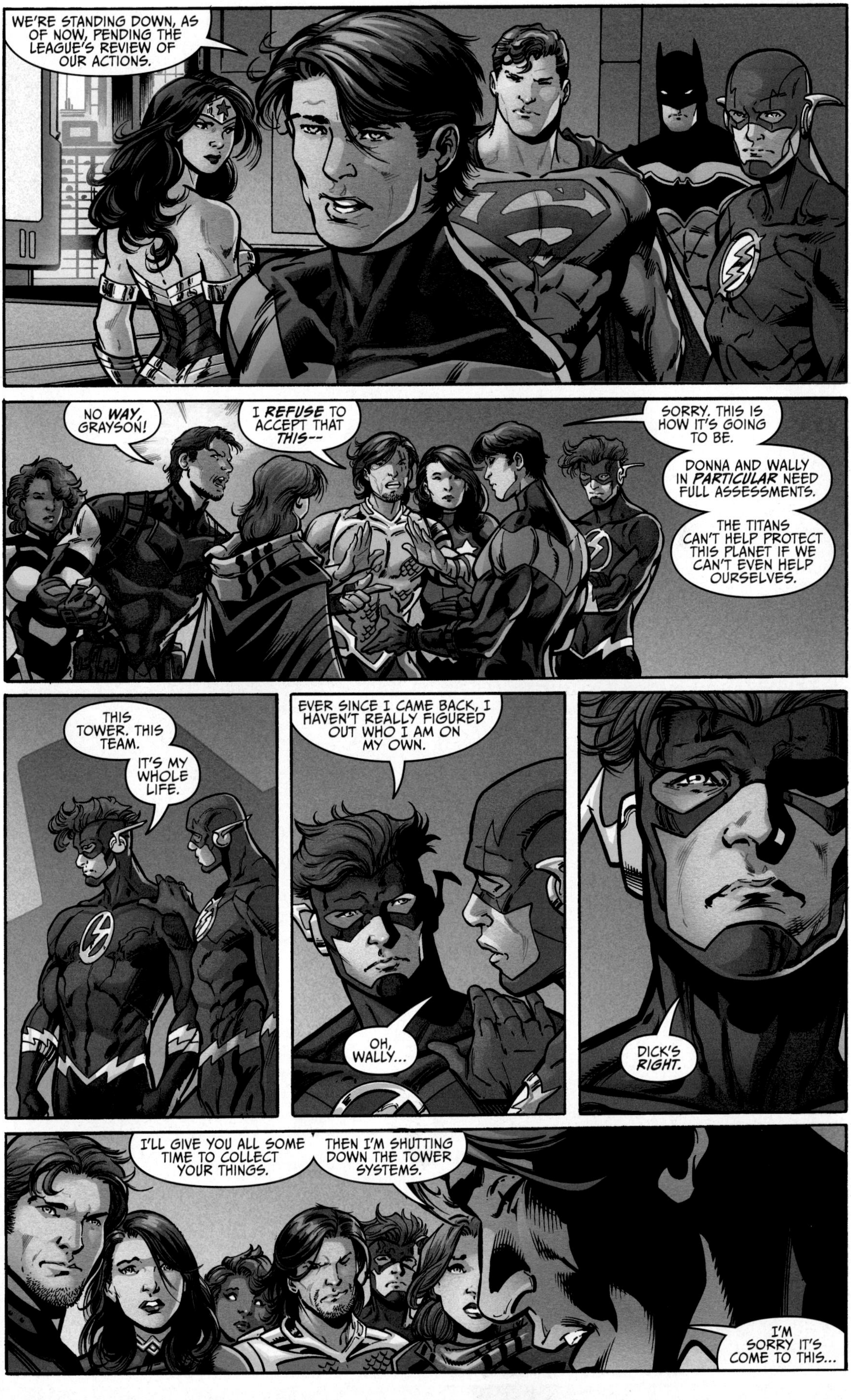

WE'RE STANDING DOWN, AS OF NOW, PENDING THE LEAGUE'S REVIEW OF OUR ACTIONS.
NO WAY, GRAYSON!
I REFUSE TO ACCEPT THAT THIS--
SORRY. THIS IS HOW IT'S GOING TO BE.
DONNA AND WALLY IN PARTICULAR NEED FULL ASSESSMENTS.
THE TITANS CAN'T HELP PROTECT THIS PLANET IF WE CAN'T EVEN HELP OURSELVES.
THIS TOWER. THIS TEAM.
IT'S MY WHOLE LIFE.
EVER SINCE I CAME BACK, I HAVEN'T REALLY FIGURED OUT WHO I AM ON MY OWN.
OH, WALLY...
DICK'S RIGHT.
I'LL GIVE YOU ALL SOME TIME TO COLLECT YOUR THINGS.
THEN I'M SHUTTING DOWN THE TOWER SYSTEMS.
I'M SORRY IT'S COME TO THIS...

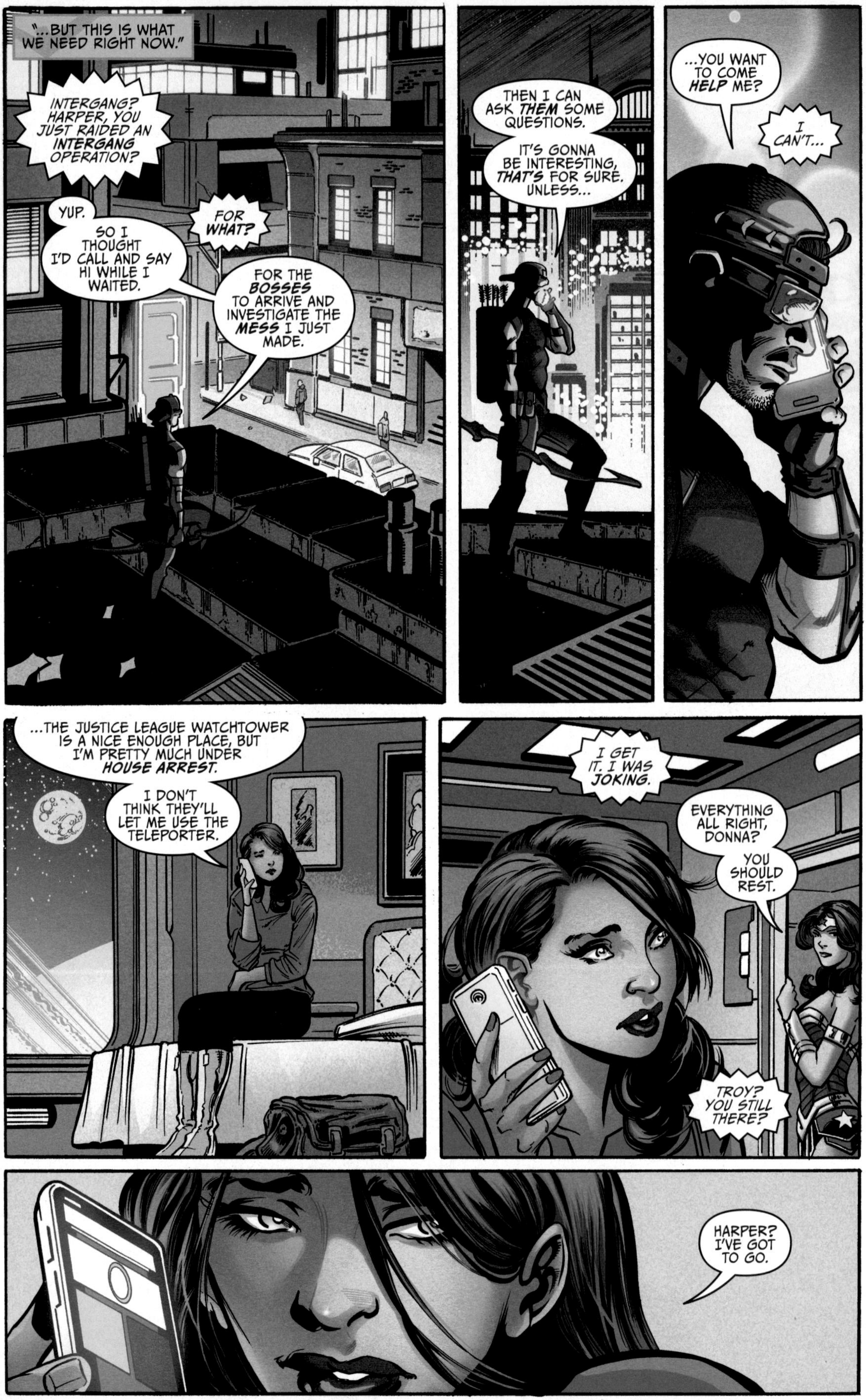
"...BUT THIS IS WHAT WE NEED RIGHT NOW."
INTERGANG? HARPER, YOU JUST RAIDED AN INTERGANG OPERATION?
YUP.
SO I THOUGHT I'D CALL AND SAY HI WHILE I WAITED.
FOR WHAT?
FOR THE BOSSES TO ARRIVE AND INVESTIGATE THE MESS I JUST MADE.
THEN I CAN ASK THEM SOME QUESTIONS.
IT'S GONNA BE INTERESTING, THAT'S FOR SURE. UNLESS...
...YOU WANT TO COME HELP ME?
I CAN'T...
...THE JUSTICE LEAGUE WATCHTOWER IS A NICE ENOUGH PLACE, BUT I'M PRETTY MUCH UNDER HOUSE ARREST.
I DON'T THINK THEY'LL LET ME USE THE TELEPORTER.
I GET IT. I WAS JOKING.
EVERYTHING ALL RIGHT, DONNA?
YOU SHOULD REST.
TROY? YOU STILL THERE?
HARPER? I'VE GOT TO GO.

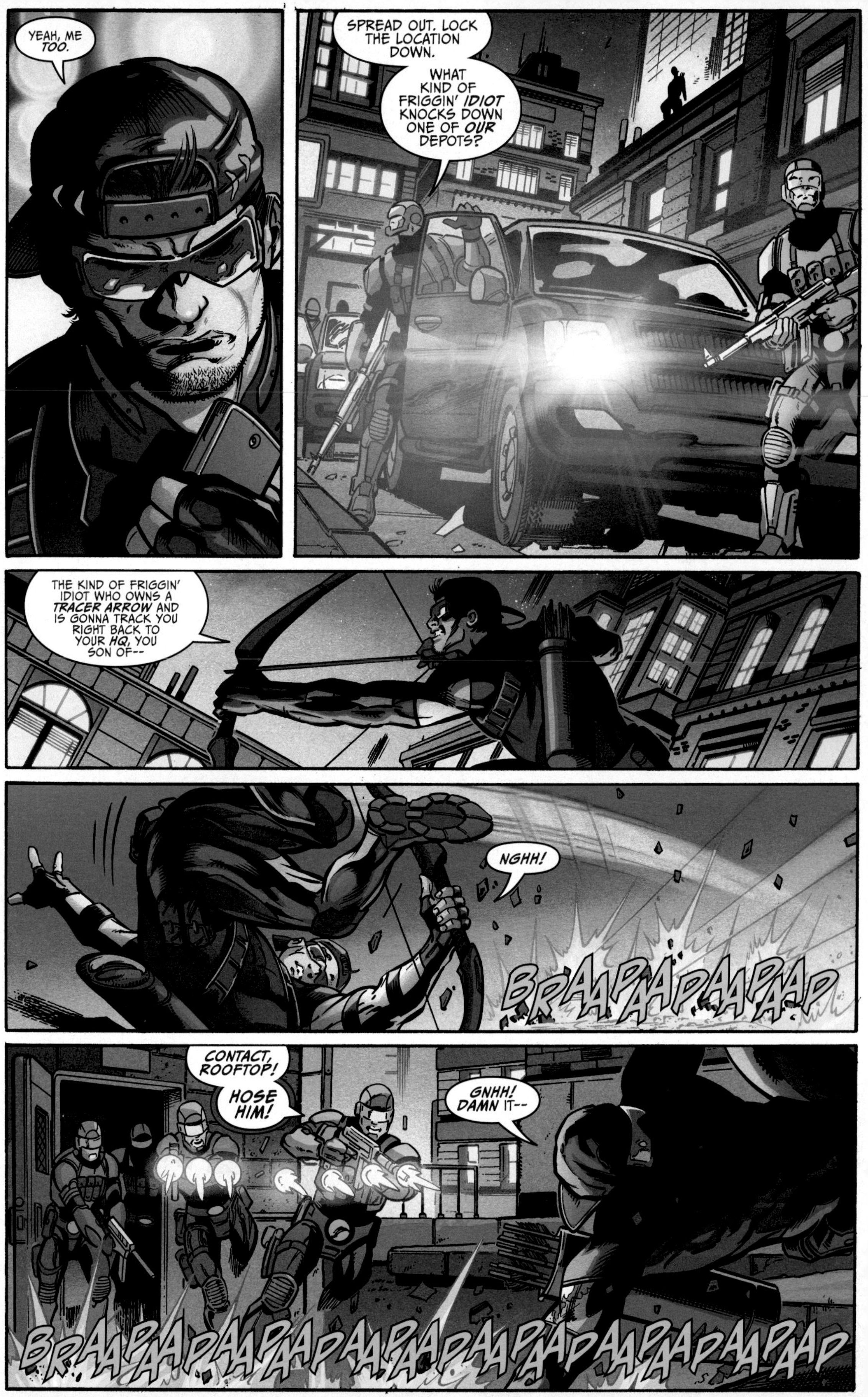
YEAH, ME TOO.
SPREAD OUT. LOCK THE LOCATION DOWN.
WHAT KIND OF FRIGGIN' IDIOT KNOCKS DOWN ONE OF OUR DEPOTS?
THE KIND OF FRIGGIN' IDIOT WHO OWNS A TRACER ARROW AND IS GONNA TRACK YOU RIGHT BACK TO YOUR HQ, YOU SON OF--
NGHH!
BRAAPAAPAAPAAP
CONTACT, ROOFTOP!
HOSE HIM!
GNHH! DAMN IT--
BRAAPAAPAAPAAPAAPAAPAAPAAPAAPAAPAAPAAP

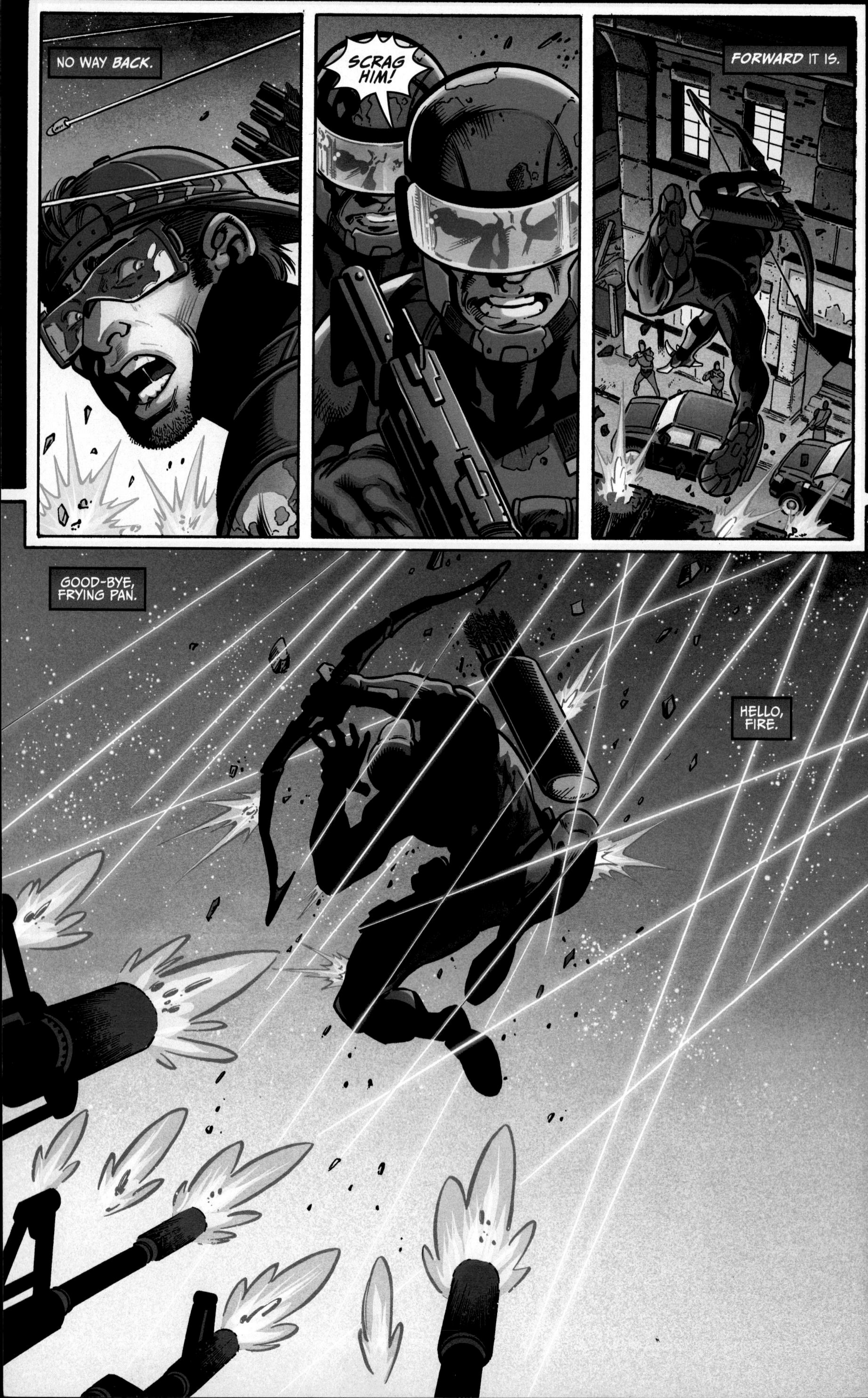
NO WAY BACK.
SCRAG HIM!
FORWARD IT IS.
GOOD-BYE, FRYING PAN.
HELLO, FIRE.

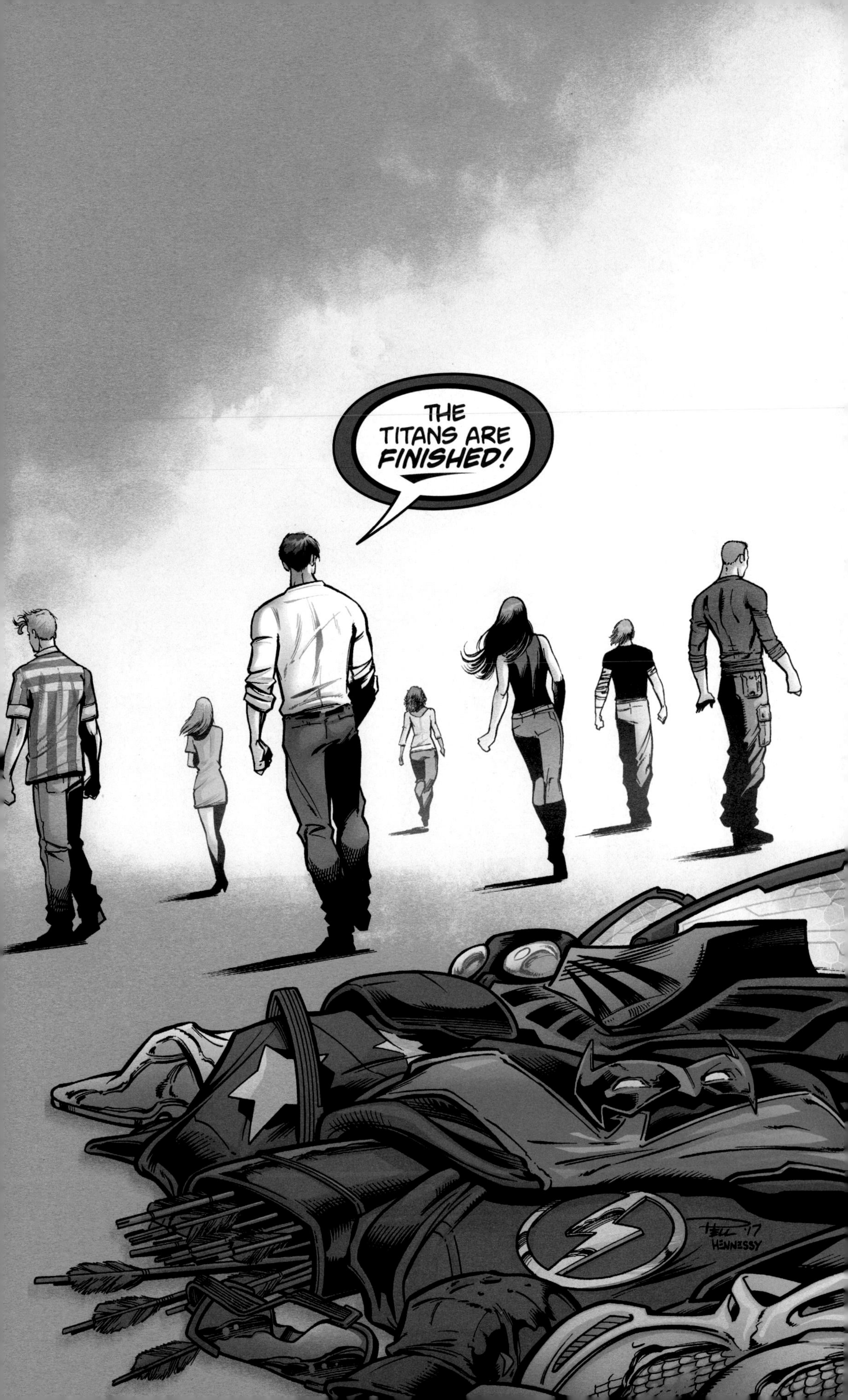
THE TITANS ARE FINISHED!

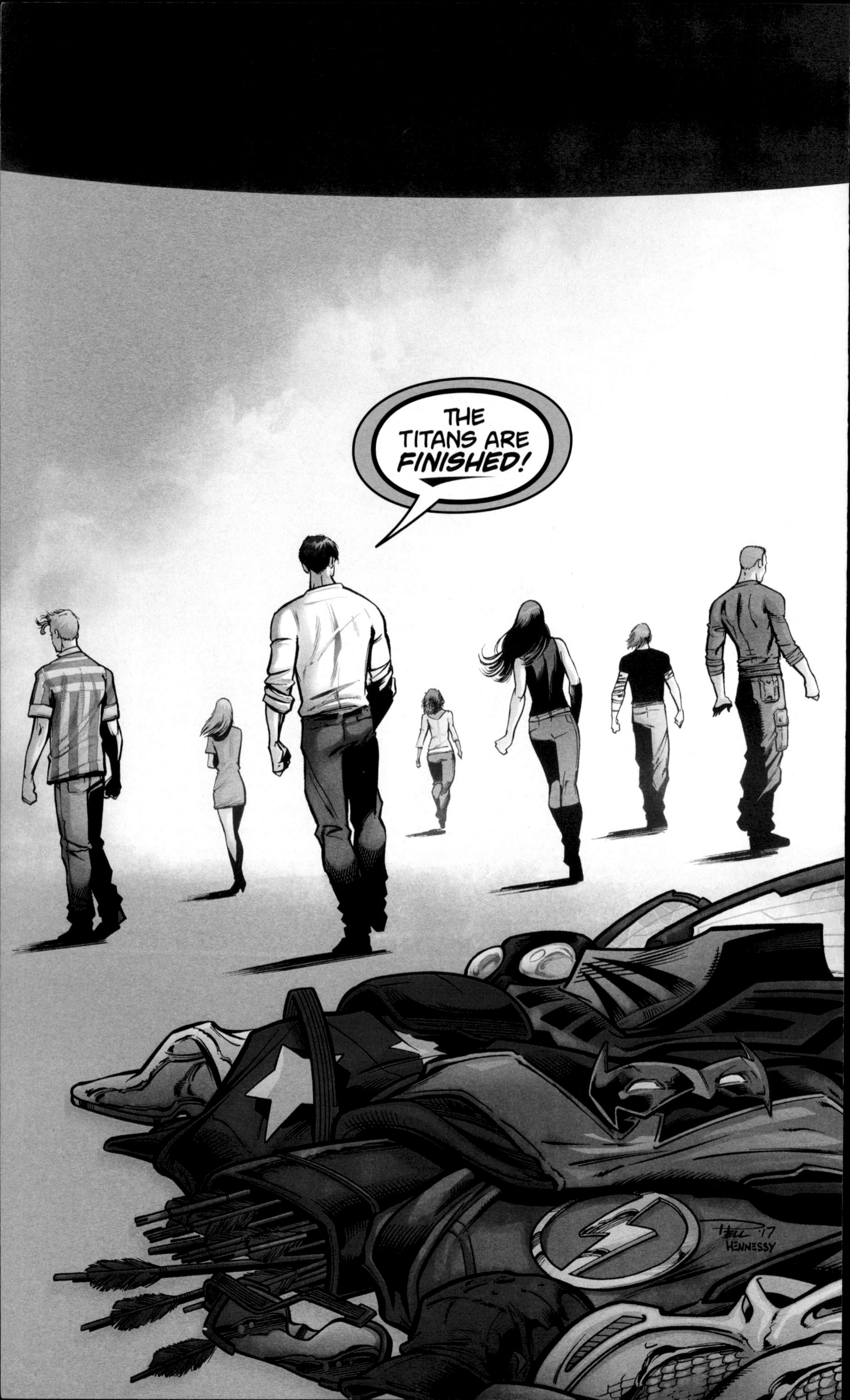
THE TITANS ARE FINISHED!
HENNESSY

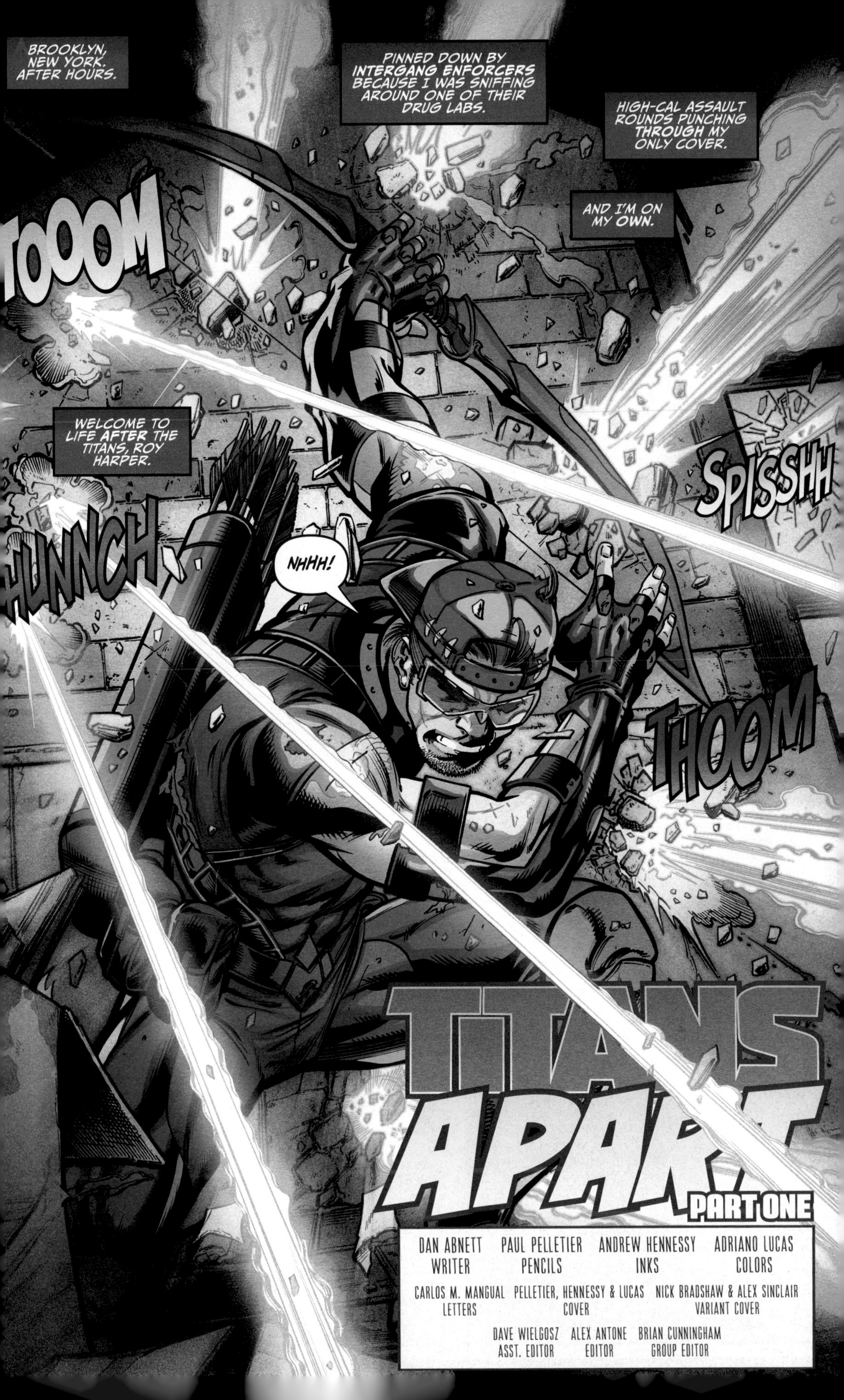
BROOKLYN, NEW YORK. AFTER HOURS.
PINNED DOWN BY INTERGANG ENFORCERS BECAUSE I WAS SNIFFING AROUND ONE OF THEIR DRUG LABS.
HIGH-CAL ASSAULT ROUNDS PUNCHING THROUGH MY ONLY COVER.
AND I'M ON MY OWN.
TOOOM
WELCOME TO LIFE AFTER THE TITANS, ROY HARPER.
SPISSHH
HUNNCH
NHHH!
THOOM
TITANS APART
PART ONE
DAN ABNETT WRITER
PAUL PELLETIER PENCILS
ANDREW HENNESSY INKS
ADRIANO LUCAS COLORS
CARLOS M. MANGUAL LETTERS
PELLETIER, HENNESSY & LUCAS COVER
NICK BRADSHAW & ALEX SINCLAIR VARIANT COVER
DAVE WIELGOSZ ASST. EDITOR
ALEX ANTONE EDITOR
BRIAN CUNNINGHAM GROUP EDITOR

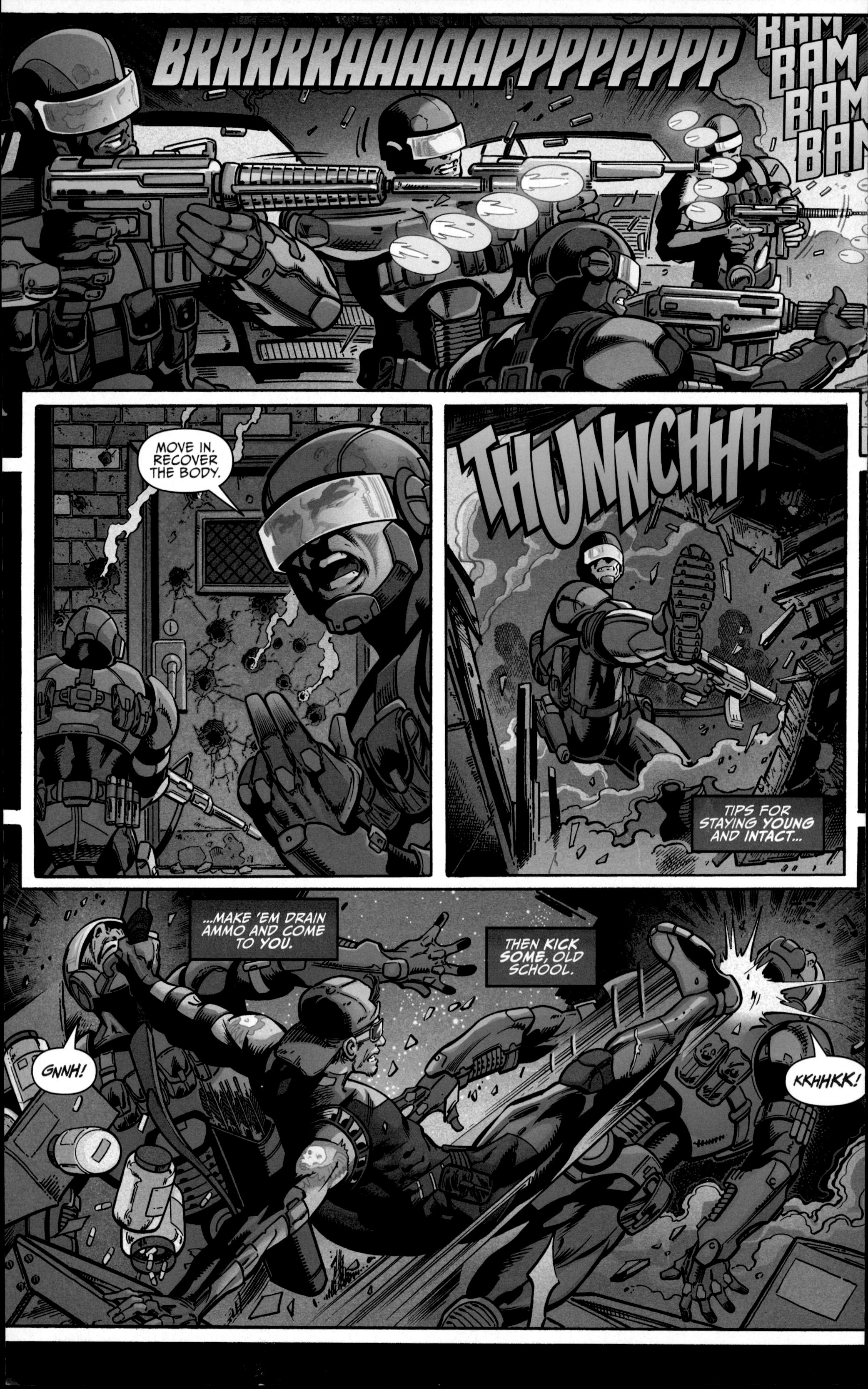
BRRRRRAAAAAAPPPPPPPP
BAM BAM BAM BAM
MOVE IN. RECOVER THE BODY.
THUNNCHHH
TIPS FOR STAYING YOUNG AND INTACT...
...MAKE 'EM DRAIN AMMO AND COME TO YOU.
THEN KICK SOME, OLD SCHOOL.
GNNH!
KKHHKK!

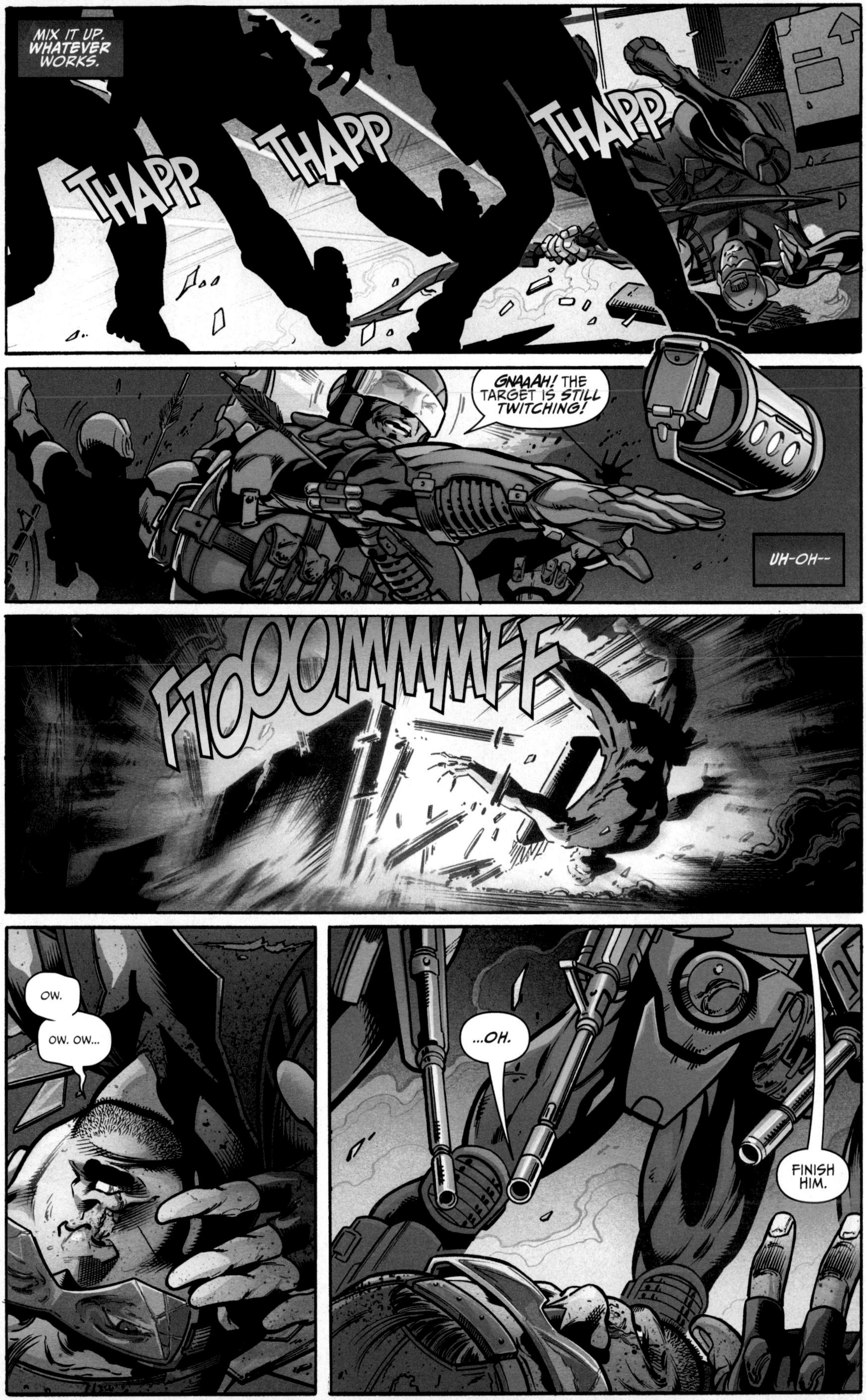
MIX IT UP. WHATEVER WORKS.
THAPP
THAPP
THAPP
GNAAAH! THE TARGET IS STILL TWITCHING!
UH-OH--
FTOOOMMMFF
OW.
OW. OW...
...OH.
FINISH HIM.

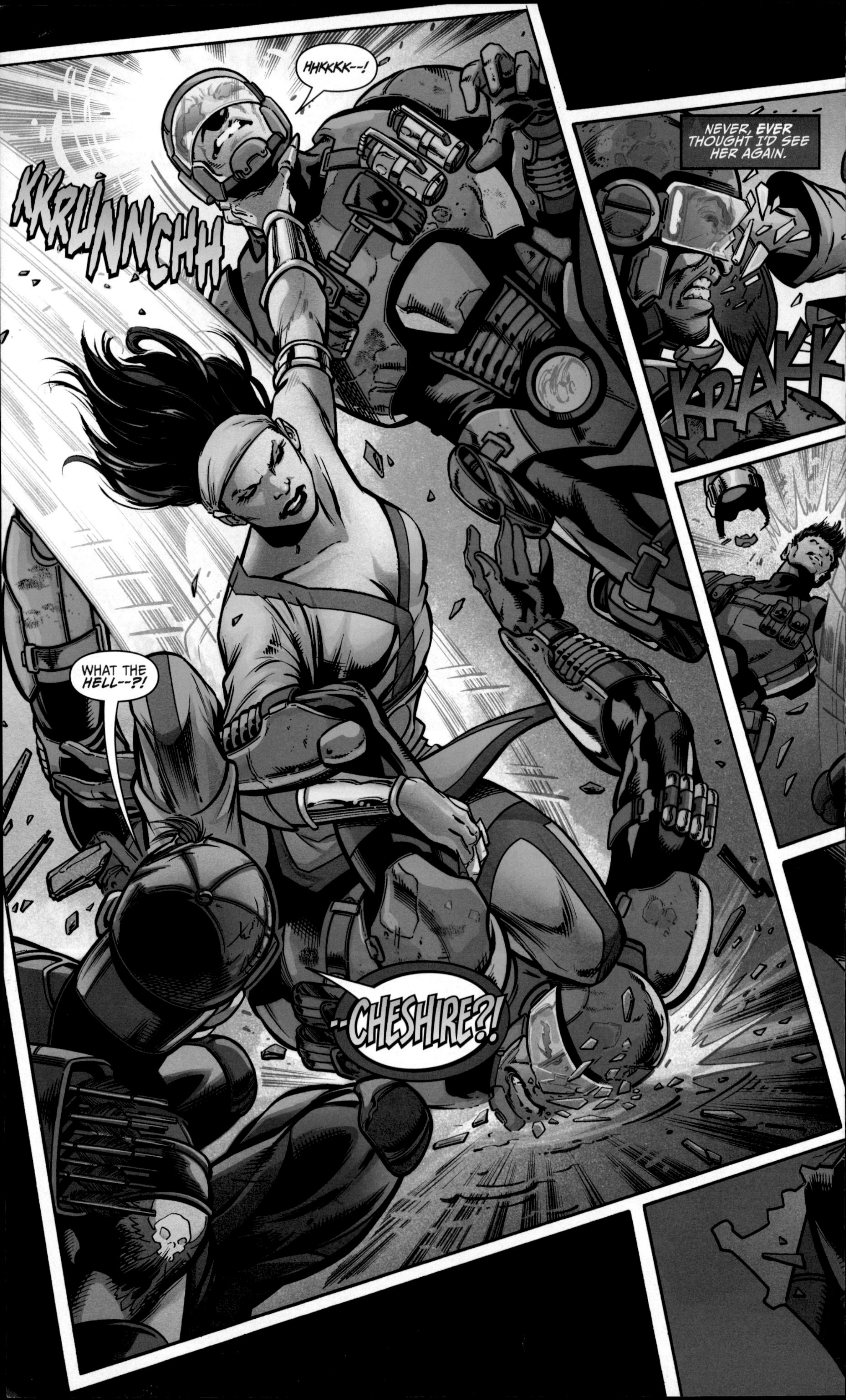

HHKKKK--!
KKRUNNCHH
WHAT THE HELL--?!
--CHESHIRE?!
NEVER, EVER THOUGHT I'D SEE HER AGAIN.
KRAKK

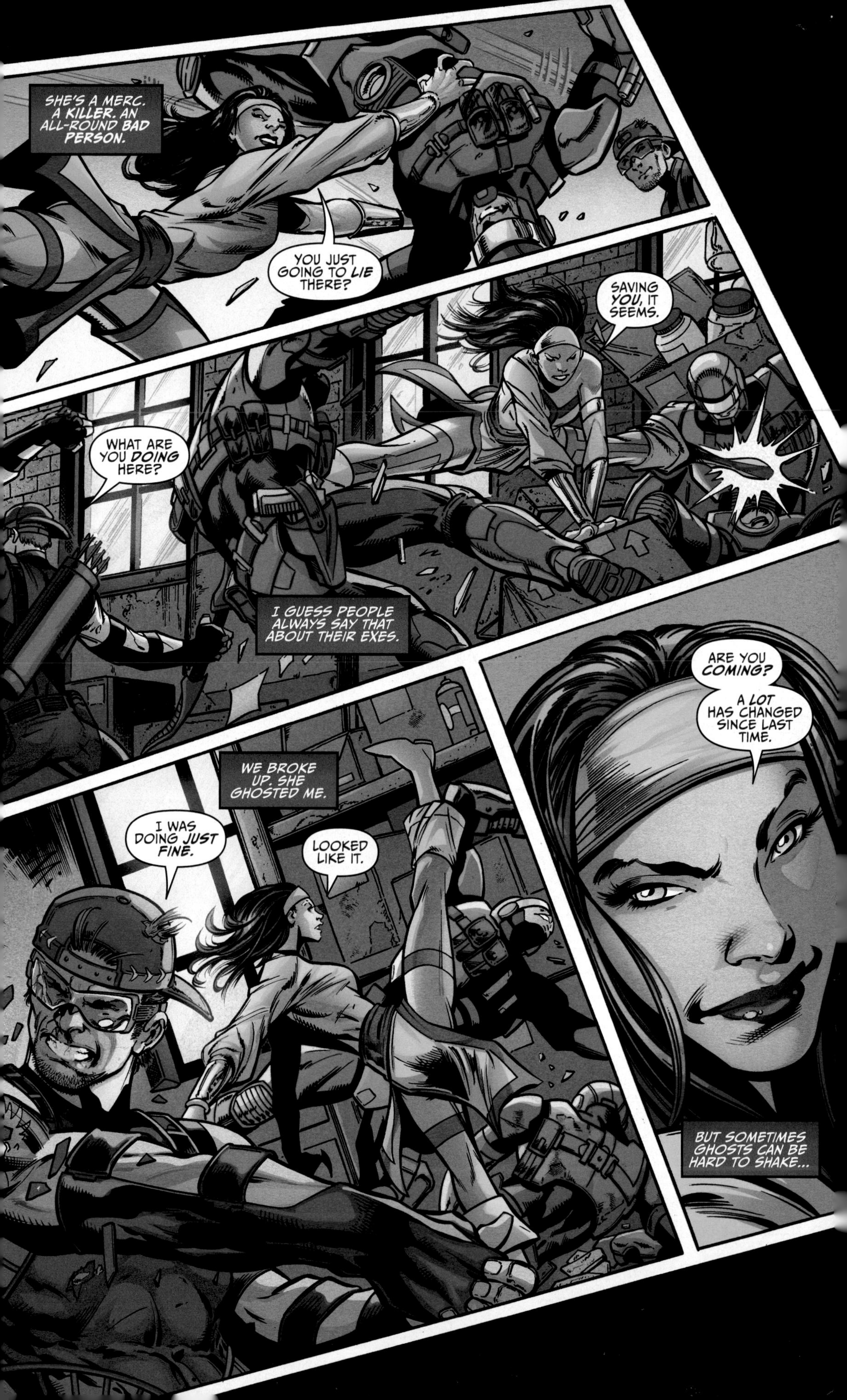
SHE'S A MERC. A KILLER. AN ALL-ROUND BAD PERSON.
YOU JUST GOING TO LIE THERE?
SAVING YOU, IT SEEMS.
WHAT ARE YOU DOING HERE?
I GUESS PEOPLE ALWAYS SAY THAT ABOUT THEIR EXES.
WE BROKE UP. SHE GHOSTED ME.
I WAS DOING JUST FINE.
LOOKED LIKE IT.
ARE YOU COMING?
A LOT HAS CHANGED SINCE LAST TIME.
BUT SOMETIMES GHOSTS CAN BE HARD TO SHAKE...

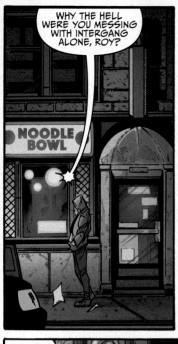

WHY THE HELL WERE YOU MESSING WITH INTERGANG ALONE, ROY?

NOODLE BOWL

I WAS GOING AFTER THE CARTEL SUPPLY LINE.

A *WAR ON DRUGS?*

CAN SOMEONE *LIKE* YOU GET THAT *CLOSE* AGAIN AND *NOT* FALL INTO THE PIT?

I KNOW WHAT I'M DOING.

BECAUSE I'VE *BEEN* THERE, I KNOW WHERE THE PIT IS.

BUT *ALONE?*

WHERE ARE YOUR *TITAN* FRIENDS?

...

ELSEWHERE.

JADE, WHY ARE YOU *REALLY* HERE?

SAME AS YOU. HITTING THE CARTELS.

A *CONSCIENCE,* SUDDENLY?

...A *PAYCHECK.*

I'VE BEEN HIRED BY A COLLECTIVE OF FAMILIES WHO LOST THEIR LOVED ONES TO DRUGS. TO OBTAIN JUSTICE THE *LAW* CAN'T PROVIDE.

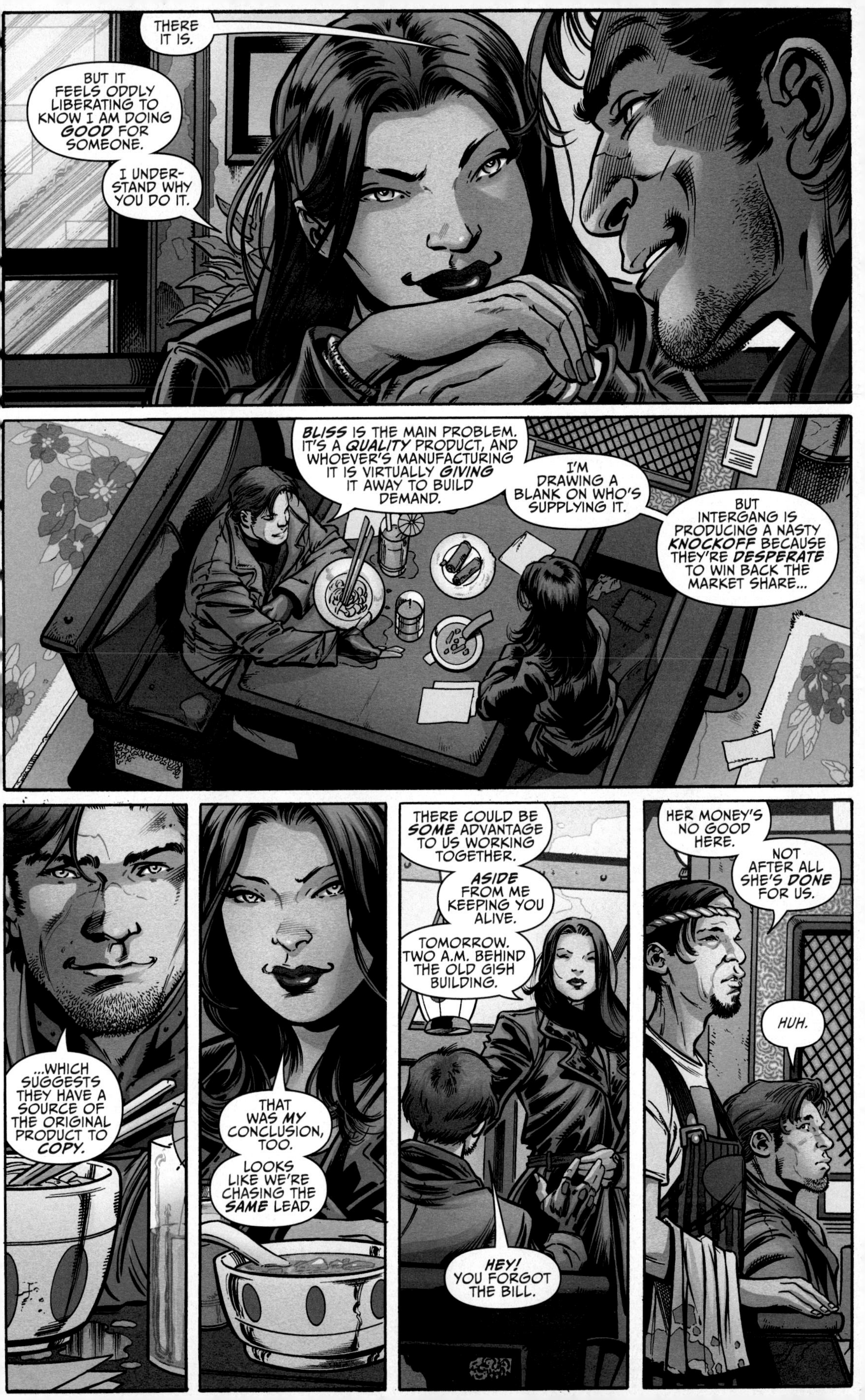
THERE IT IS.
BUT IT FEELS ODDLY LIBERATING TO KNOW I AM DOING GOOD FOR SOMEONE.
I UNDER-STAND WHY YOU DO IT.
BLISS IS THE MAIN PROBLEM. IT'S A QUALITY PRODUCT, AND WHOEVER'S MANUFACTURING IT IS VIRTUALLY GIVING IT AWAY TO BUILD DEMAND.
I'M DRAWING A BLANK ON WHO'S SUPPLYING IT.
BUT INTERGANG IS PRODUCING A NASTY KNOCKOFF BECAUSE THEY'RE DESPERATE TO WIN BACK THE MARKET SHARE...
...WHICH SUGGESTS THEY HAVE A SOURCE OF THE ORIGINAL PRODUCT TO COPY.
THAT WAS MY CONCLUSION, TOO.
LOOKS LIKE WE'RE CHASING THE SAME LEAD.
THERE COULD BE SOME ADVANTAGE TO US WORKING TOGETHER.
ASIDE FROM ME KEEPING YOU ALIVE.
TOMORROW. TWO A.M. BEHIND THE OLD GISH BUILDING.
HEY! YOU FORGOT THE BILL.
HER MONEY'S NO GOOD HERE.
NOT AFTER ALL SHE'S DONE FOR US.
HUH.

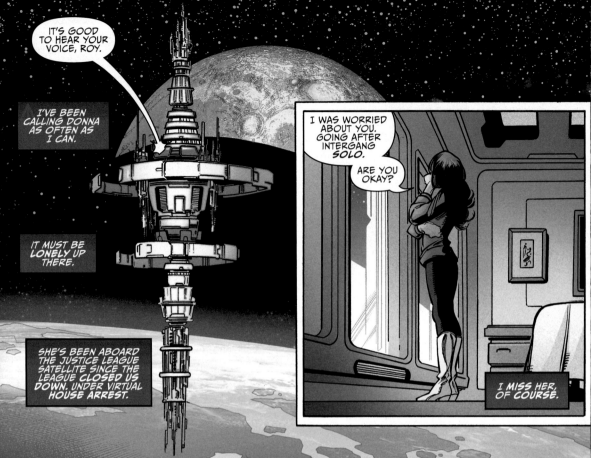

IT'S GOOD TO HEAR YOUR VOICE, ROY.

I'VE BEEN CALLING DONNA AS OFTEN AS I CAN.

IT MUST BE LONELY UP THERE.

SHE'S BEEN ABOARD THE JUSTICE LEAGUE SATELLITE SINCE THE LEAGUE *CLOSED US DOWN.* UNDER VIRTUAL HOUSE ARREST.

I WAS WORRIED ABOUT YOU. GOING AFTER INTERGANG *SOLO.*

ARE YOU OKAY?

I *MISS* HER, OF *COURSE.*

BUT I'M STARTING TO WONDER IF MY CALLS ARE JUST MAKING THINGS *WORSE.*

I'M *FINE,* DONNA.

I KNOW YOU'D BE DOWN HERE *HELPING* ME IF YOU COULD. THE LEAGUE JUST WANTS TO KNOW WHERE YOU *ARE,* IN CASE--

I TURN INTO TROIA?

THEY'RE WORRIED ABOUT *ALL* OF US GOING OFF THE RAILS, HARPER.

THAT'S WHY THEY *BENCHED* US!

SORRY.

I FEEL SO *USELESS* HERE.

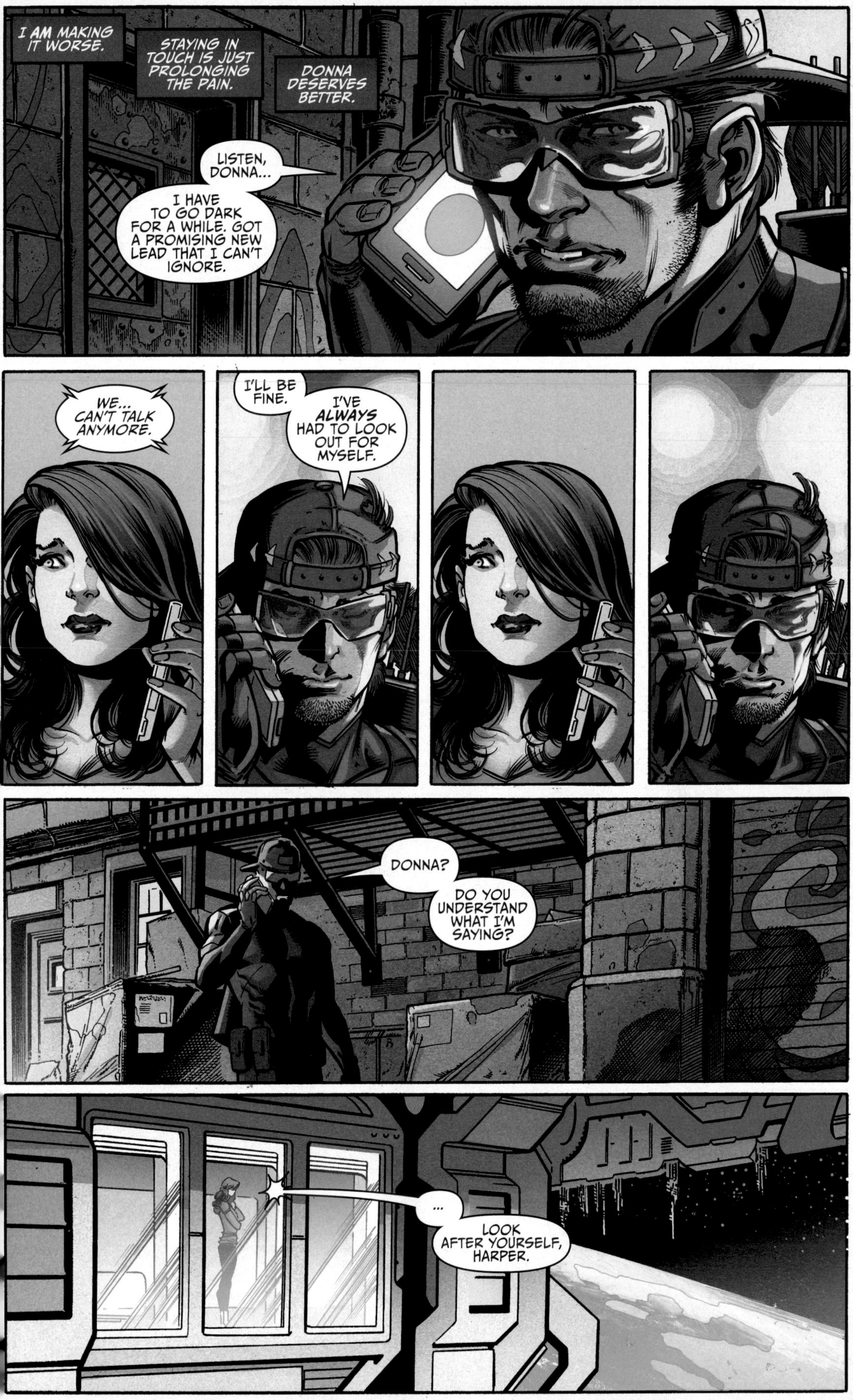

I AM MAKING IT WORSE.
STAYING IN TOUCH IS JUST PROLONGING THE PAIN.
DONNA DESERVES BETTER.
LISTEN, DONNA...
I HAVE TO GO DARK FOR A WHILE. GOT A PROMISING NEW LEAD THAT I CAN'T IGNORE.
WE... CAN'T TALK ANYMORE.
I'LL BE FINE.
I'VE ALWAYS HAD TO LOOK OUT FOR MYSELF.
DONNA?
DO YOU UNDERSTAND WHAT I'M SAYING?
...
LOOK AFTER YOURSELF, HARPER.

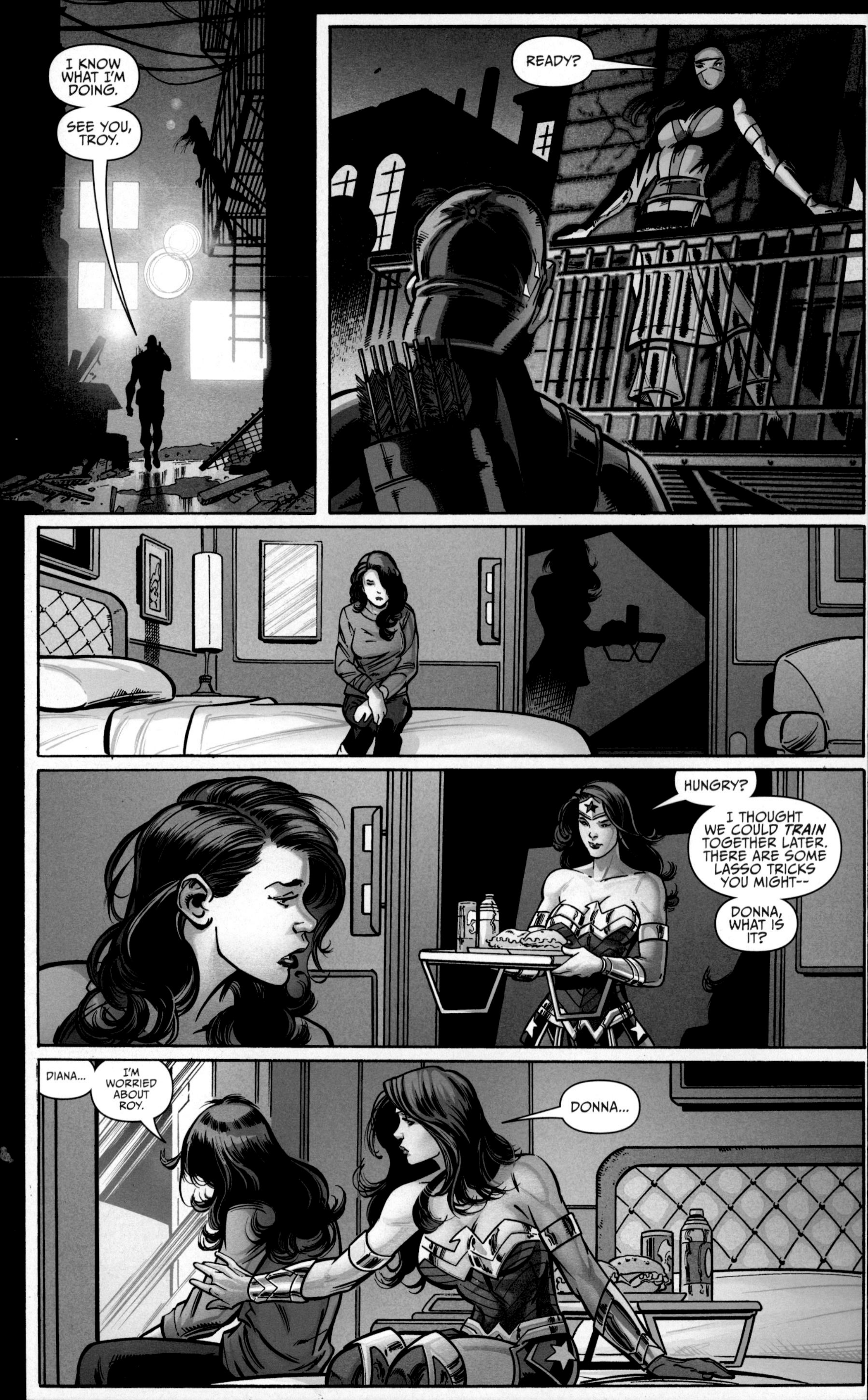
I KNOW WHAT I'M DOING.
SEE YOU, TROY.
READY?
HUNGRY?
I THOUGHT WE COULD *TRAIN* TOGETHER LATER. THERE ARE SOME LASSO TRICKS YOU MIGHT--
DONNA, WHAT IS IT?
DIANA...
I'M WORRIED ABOUT ROY.
DONNA...

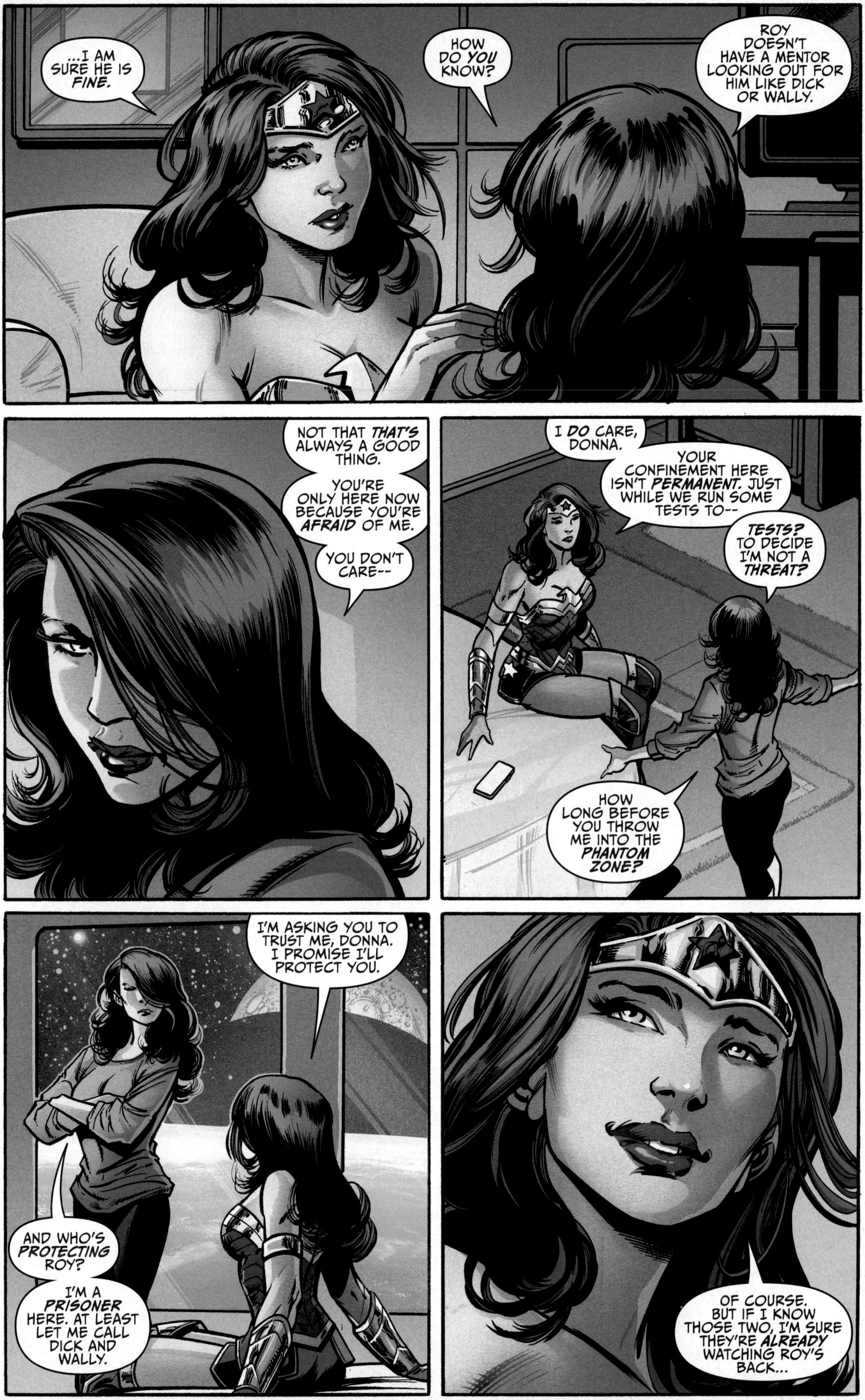
...I AM SURE HE IS *FINE.*
HOW DO *YOU* KNOW?
ROY DOESN'T HAVE A MENTOR LOOKING OUT FOR HIM LIKE DICK OR WALLY.
NOT THAT *THAT'S* ALWAYS A GOOD THING.
YOU'RE ONLY HERE NOW BECAUSE YOU'RE *AFRAID* OF ME.
YOU DON'T CARE--
I *DO* CARE, DONNA.
YOUR CONFINEMENT HERE ISN'T *PERMANENT.* JUST WHILE WE RUN SOME TESTS TO--
TESTS? TO DECIDE I'M NOT A *THREAT?*
HOW LONG BEFORE YOU THROW ME INTO THE *PHANTOM ZONE?*
I'M ASKING YOU TO TRUST ME, DONNA. I PROMISE I'LL PROTECT YOU.
AND WHO'S *PROTECTING* ROY?
I'M A *PRISONER* HERE. AT LEAST LET ME CALL DICK AND WALLY.
OF COURSE. BUT IF I KNOW THOSE TWO, I'M SURE THEY'RE *ALREADY* WATCHING ROY'S BACK...

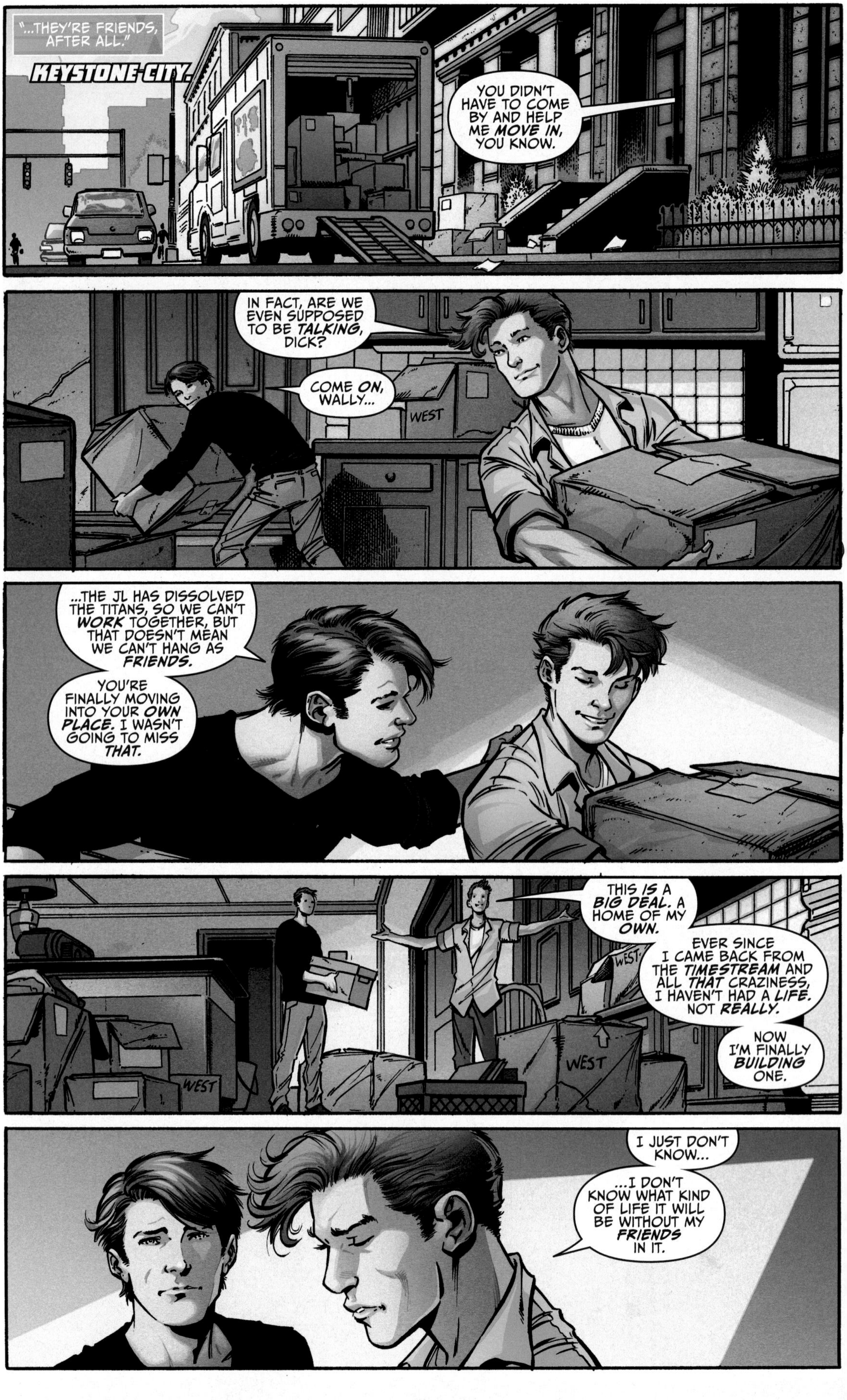
"...THEY'RE FRIENDS, AFTER ALL."
KEYSTONE CITY.
YOU DIDN'T HAVE TO COME BY AND HELP ME MOVE IN, YOU KNOW.
IN FACT, ARE WE EVEN SUPPOSED TO BE TALKING, DICK?
COME ON, WALLY...
WEST
...THE JL HAS DISSOLVED THE TITANS, SO WE CAN'T WORK TOGETHER, BUT THAT DOESN'T MEAN WE CAN'T HANG AS FRIENDS.
YOU'RE FINALLY MOVING INTO YOUR OWN PLACE. I WASN'T GOING TO MISS THAT.
THIS IS A BIG DEAL. A HOME OF MY OWN.
EVER SINCE I CAME BACK FROM THE TIMESTREAM AND ALL THAT CRAZINESS, I HAVEN'T HAD A LIFE. NOT REALLY.
NOW I'M FINALLY BUILDING ONE.
WEST
WEST
WEST
I JUST DON'T KNOW...
...I DON'T KNOW WHAT KIND OF LIFE IT WILL BE WITHOUT MY FRIENDS IN IT.

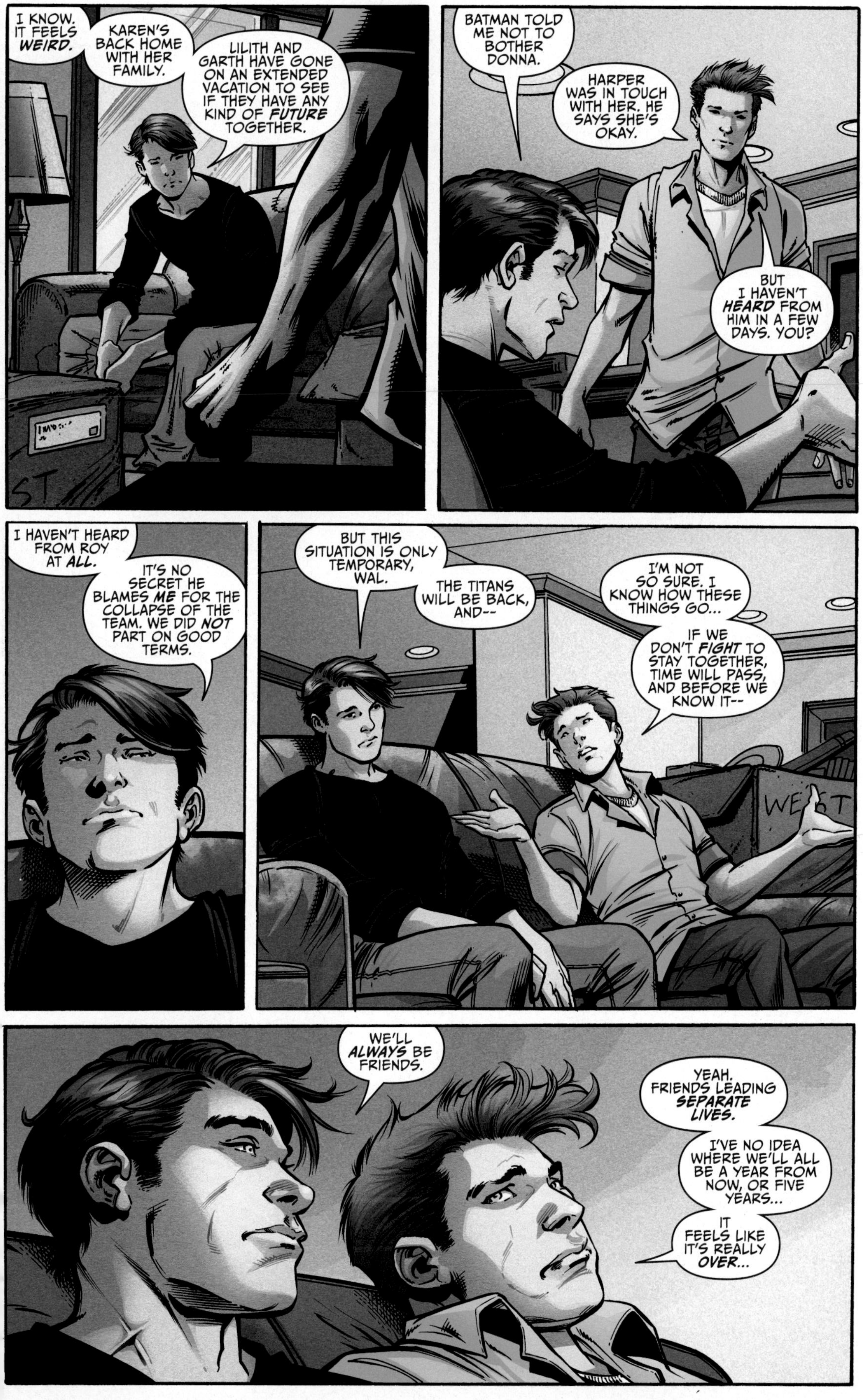
I KNOW. IT FEELS WEIRD.
KAREN'S BACK HOME WITH HER FAMILY.
LILITH AND GARTH HAVE GONE ON AN EXTENDED VACATION TO SEE IF THEY HAVE ANY KIND OF FUTURE TOGETHER.
BATMAN TOLD ME NOT TO BOTHER DONNA.
HARPER WAS IN TOUCH WITH HER. HE SAYS SHE'S OKAY.
BUT I HAVEN'T HEARD FROM HIM IN A FEW DAYS. YOU?
I HAVEN'T HEARD FROM ROY AT ALL.
IT'S NO SECRET HE BLAMES ME FOR THE COLLAPSE OF THE TEAM. WE DID NOT PART ON GOOD TERMS.
BUT THIS SITUATION IS ONLY TEMPORARY, WAL.
THE TITANS WILL BE BACK, AND--
I'M NOT SO SURE. I KNOW HOW THESE THINGS GO...
IF WE DON'T FIGHT TO STAY TOGETHER, TIME WILL PASS, AND BEFORE WE KNOW IT--
WE'LL ALWAYS BE FRIENDS.
YEAH. FRIENDS LEADING SEPARATE LIVES.
I'VE NO IDEA WHERE WE'LL ALL BE A YEAR FROM NOW, OR FIVE YEARS...
IT FEELS LIKE IT'S REALLY OVER...

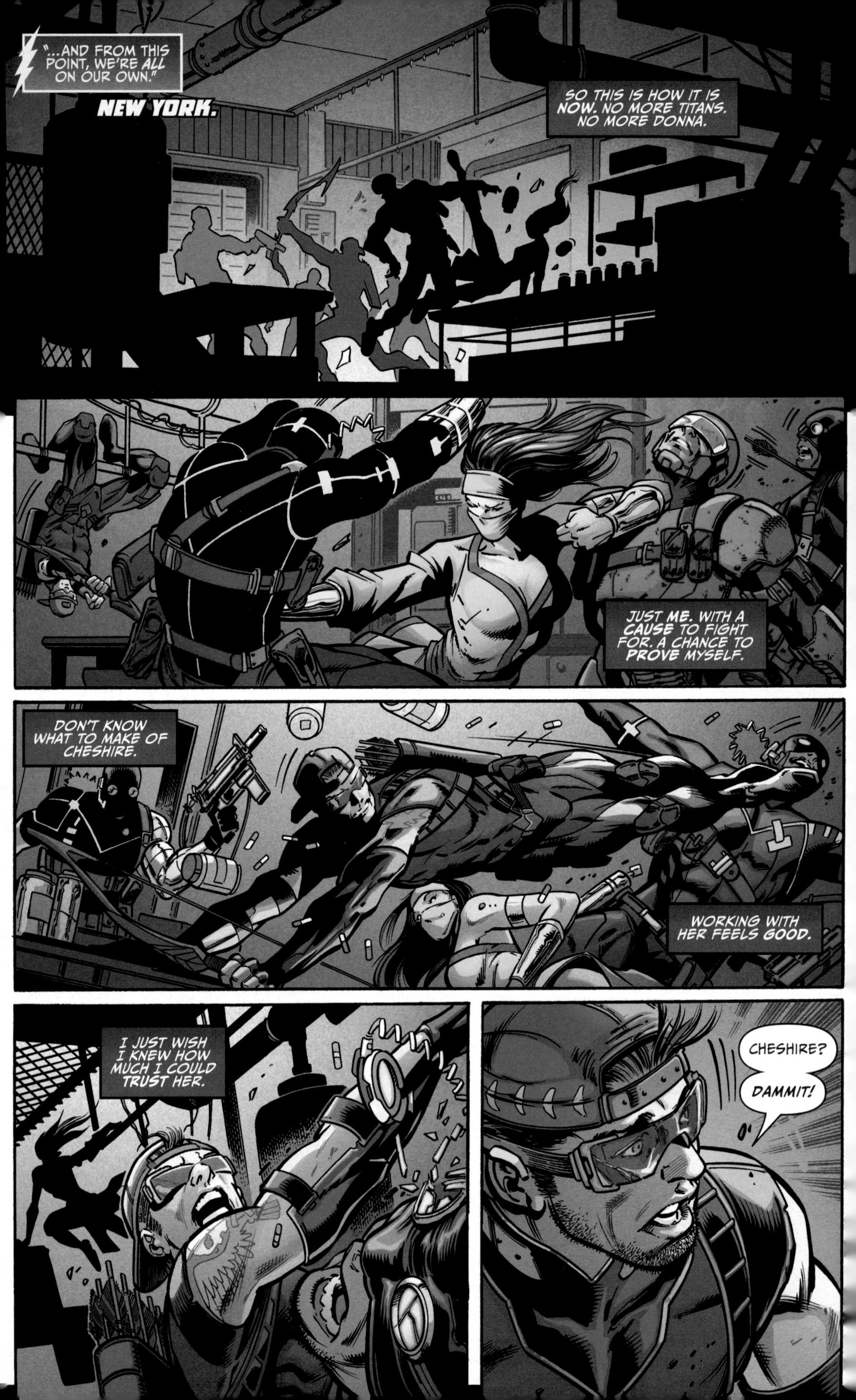
"...AND FROM THIS POINT, WE'RE ALL ON OUR OWN."
NEW YORK.
SO THIS IS HOW IT IS NOW. NO MORE TITANS. NO MORE DONNA.
JUST ME. WITH A CAUSE TO FIGHT FOR. A CHANCE TO PROVE MYSELF.
DON'T KNOW WHAT TO MAKE OF CHESHIRE.
WORKING WITH HER FEELS GOOD.
I JUST WISH I KNEW HOW MUCH I COULD TRUST HER.
CHESHIRE?
DAMMIT!

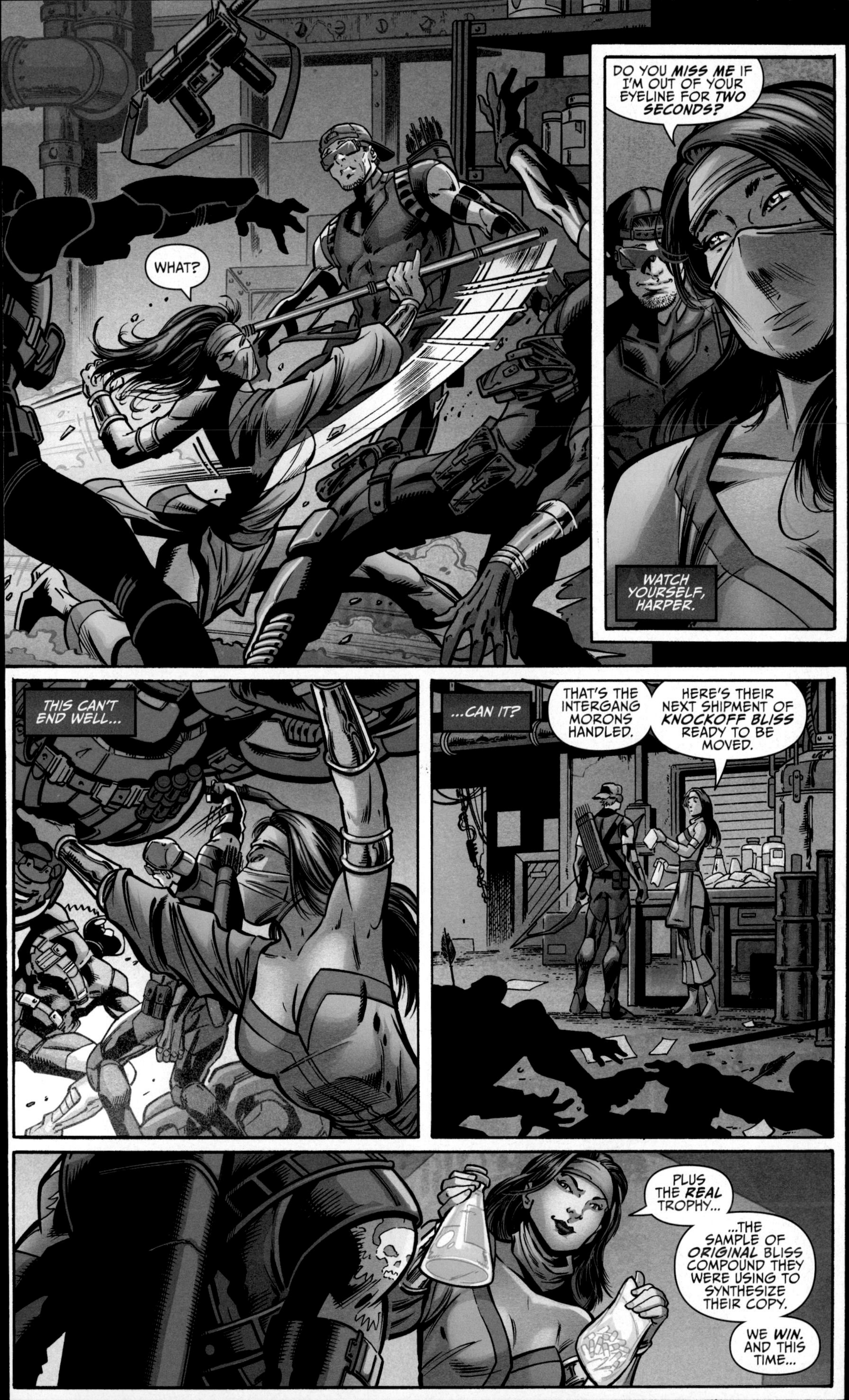
WHAT?
DO YOU MISS ME IF I'M OUT OF YOUR EYELINE FOR TWO SECONDS?
WATCH YOURSELF, HARPER.
THIS CAN'T END WELL...
...CAN IT?
THAT'S THE INTERGANG MORONS HANDLED.
HERE'S THEIR NEXT SHIPMENT OF KNOCKOFF BLISS READY TO BE MOVED.
PLUS THE REAL TROPHY...
...THE SAMPLE OF ORIGINAL BLISS COMPOUND THEY WERE USING TO SYNTHESIZE THEIR COPY.
WE WIN. AND THIS TIME...

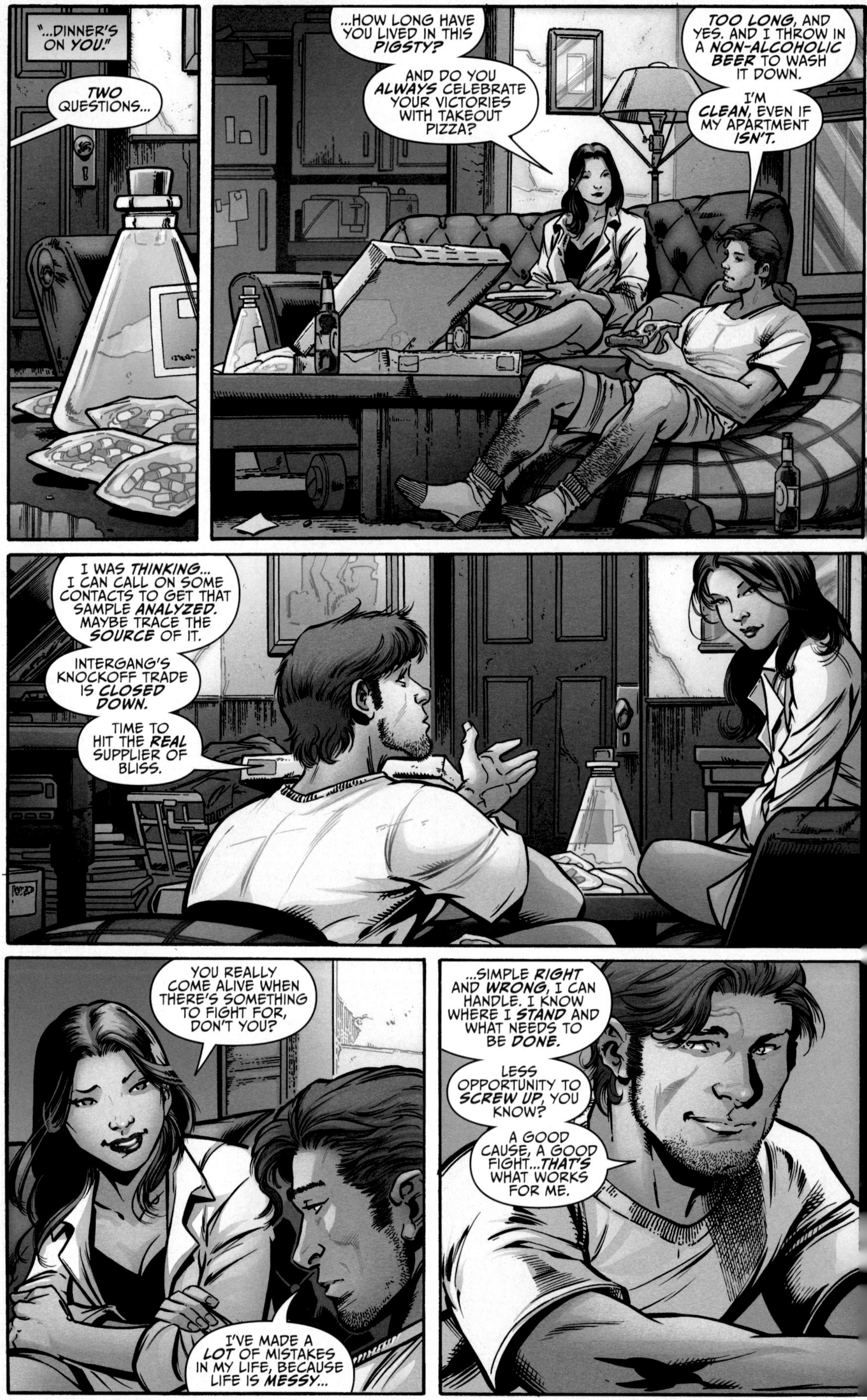

"...DINNER'S ON YOU."
TWO QUESTIONS...
...HOW LONG HAVE YOU LIVED IN THIS PIGSTY?
AND DO YOU ALWAYS CELEBRATE YOUR VICTORIES WITH TAKEOUT PIZZA?
TOO LONG, AND YES. AND I THROW IN A NON-ALCOHOLIC BEER TO WASH IT DOWN.
I'M CLEAN, EVEN IF MY APARTMENT ISN'T.
I WAS THINKING... I CAN CALL ON SOME CONTACTS TO GET THAT SAMPLE ANALYZED. MAYBE TRACE THE SOURCE OF IT.
INTERGANG'S KNOCKOFF TRADE IS CLOSED DOWN.
TIME TO HIT THE REAL SUPPLIER OF BLISS.
YOU REALLY COME ALIVE WHEN THERE'S SOMETHING TO FIGHT FOR, DON'T YOU?
I'VE MADE A LOT OF MISTAKES IN MY LIFE, BECAUSE LIFE IS MESSY...
...SIMPLE RIGHT AND WRONG, I CAN HANDLE. I KNOW WHERE I STAND AND WHAT NEEDS TO BE DONE.
LESS OPPORTUNITY TO SCREW UP, YOU KNOW?
A GOOD CAUSE, A GOOD FIGHT...THAT'S WHAT WORKS FOR ME.

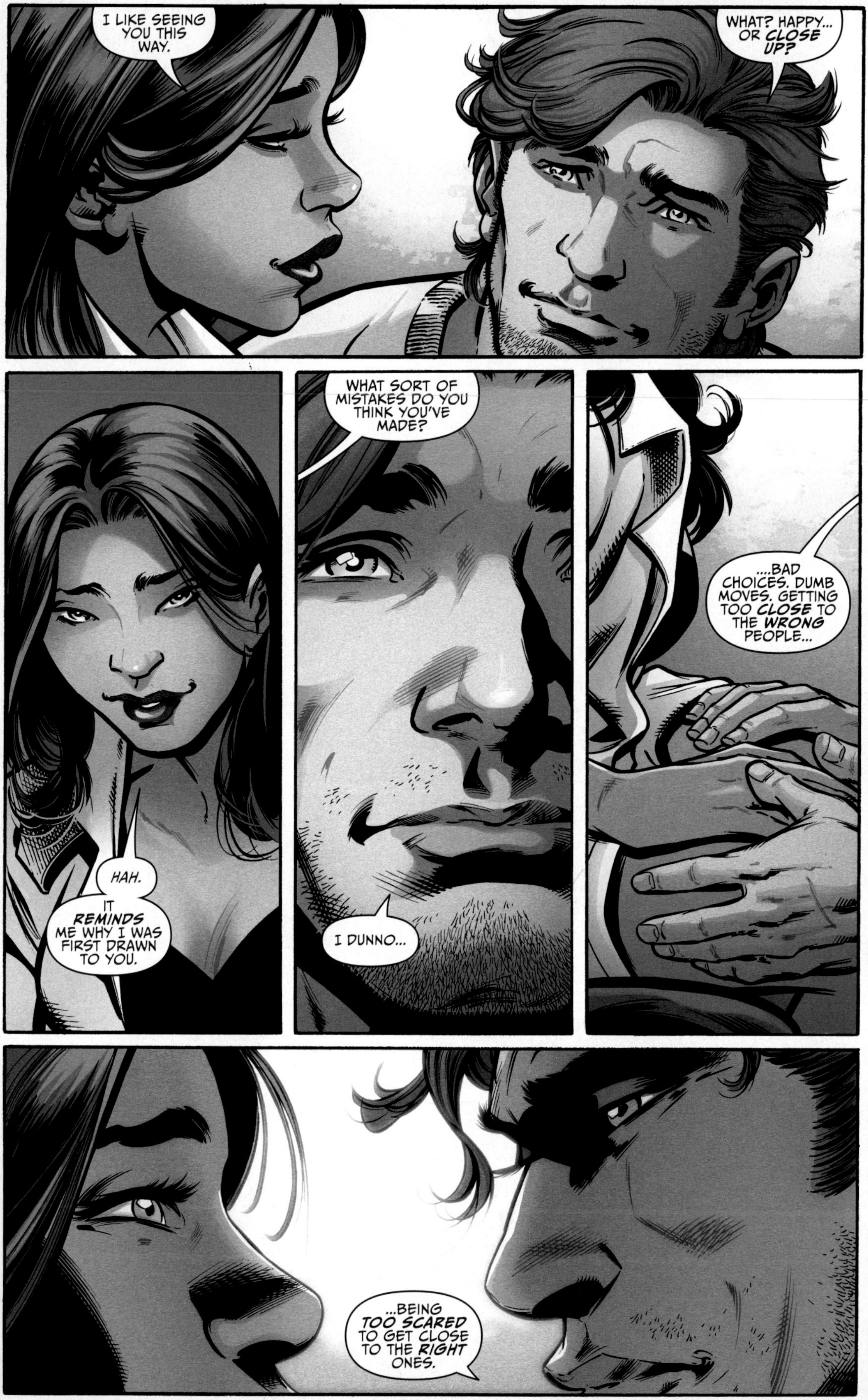
I LIKE SEEING YOU THIS WAY.
WHAT? HAPPY... OR CLOSE UP?
HAH.
IT REMINDS ME WHY I WAS FIRST DRAWN TO YOU.
WHAT SORT OF MISTAKES DO YOU THINK YOU'VE MADE?
I DUNNO...
....BAD CHOICES. DUMB MOVES. GETTING TOO CLOSE TO THE WRONG PEOPLE...
...BEING TOO SCARED TO GET CLOSE TO THE RIGHT ONES.

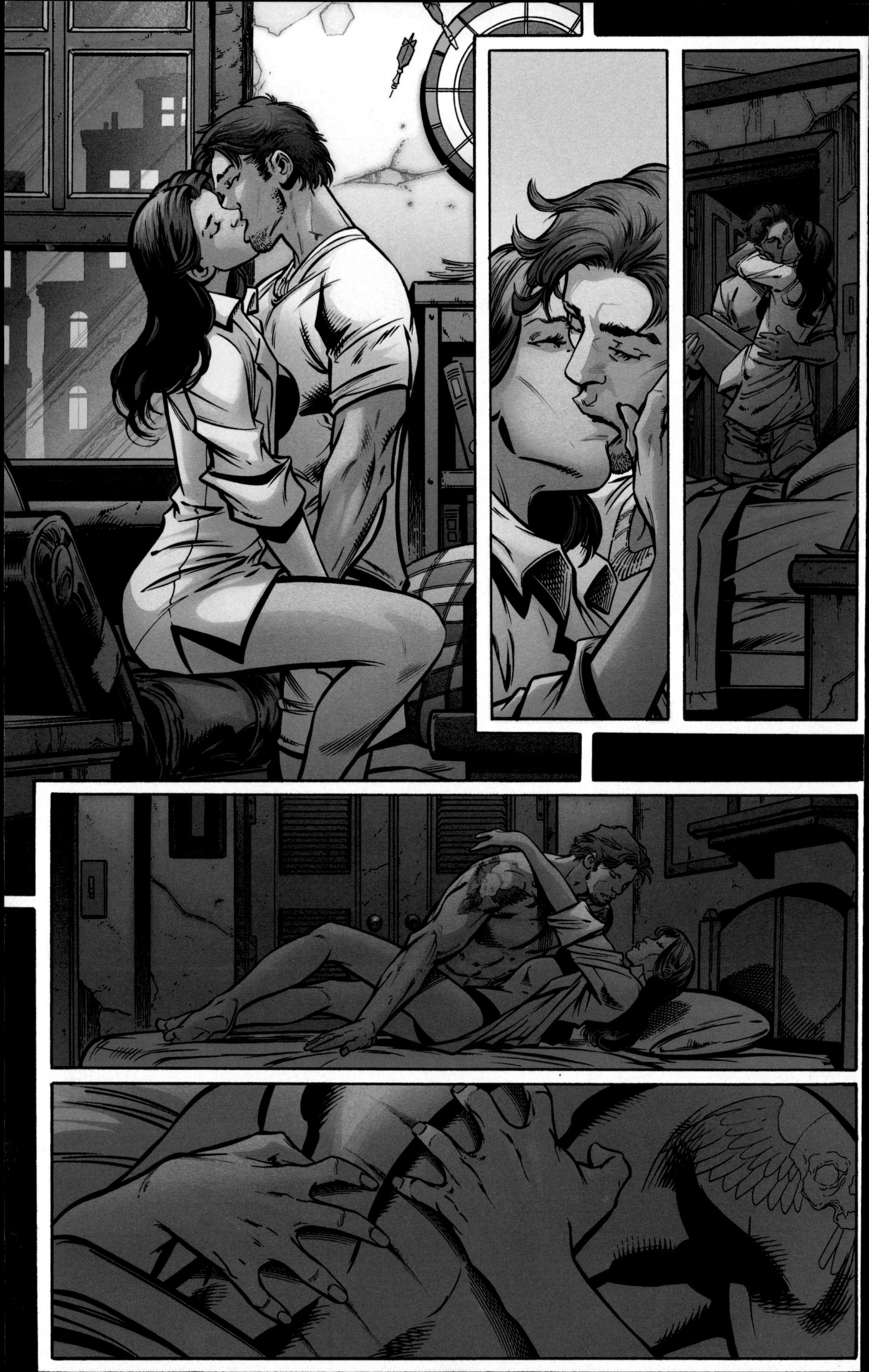

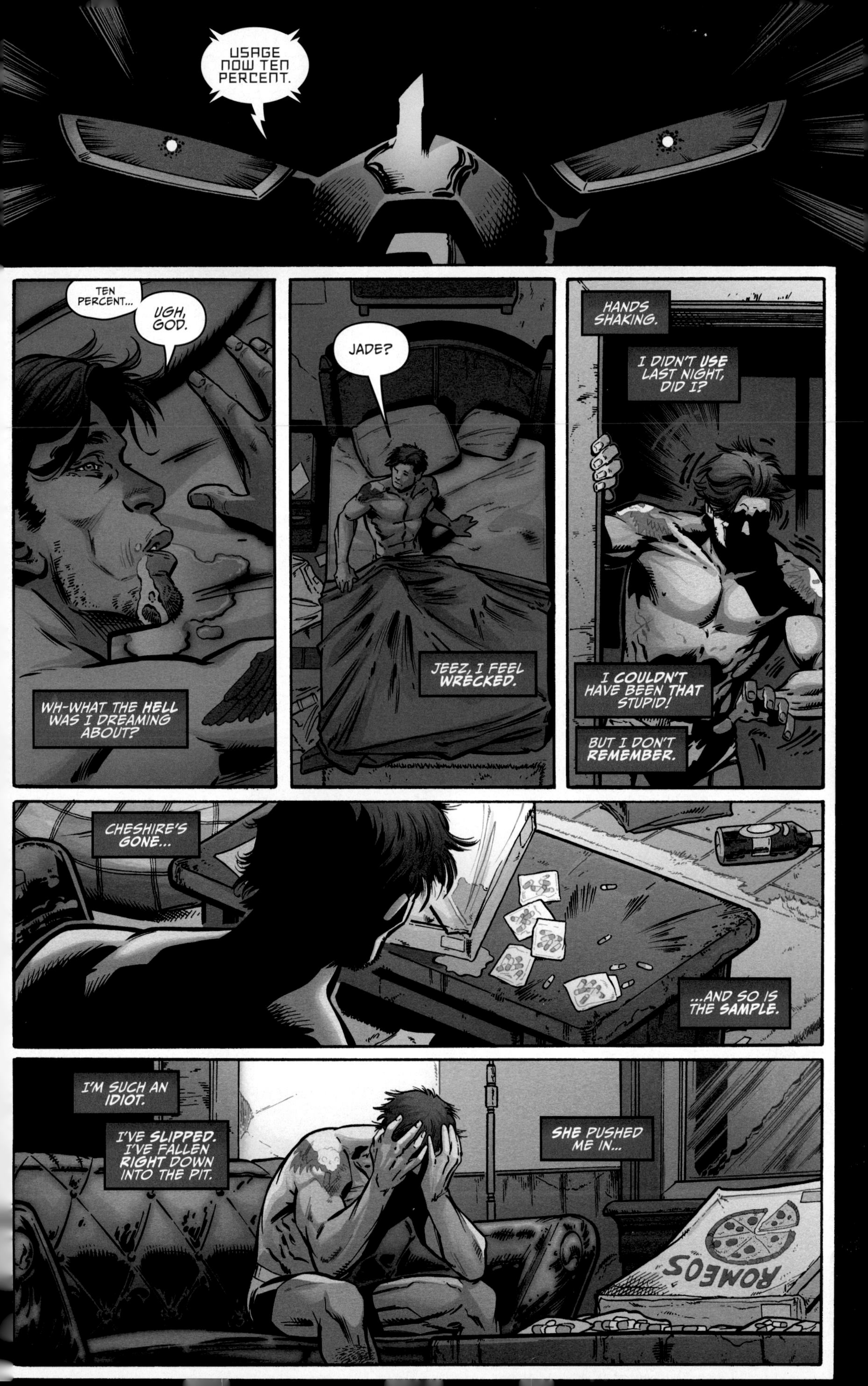
USAGE NOW TEN PERCENT.
TEN PERCENT...
UGH, GOD.
WH-WHAT THE HELL WAS I DREAMING ABOUT?
JADE?
JEEZ, I FEEL WRECKED.
HANDS SHAKING.
I DIDN'T USE LAST NIGHT, DID I?
I COULDN'T HAVE BEEN THAT STUPID!
BUT I DON'T REMEMBER.
CHESHIRE'S GONE...
...AND SO IS THE SAMPLE.
I'M SUCH AN IDIOT.
I'VE SLIPPED. I'VE FALLEN RIGHT DOWN INTO THE PIT.
SHE PUSHED ME IN...
ROMEOS

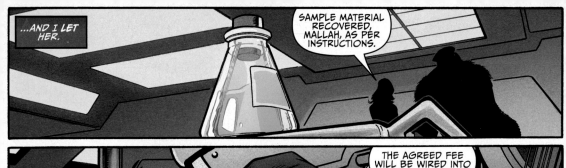

...AND I LET HER.

SAMPLE MATERIAL RECOVERED, MALLAH, AS PER INSTRUCTIONS.

THE AGREED FEE WILL BE WIRED INTO YOUR ACCOUNT, CHESHIRE.

YOU HEAR THAT, *BRAIN*, MY OLD SO-AND-SO? THE MISSING SAMPLE HAS BEEN RETURNED SAFE AND S--

I HEARD, MALLAH. I HEAR *EVERY-THING*.

WERE THERE ANY COMPLICA-TIONS?

JUST A LITTLE PIECE OF THE *PAST* I HAD TO DEAL WITH...

...BUT I'M *NOT* ONE FOR SENTIMENT.

THAT *PAST* WON'T TROUBLE US AGAIN. IT'S TAKEN A LITTLE *TRIP*, AND IT WON'T BE BACK.

MAKE SURE OF IT.

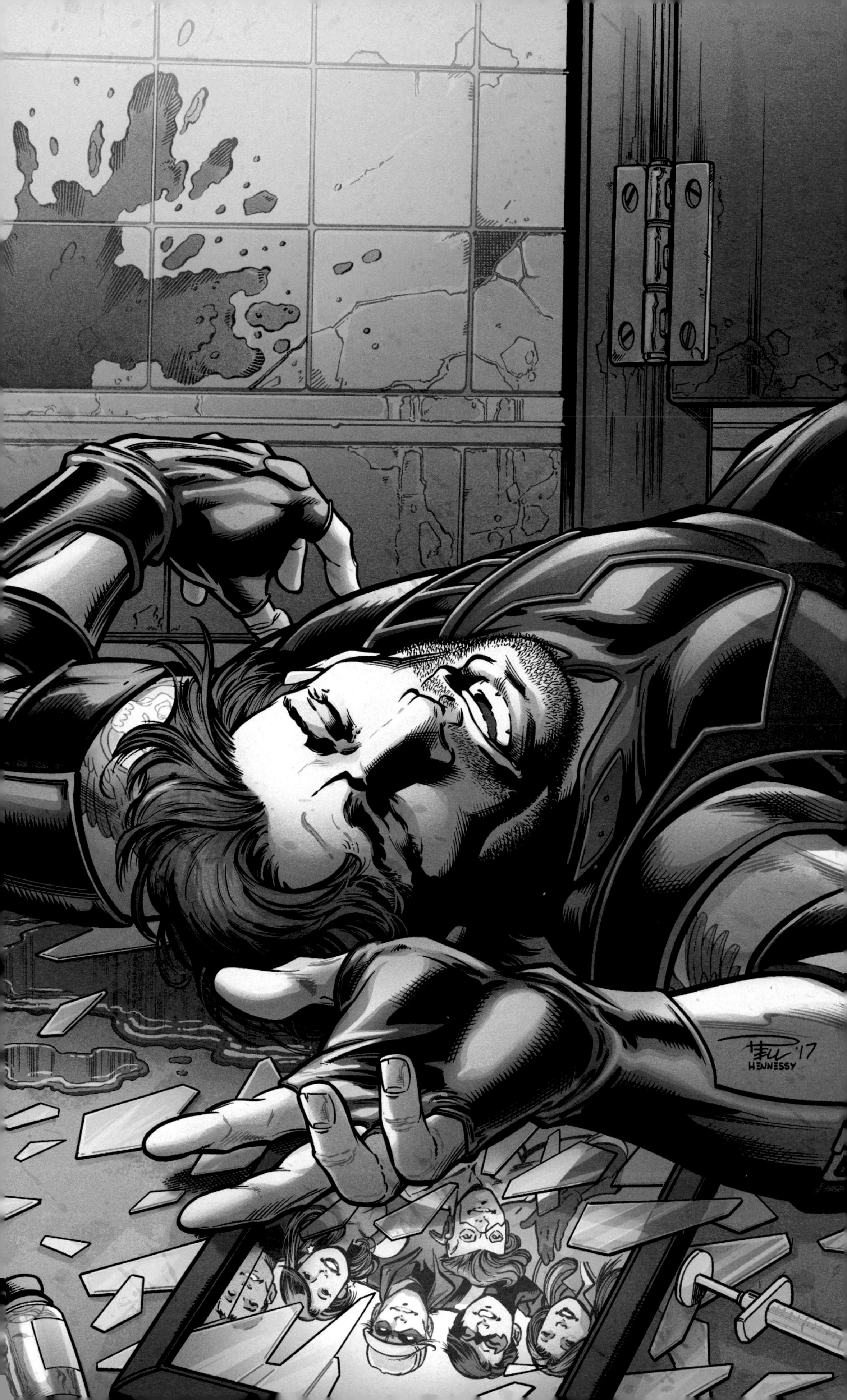
'17
HENNESSY

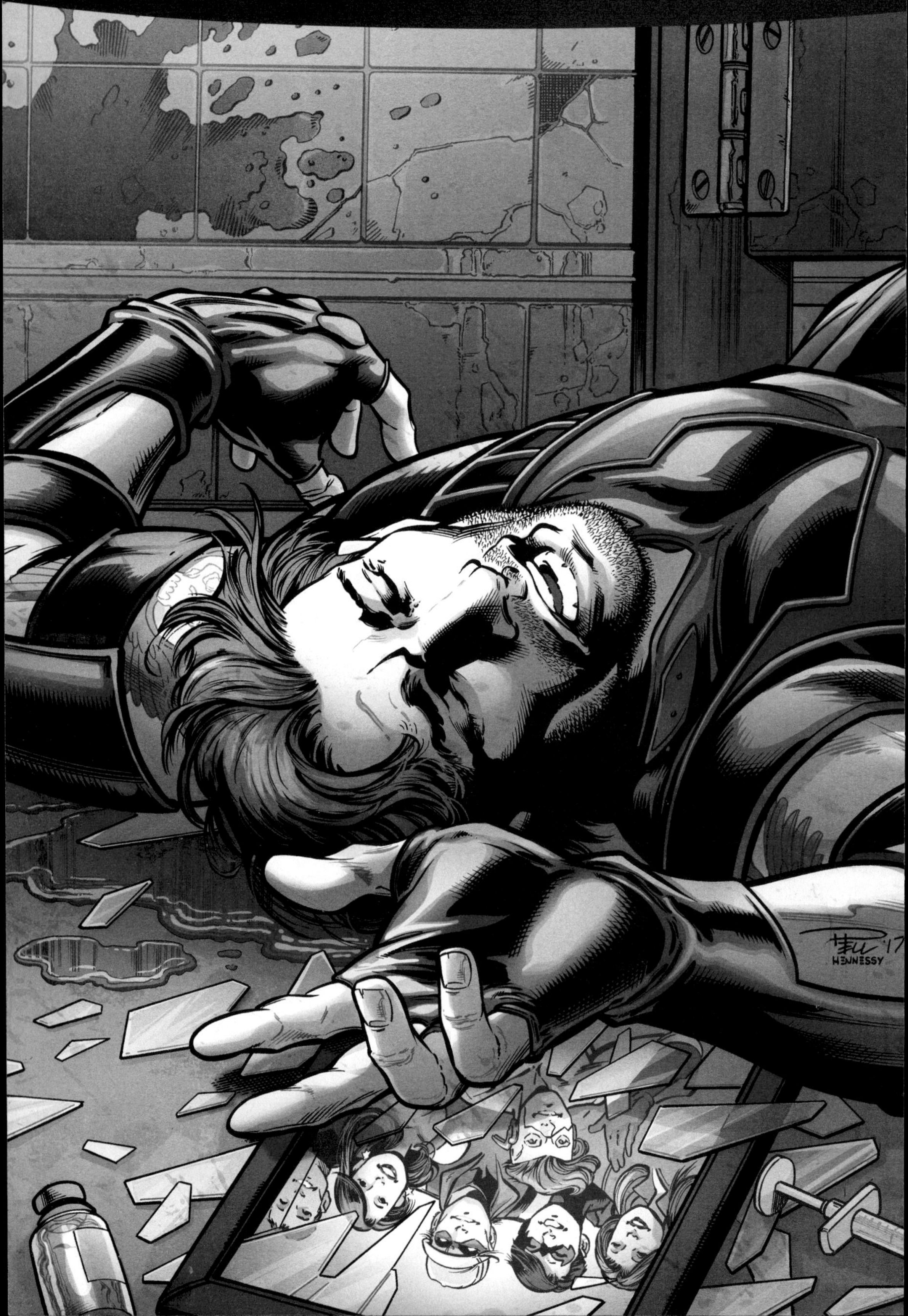
HENNESSY

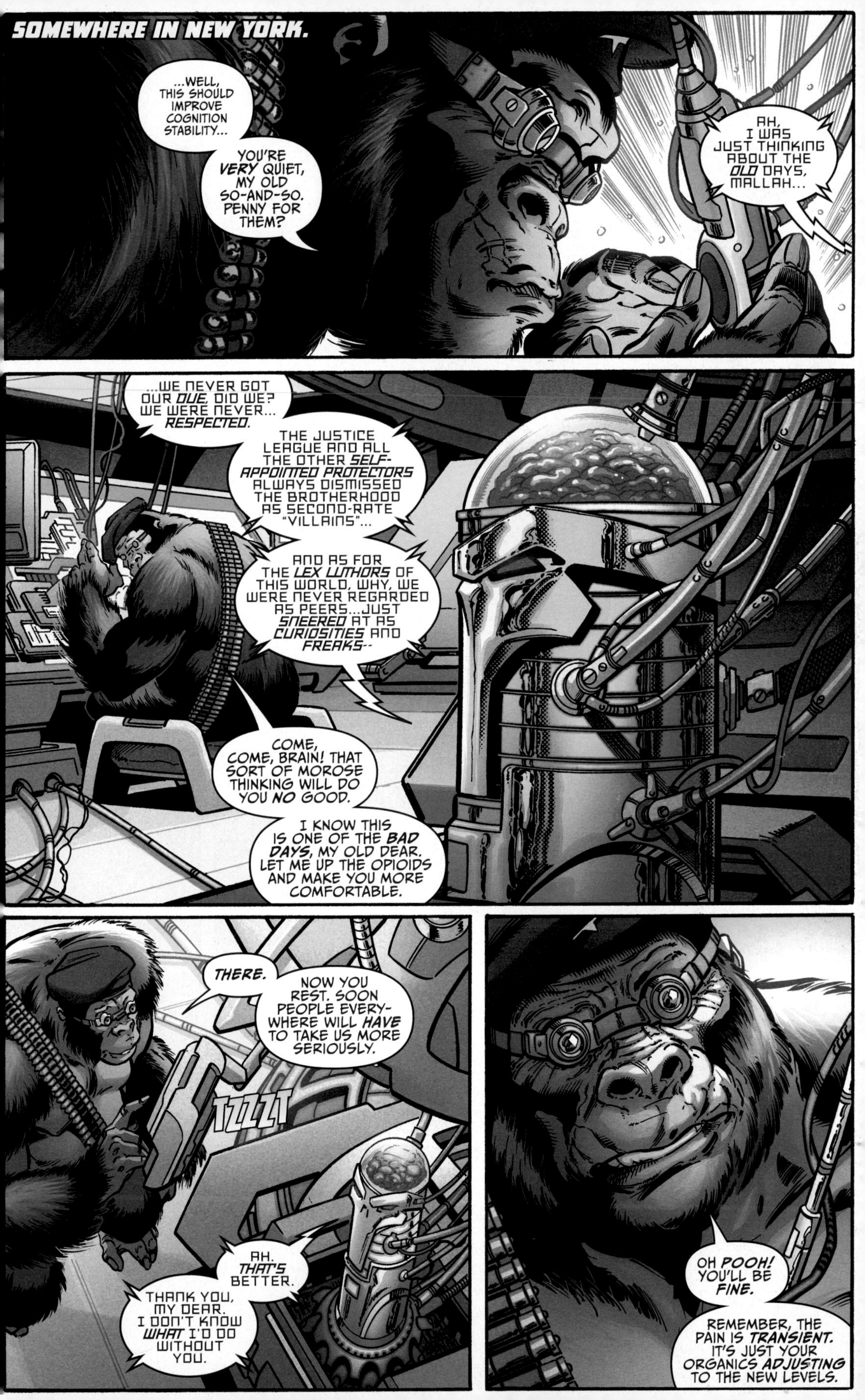
SOMEWHERE IN NEW YORK.
...WELL, THIS SHOULD IMPROVE COGNITION STABILITY...
YOU'RE VERY QUIET, MY OLD SO-AND-SO. PENNY FOR THEM?
AH, I WAS JUST THINKING ABOUT THE OLD DAYS, MALLAH...
...WE NEVER GOT OUR DUE, DID WE? WE WERE NEVER... RESPECTED.
THE JUSTICE LEAGUE AND ALL THE OTHER SELF-APPOINTED PROTECTORS ALWAYS DISMISSED THE BROTHERHOOD AS SECOND-RATE "VILLAINS"...
AND AS FOR THE LEX LUTHORS OF THIS WORLD, WHY, WE WERE NEVER REGARDED AS PEERS...JUST SNEERED AT AS CURIOSITIES AND FREAKS--
COME, COME, BRAIN! THAT SORT OF MOROSE THINKING WILL DO YOU NO GOOD.
I KNOW THIS IS ONE OF THE BAD DAYS, MY OLD DEAR. LET ME UP THE OPIOIDS AND MAKE YOU MORE COMFORTABLE.
THERE.
NOW YOU REST. SOON PEOPLE EVERY-WHERE WILL HAVE TO TAKE US MORE SERIOUSLY.
TZZZT
AH. THAT'S BETTER.
THANK YOU, MY DEAR. I DON'T KNOW WHAT I'D DO WITHOUT YOU.
OH POOH! YOU'LL BE FINE.
REMEMBER, THE PAIN IS TRANSIENT. IT'S JUST YOUR ORGANICS ADJUSTING TO THE NEW LEVELS.

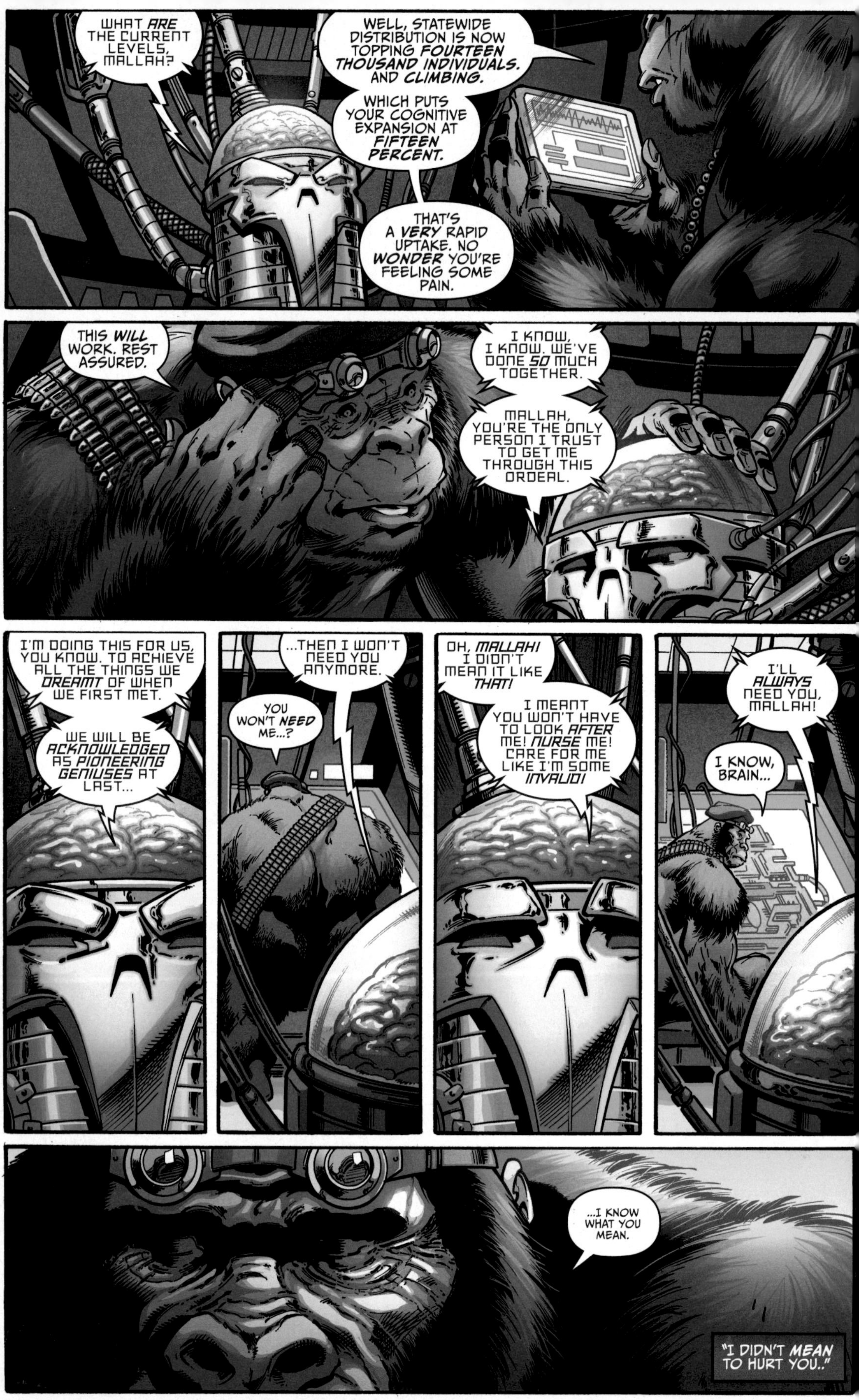
WHAT ARE THE CURRENT LEVELS, MALLAH?
WELL, STATEWIDE DISTRIBUTION IS NOW TOPPING FOURTEEN THOUSAND INDIVIDUALS. AND CLIMBING.
WHICH PUTS YOUR COGNITIVE EXPANSION AT FIFTEEN PERCENT.
THAT'S A VERY RAPID UPTAKE. NO WONDER YOU'RE FEELING SOME PAIN.
THIS WILL WORK. REST ASSURED.
I KNOW, I KNOW. WE'VE DONE SO MUCH TOGETHER.
MALLAH, YOU'RE THE ONLY PERSON I TRUST TO GET ME THROUGH THIS ORDEAL.
I'M DOING THIS FOR US, YOU KNOW. TO ACHIEVE ALL THE THINGS WE DREAMT OF WHEN WE FIRST MET.
WE WILL BE ACKNOWLEDGED AS PIONEERING GENIUSES AT LAST...
...THEN I WON'T NEED YOU ANYMORE.
YOU WON'T NEED ME...?
OH, MALLAH! I DIDN'T MEAN IT LIKE THAT!
I MEANT YOU WON'T HAVE TO LOOK AFTER ME! NURSE ME! CARE FOR ME LIKE I'M SOME INVALID!
I'LL ALWAYS NEED YOU, MALLAH!
I KNOW, BRAIN...
...I KNOW WHAT YOU MEAN.
"I DIDN'T MEAN TO HURT YOU.."

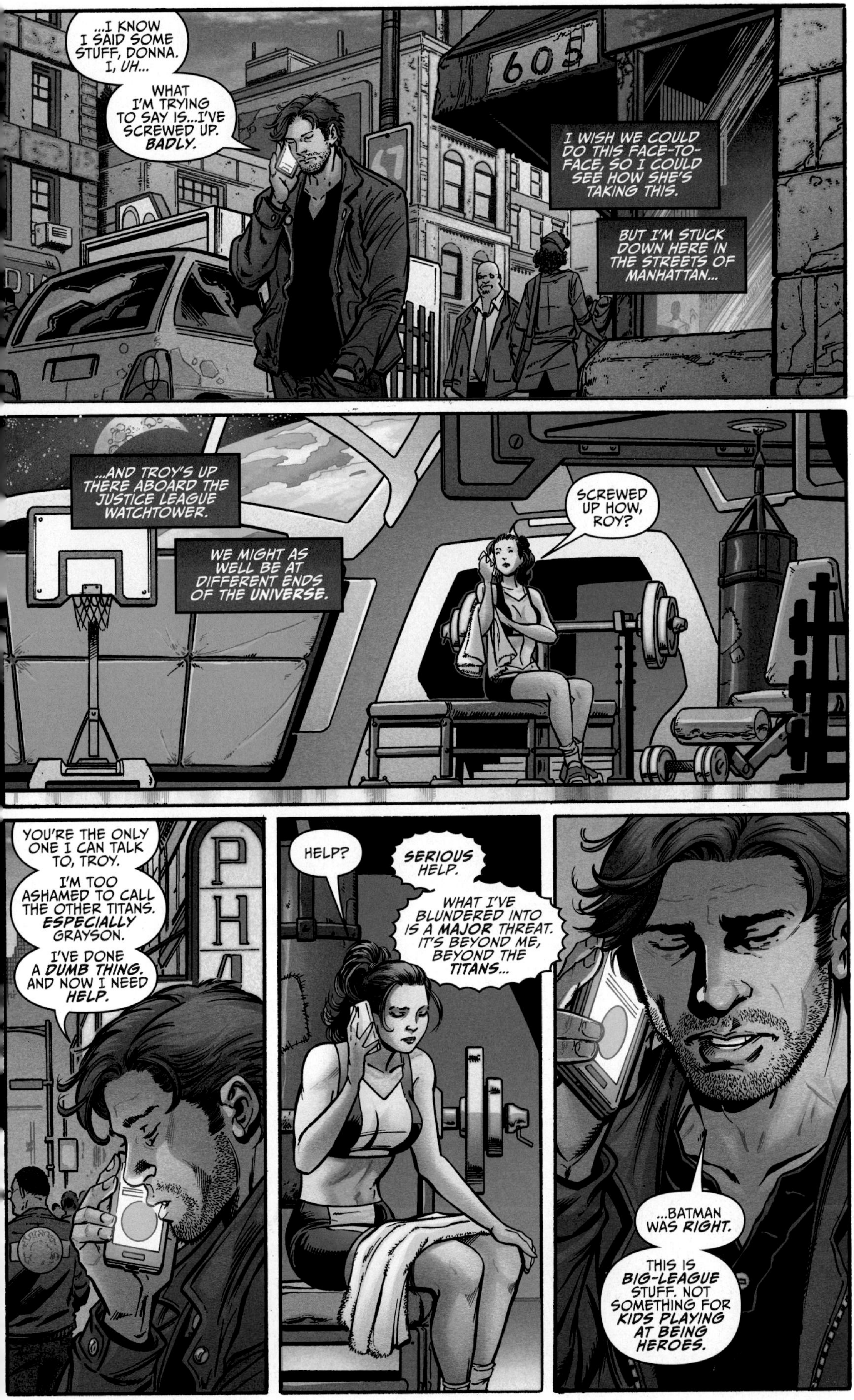
...I KNOW I SAID SOME STUFF, DONNA. I, UH...
WHAT I'M TRYING TO SAY IS...I'VE SCREWED UP. BADLY.
605
I WISH WE COULD DO THIS FACE-TO-FACE, SO I COULD SEE HOW SHE'S TAKING THIS.
BUT I'M STUCK DOWN HERE IN THE STREETS OF MANHATTAN...
...AND TROY'S UP THERE ABOARD THE JUSTICE LEAGUE WATCHTOWER.
WE MIGHT AS WELL BE AT DIFFERENT ENDS OF THE UNIVERSE.
SCREWED UP HOW, ROY?
YOU'RE THE ONLY ONE I CAN TALK TO, TROY.
I'M TOO ASHAMED TO CALL THE OTHER TITANS. ESPECIALLY GRAYSON.
I'VE DONE A DUMB THING. AND NOW I NEED HELP.
HELP?
SERIOUS HELP.
WHAT I'VE BLUNDERED INTO IS A MAJOR THREAT. IT'S BEYOND ME, BEYOND THE TITANS...
...BATMAN WAS RIGHT.
THIS IS BIG-LEAGUE STUFF. NOT SOMETHING FOR KIDS PLAYING AT BEING HEROES.

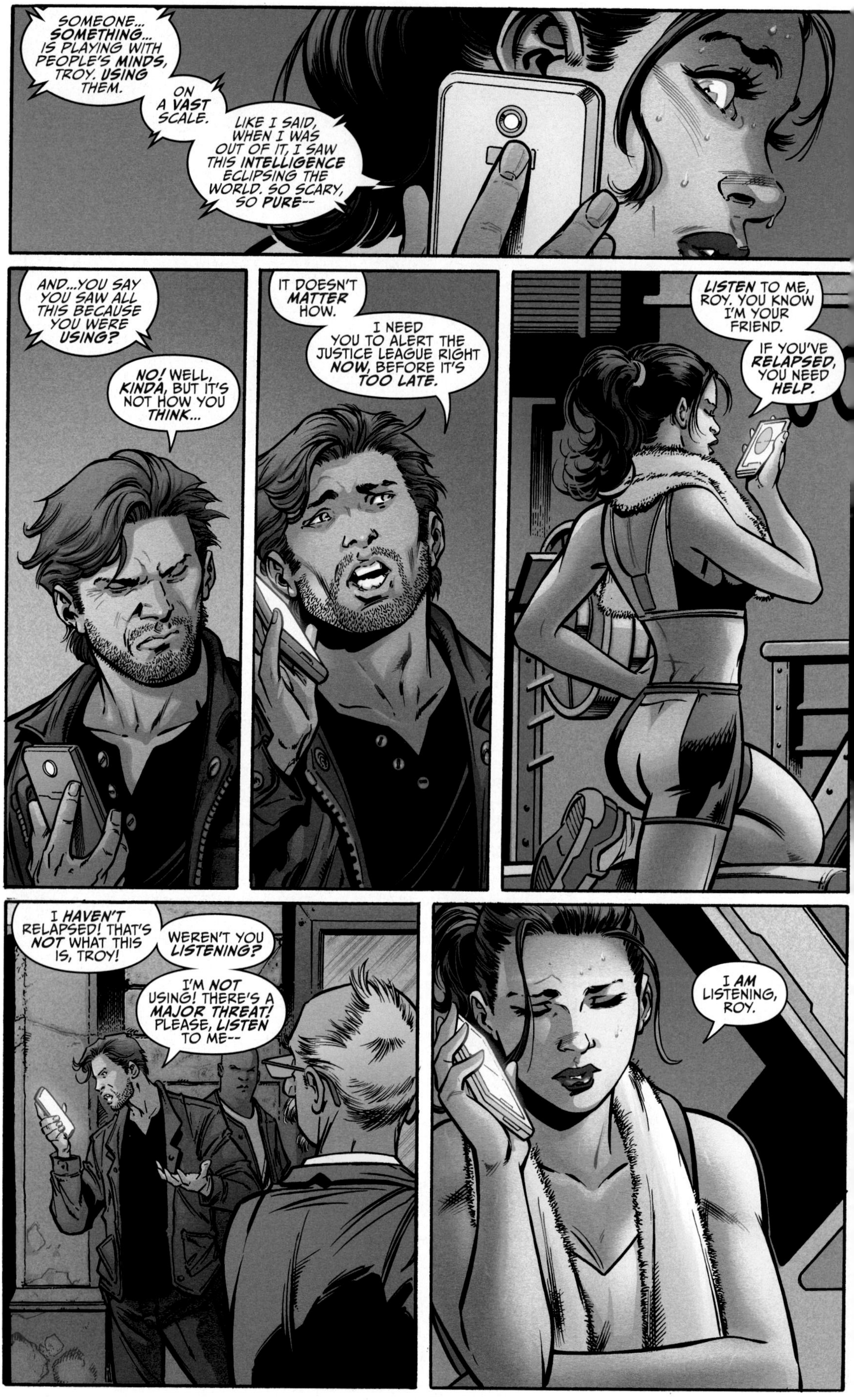
SOMEONE... SOMETHING... IS PLAYING WITH PEOPLE'S MINDS, TROY. USING THEM.
ON A VAST SCALE.
LIKE I SAID, WHEN I WAS OUT OF IT, I SAW THIS INTELLIGENCE ECLIPSING THE WORLD. SO SCARY, SO PURE--
AND...YOU SAY YOU SAW ALL THIS BECAUSE YOU WERE USING?
NO! WELL, KINDA, BUT IT'S NOT HOW YOU THINK...
IT DOESN'T MATTER HOW.
I NEED YOU TO ALERT THE JUSTICE LEAGUE RIGHT NOW, BEFORE IT'S TOO LATE.
LISTEN TO ME, ROY. YOU KNOW I'M YOUR FRIEND.
IF YOU'VE RELAPSED, YOU NEED HELP.
I HAVEN'T RELAPSED! THAT'S NOT WHAT THIS IS, TROY!
WEREN'T YOU LISTENING?
I'M NOT USING! THERE'S A MAJOR THREAT! PLEASE, LISTEN TO ME--
I AM LISTENING, ROY.

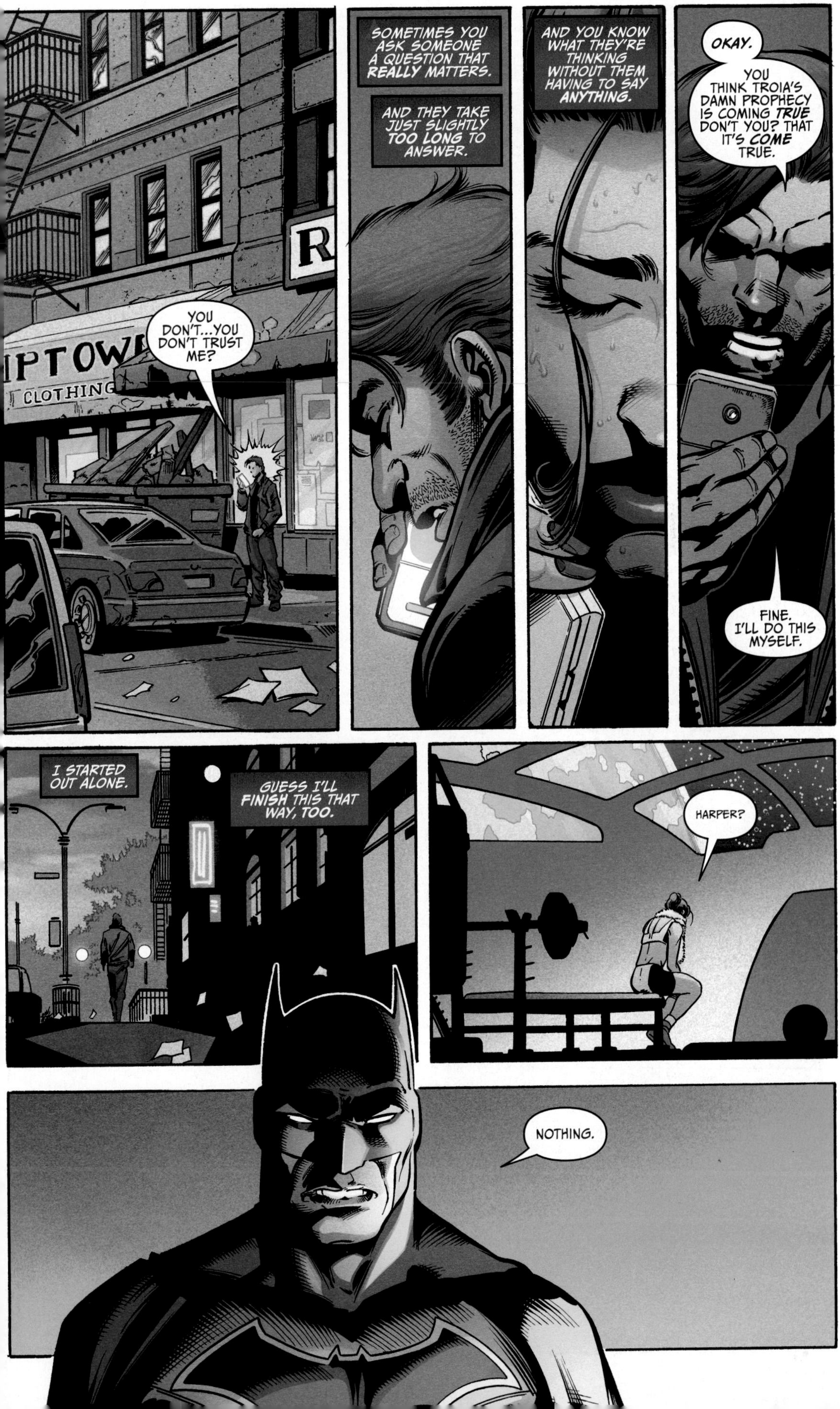

IPTOWN
CLOTHING
YOU DON'T...YOU DON'T TRUST ME?
SOMETIMES YOU ASK SOMEONE A QUESTION THAT REALLY MATTERS.
AND THEY TAKE JUST SLIGHTLY TOO LONG TO ANSWER.
AND YOU KNOW WHAT THEY'RE THINKING WITHOUT THEM HAVING TO SAY ANYTHING.
OKAY.
YOU THINK TROIA'S DAMN PROPHECY IS COMING TRUE DON'T YOU? THAT IT'S COME TRUE.
FINE. I'LL DO THIS MYSELF.
I STARTED OUT ALONE.
GUESS I'LL FINISH THIS THAT WAY, TOO.
HARPER?
NOTHING.

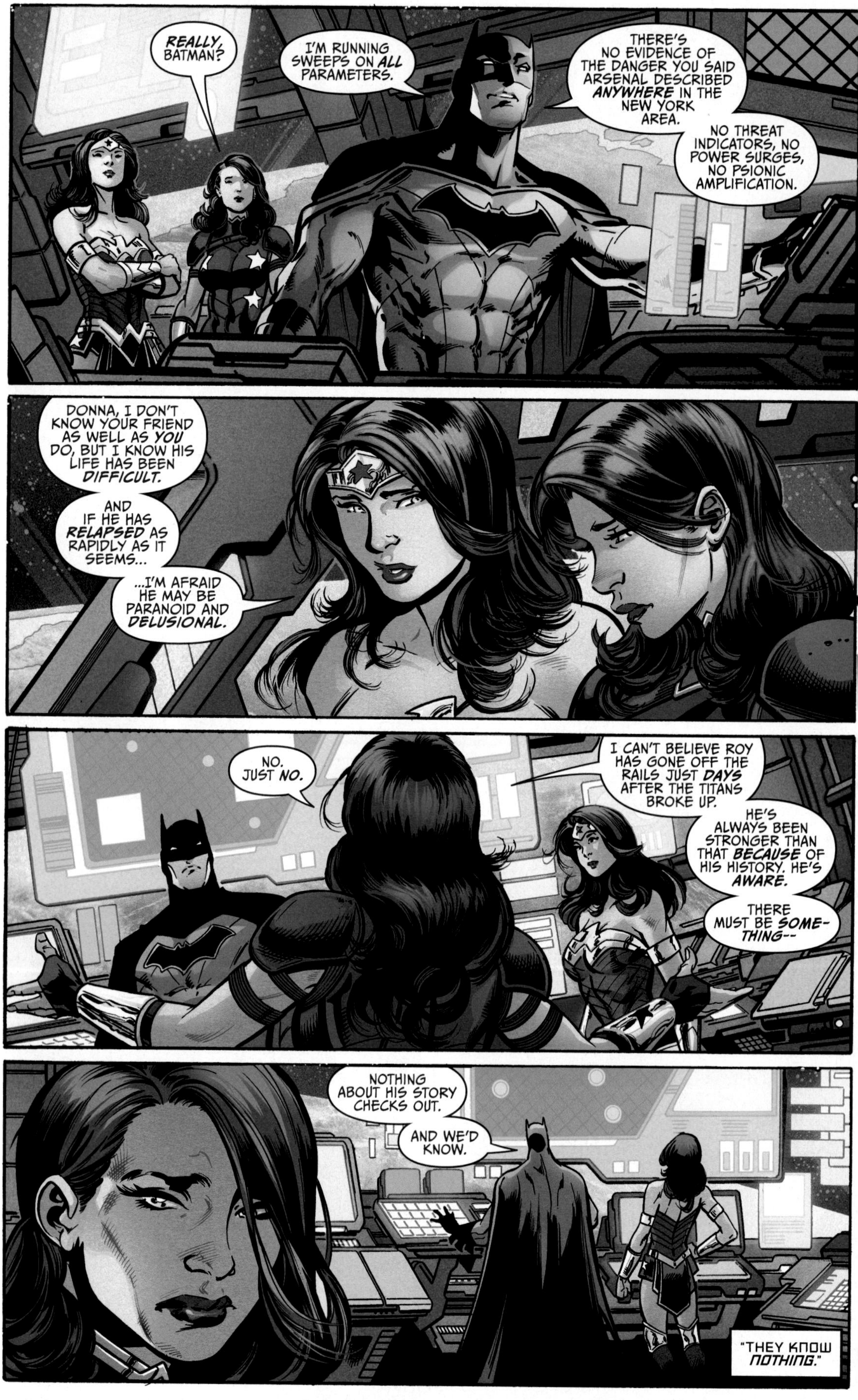

REALLY, BATMAN?
I'M RUNNING SWEEPS ON ALL PARAMETERS.
THERE'S NO EVIDENCE OF THE DANGER YOU SAID ARSENAL DESCRIBED ANYWHERE IN THE NEW YORK AREA.
NO THREAT INDICATORS, NO POWER SURGES, NO PSIONIC AMPLIFICATION.
DONNA, I DON'T KNOW YOUR FRIEND AS WELL AS YOU DO, BUT I KNOW HIS LIFE HAS BEEN DIFFICULT.
AND IF HE HAS RELAPSED AS RAPIDLY AS IT SEEMS...
...I'M AFRAID HE MAY BE PARANOID AND DELUSIONAL.
NO. JUST NO.
I CAN'T BELIEVE ROY HAS GONE OFF THE RAILS JUST DAYS AFTER THE TITANS BROKE UP.
HE'S ALWAYS BEEN STRONGER THAN THAT BECAUSE OF HIS HISTORY. HE'S AWARE.
THERE MUST BE SOME-THING--
NOTHING ABOUT HIS STORY CHECKS OUT.
AND WE'D KNOW.
"THEY KNOW NOTHING."

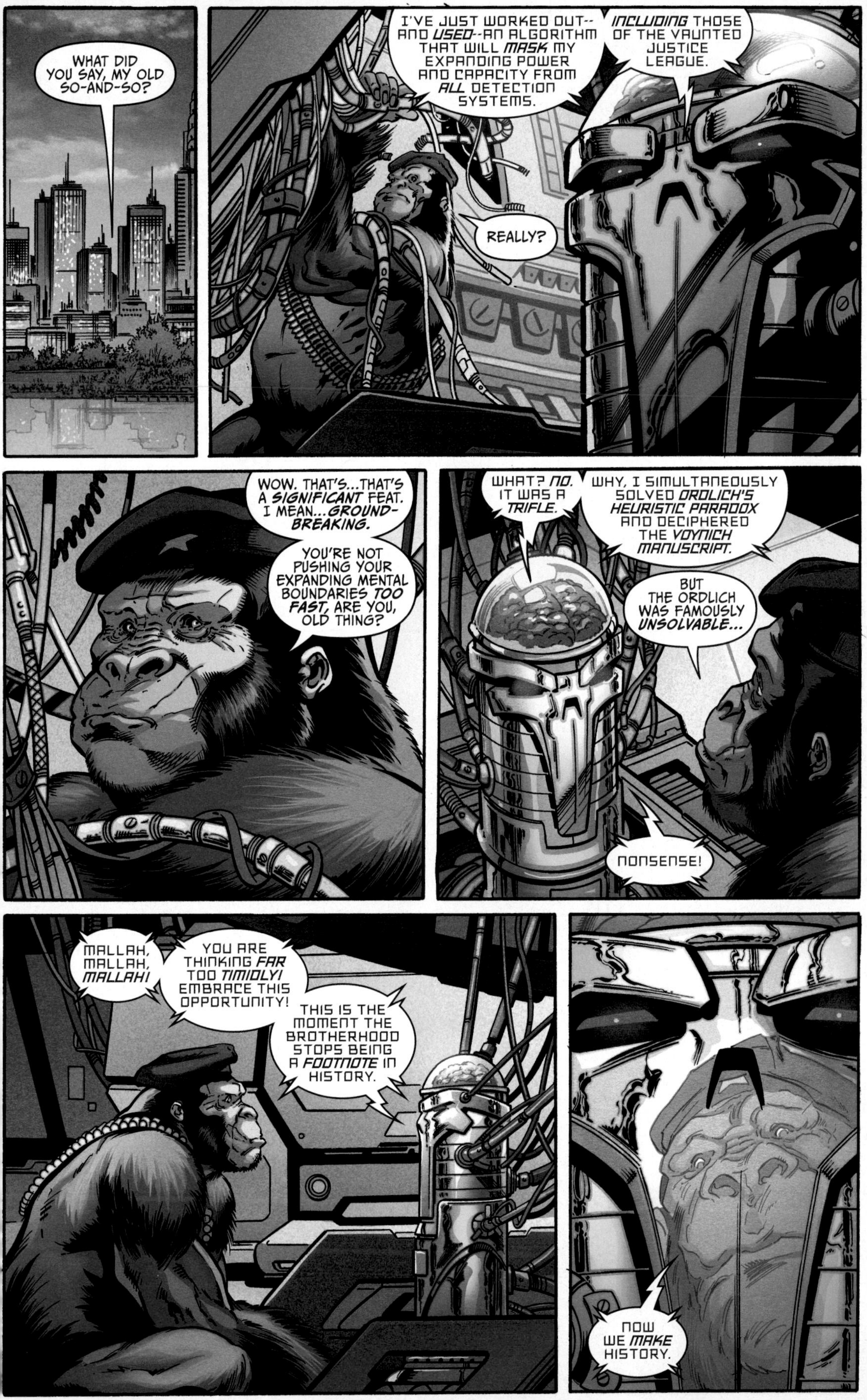
WHAT DID YOU SAY, MY OLD SO-AND-SO?
I'VE JUST WORKED OUT--AND USED--AN ALGORITHM THAT WILL MASK MY EXPANDING POWER AND CAPACITY FROM ALL DETECTION SYSTEMS.
INCLUDING THOSE OF THE VAUNTED JUSTICE LEAGUE.
REALLY?
WOW. THAT'S...THAT'S A SIGNIFICANT FEAT. I MEAN...GROUND-BREAKING.
YOU'RE NOT PUSHING YOUR EXPANDING MENTAL BOUNDARIES TOO FAST, ARE YOU, OLD THING?
WHAT? NO. IT WAS A TRIFLE.
WHY, I SIMULTANEOUSLY SOLVED ORDLICH'S HEURISTIC PARADOX AND DECIPHERED THE VOYNICH MANUSCRIPT.
BUT THE ORDLICH WAS FAMOUSLY UNSOLVABLE...
NONSENSE!
MALLAH, MALLAH, MALLAH!
YOU ARE THINKING FAR TOO TIMIDLY! EMBRACE THIS OPPORTUNITY!
THIS IS THE MOMENT THE BROTHERHOOD STOPS BEING A FOOTNOTE IN HISTORY.
NOW WE MAKE HISTORY.

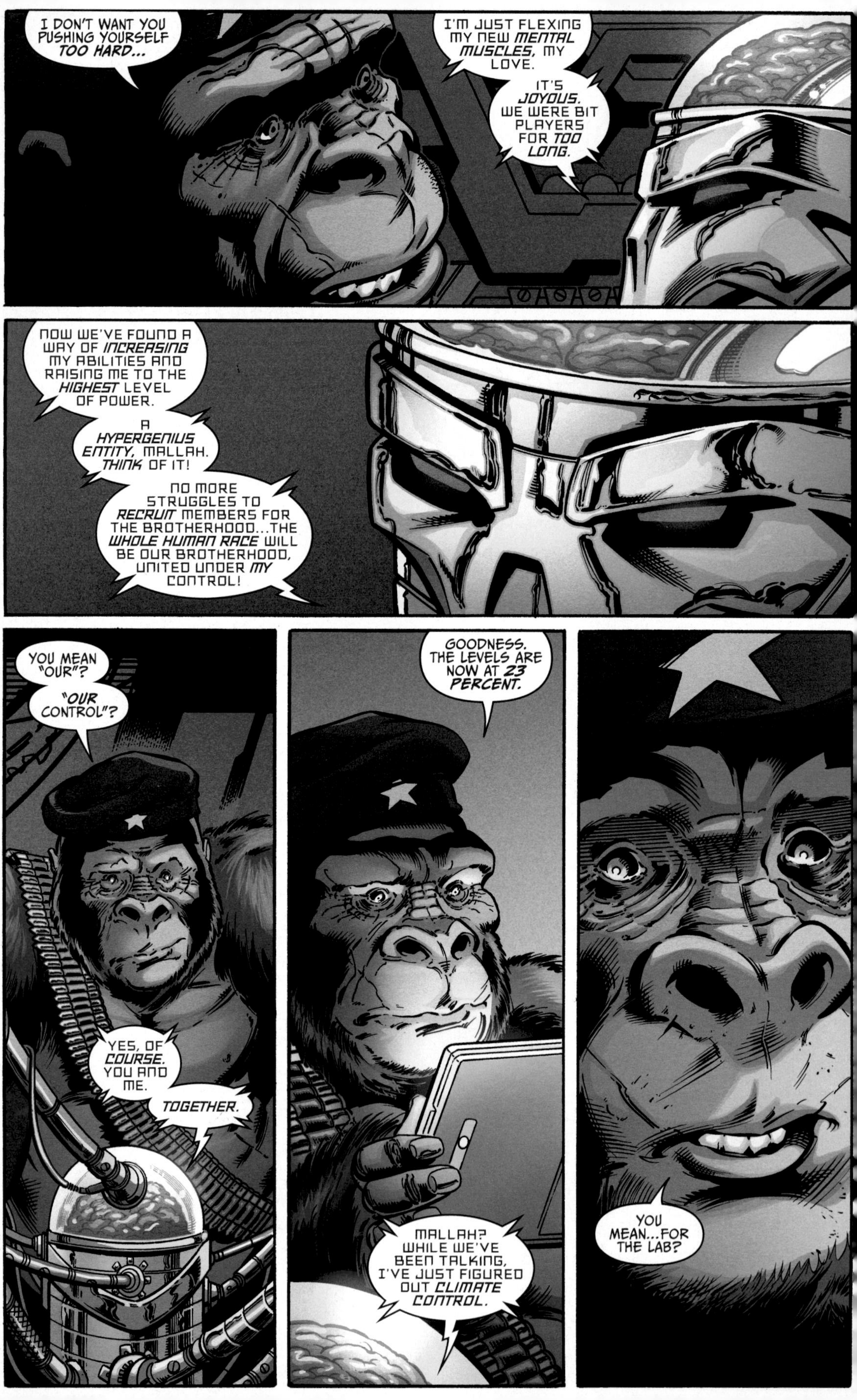
I DON'T WANT YOU PUSHING YOURSELF TOO HARD...
I'M JUST FLEXING MY NEW MENTAL MUSCLES, MY LOVE.
IT'S JOYOUS. WE WERE BIT PLAYERS FOR TOO LONG.
NOW WE'VE FOUND A WAY OF INCREASING MY ABILITIES AND RAISING ME TO THE HIGHEST LEVEL OF POWER.
A HYPERGENIUS ENTITY, MALLAH. THINK OF IT!
NO MORE STRUGGLES TO RECRUIT MEMBERS FOR THE BROTHERHOOD...THE WHOLE HUMAN RACE WILL BE OUR BROTHERHOOD, UNITED UNDER MY CONTROL!
YOU MEAN "OUR"?
"OUR CONTROL"?
YES, OF COURSE. YOU AND ME.
TOGETHER.
GOODNESS. THE LEVELS ARE NOW AT 23 PERCENT.
MALLAH? WHILE WE'VE BEEN TALKING, I'VE JUST FIGURED OUT CLIMATE CONTROL.
YOU MEAN...FOR THE LAB?

"NO."

KKKAAA KZZZZ KZZKK OOOOO OOOOON

NO, BUT HE'S ON HIS WAY--

OKAY, HE'S *HERE* NOW.

DICK?

NO, I--

DONNA, I'LL EXPLAIN IT *ALL* TO WALLY.

YES.

YES.

RELAX. WE'LL *HANDLE* IT.

I'D DO IT MYSELF, GRAYSON, BUT I'M BASICALLY A *PRISONER* UP HERE.

I'LL CALL YOU BACK.

WHAT'S GOING ON, DICK? ARE WE GETTING BACK *TOGETHER?*

NO. BUT WE NEED TO HELP A FRIEND...

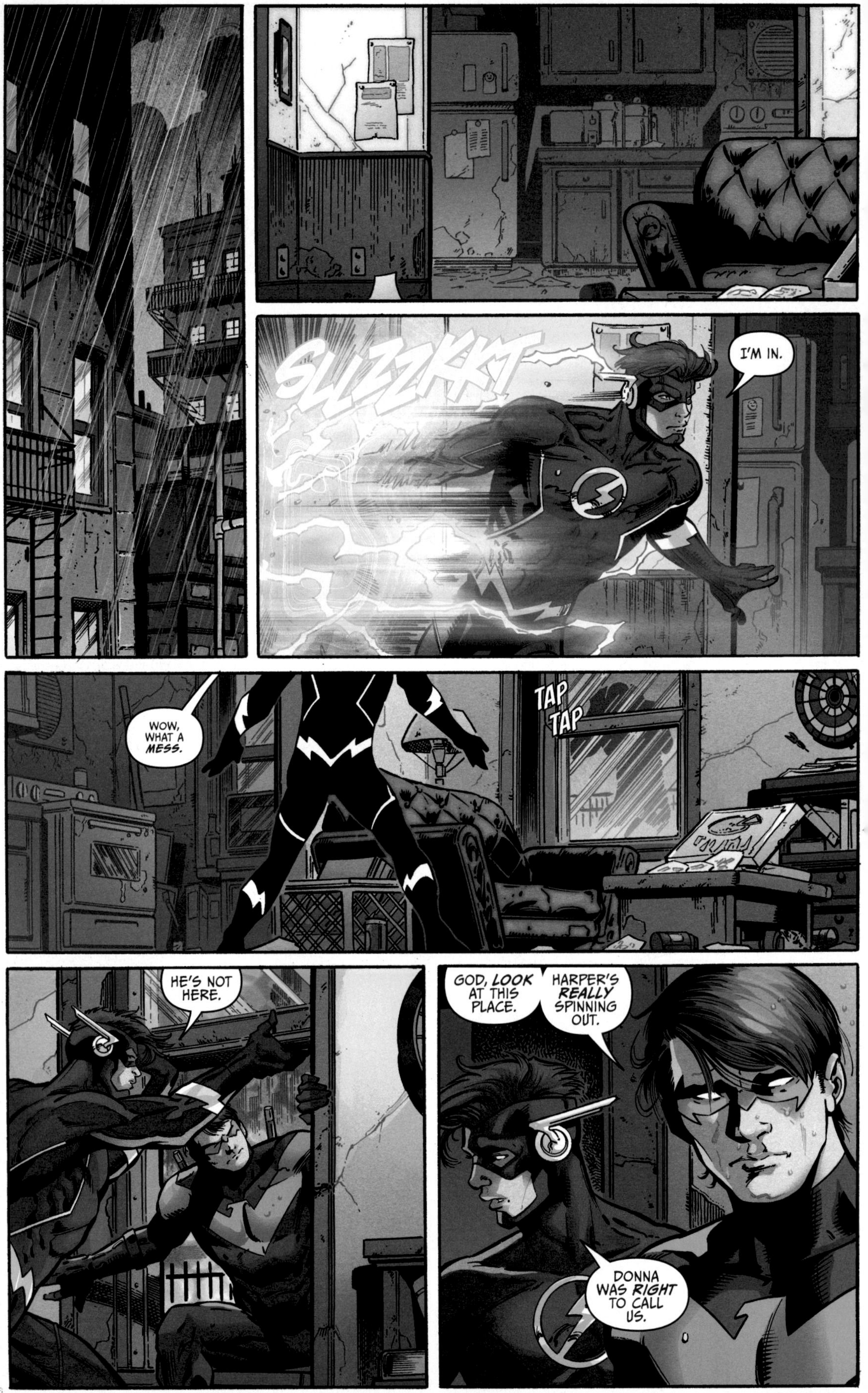
SLIZZKKT
I'M IN.
WOW, WHAT A MESS.
TAP TAP
HE'S NOT HERE.
GOD, LOOK AT THIS PLACE.
HARPER'S REALLY SPINNING OUT.
DONNA WAS RIGHT TO CALL US.

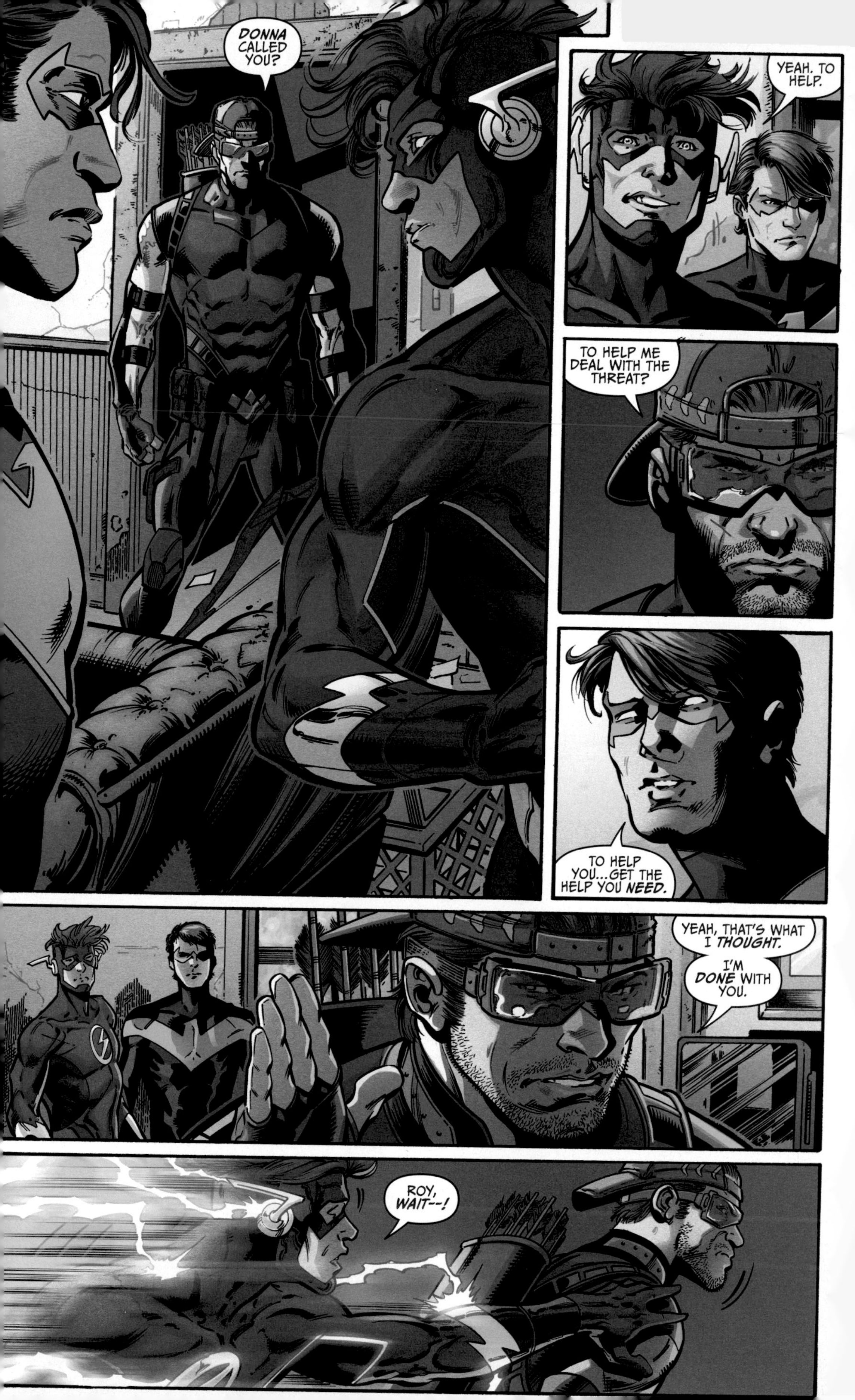
DONNA CALLED YOU?
YEAH. TO HELP.
TO HELP ME DEAL WITH THE THREAT?
TO HELP YOU...GET THE HELP YOU NEED.
YEAH, THAT'S WHAT I THOUGHT.
I'M DONE WITH YOU.
ROY, WAIT--!

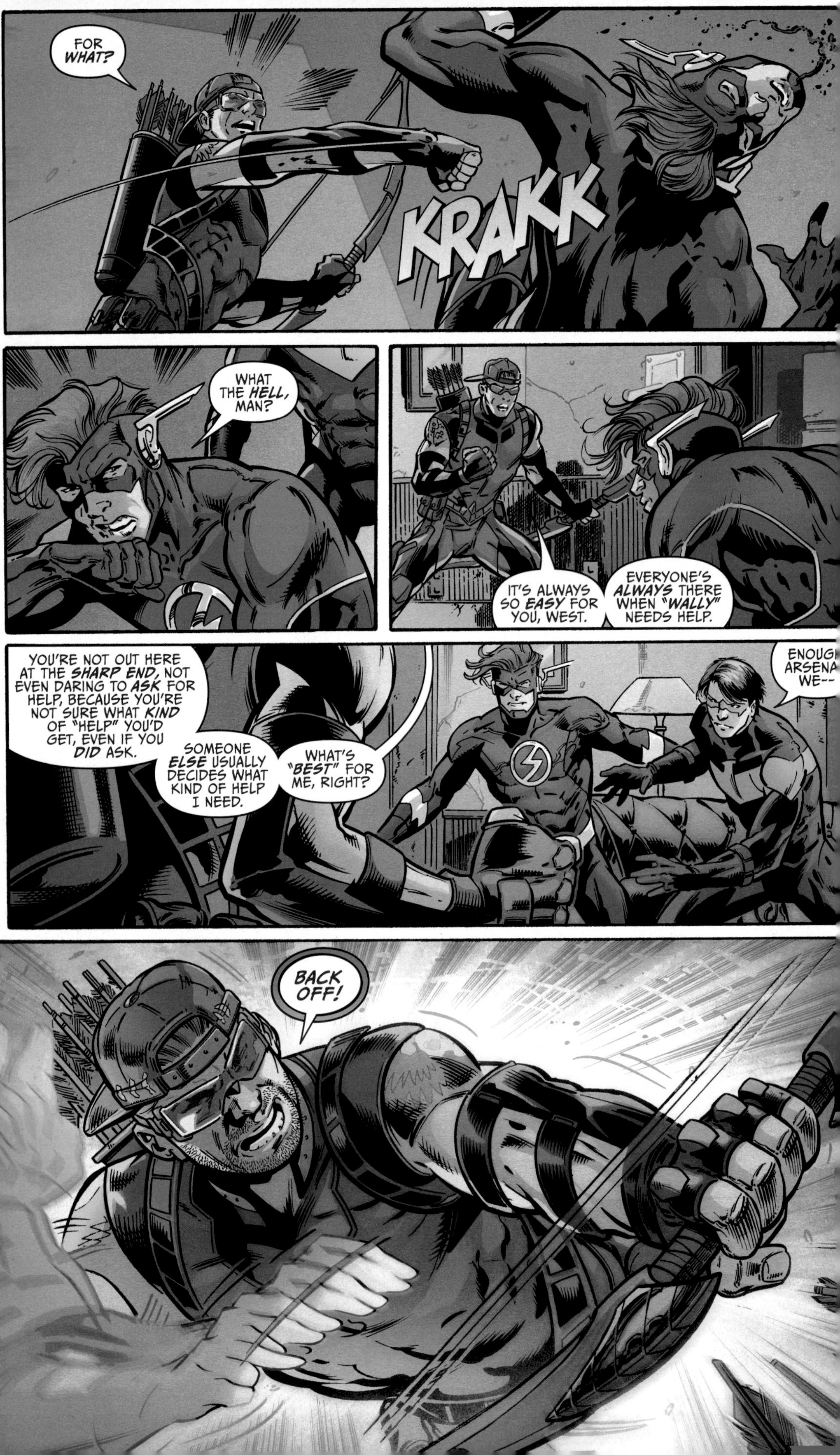
FOR *WHAT?*
KRAKK
WHAT THE *HELL*, MAN?
IT'S ALWAYS SO *EASY* FOR YOU, WEST.
EVERYONE'S *ALWAYS* THERE WHEN *"WALLY"* NEEDS HELP.
YOU'RE NOT OUT HERE AT THE *SHARP END*, NOT EVEN DARING TO *ASK* FOR HELP, BECAUSE YOU'RE NOT SURE WHAT *KIND* OF "HELP" YOU'D GET, EVEN IF YOU *DID* ASK.
SOMEONE *ELSE* USUALLY DECIDES WHAT KIND OF HELP I NEED.
WHAT'S *"BEST"* FOR ME, RIGHT?
ENOUG ARSENA WE--
BACK OFF!

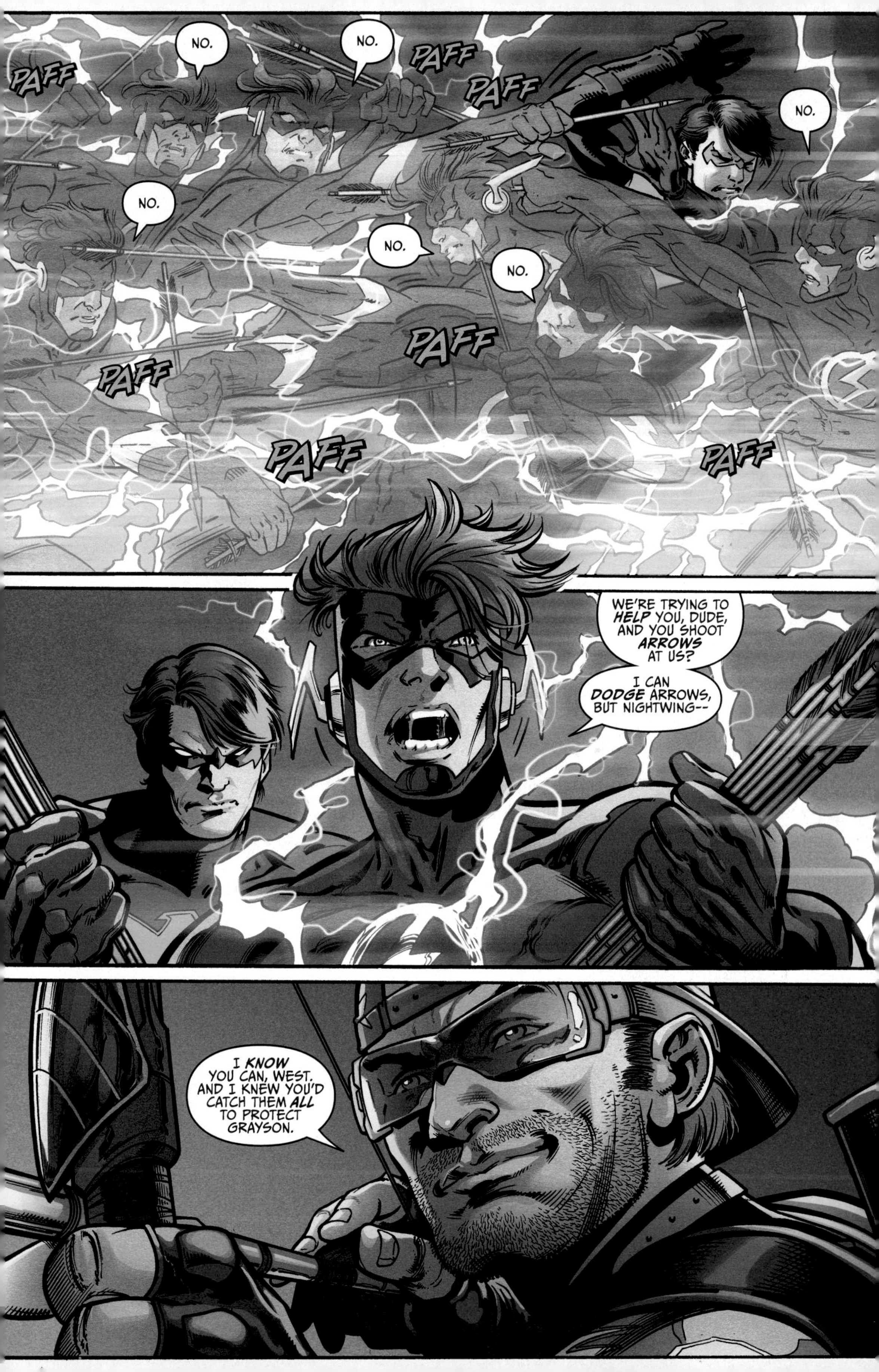
PAFF
NO.
NO.
PAFF
PAFF
NO.
NO.
NO.
NO.
PAFF
PAFF
PAFF
PAFF
WE'RE TRYING TO HELP YOU, DUDE, AND YOU SHOOT ARROWS AT US?
I CAN DODGE ARROWS, BUT NIGHTWING--
I KNOW YOU CAN, WEST. AND I KNEW YOU'D CATCH THEM ALL TO PROTECT GRAYSON.

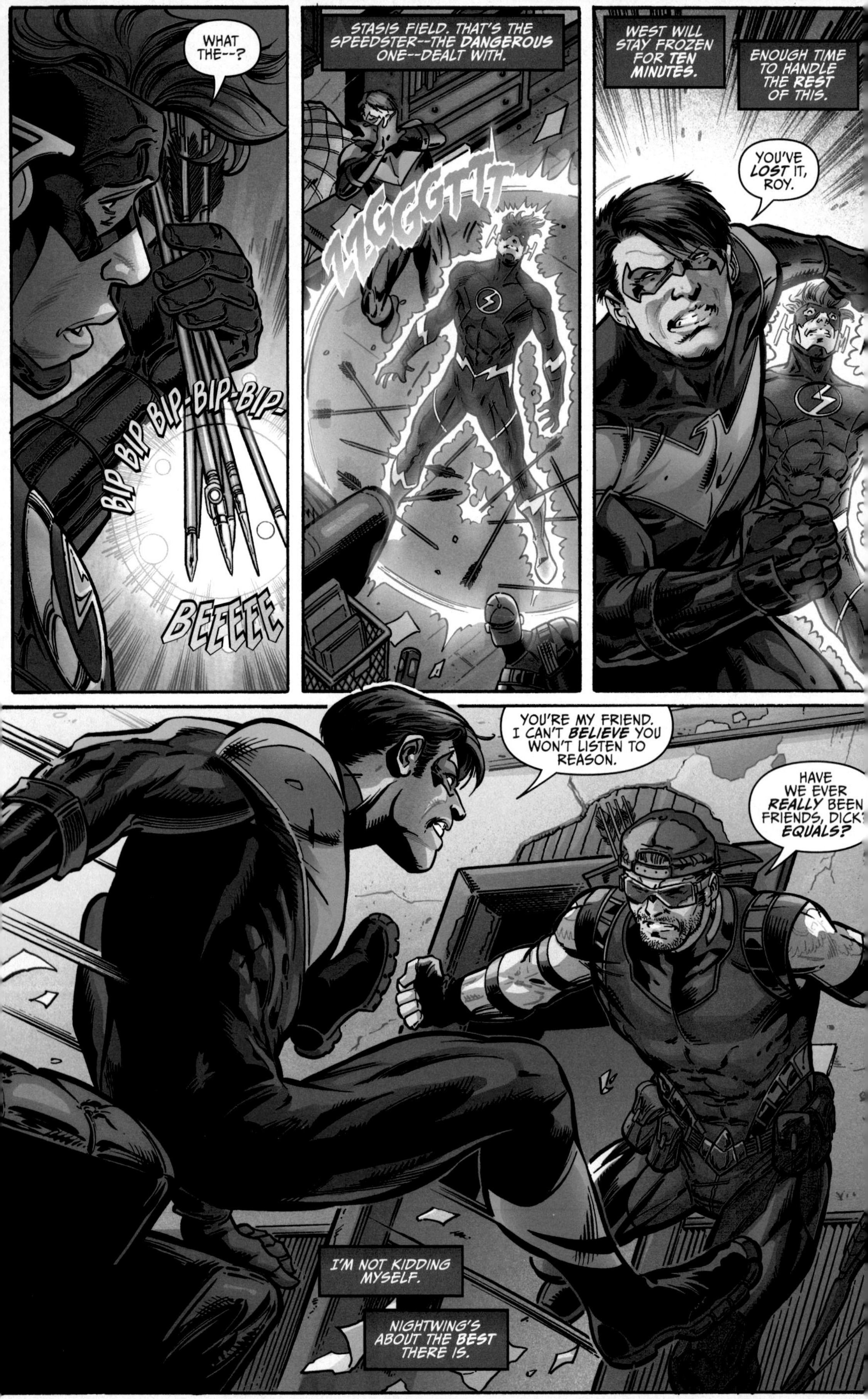
WHAT THE--?
BIP BIP BIP-BIP-BIP-
BEEEEE
STASIS FIELD. THAT'S THE SPEEDSTER--THE DANGEROUS ONE--DEALT WITH.
ZZGGGTTT
WEST WILL STAY FROZEN FOR TEN MINUTES.
ENOUGH TIME TO HANDLE THE REST OF THIS.
YOU'VE LOST IT, ROY.
YOU'RE MY FRIEND. I CAN'T BELIEVE YOU WON'T LISTEN TO REASON.
HAVE WE EVER REALLY BEEN FRIENDS, DICK? EQUALS?
I'M NOT KIDDING MYSELF.
NIGHTWING'S ABOUT THE BEST THERE IS.

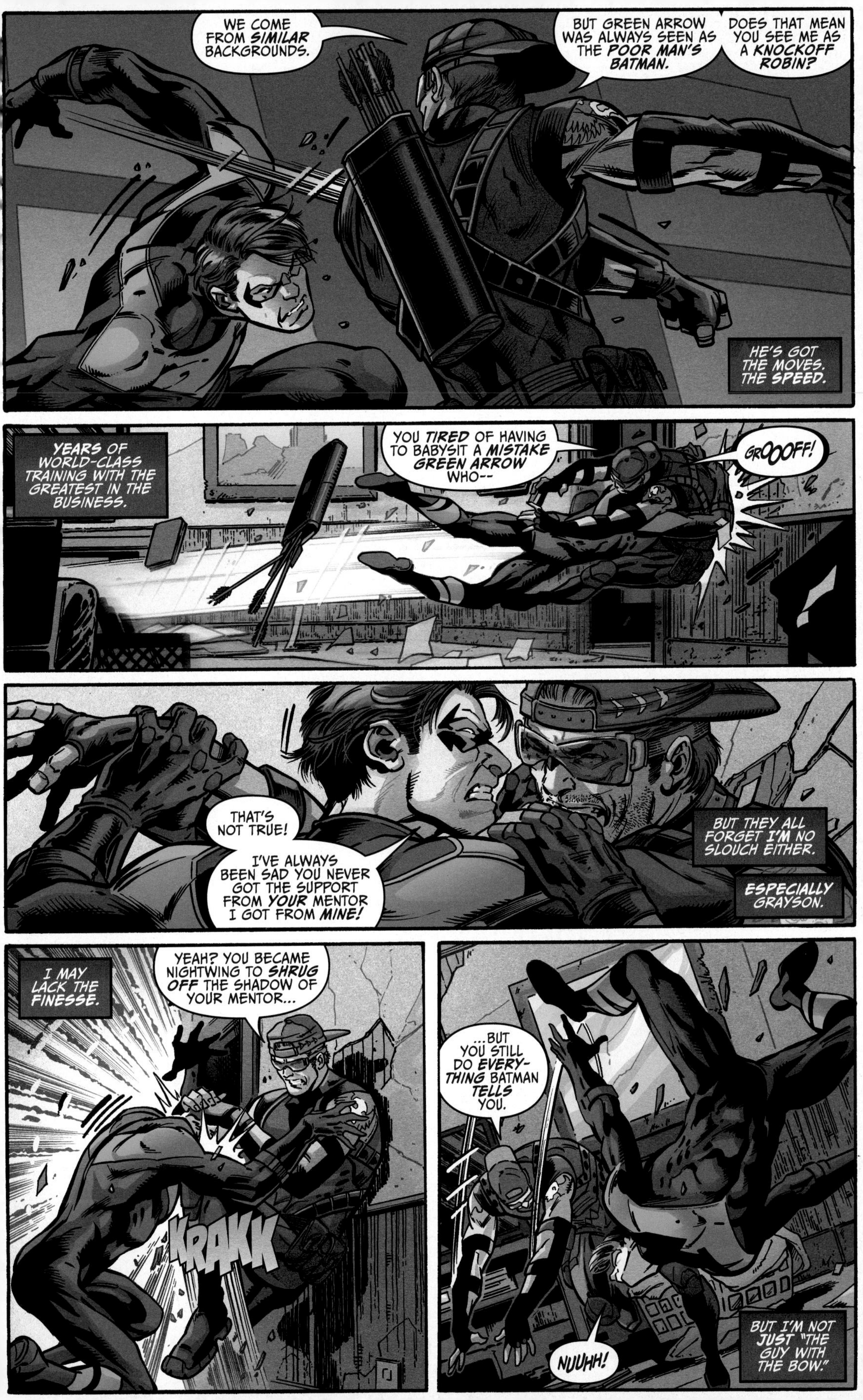
WE COME FROM SIMILAR BACKGROUNDS.
BUT GREEN ARROW WAS ALWAYS SEEN AS THE POOR MAN'S BATMAN.
DOES THAT MEAN YOU SEE ME AS A KNOCKOFF ROBIN?
HE'S GOT THE MOVES. THE SPEED.
YEARS OF WORLD-CLASS TRAINING WITH THE GREATEST IN THE BUSINESS.
YOU TIRED OF HAVING TO BABYSIT A MISTAKE GREEN ARROW WHO--
GROOOFF!
THAT'S NOT TRUE!
I'VE ALWAYS BEEN SAD YOU NEVER GOT THE SUPPORT FROM YOUR MENTOR I GOT FROM MINE!
BUT THEY ALL FORGET I'M NO SLOUCH EITHER.
ESPECIALLY GRAYSON.
I MAY LACK THE FINESSE.
YEAH? YOU BECAME NIGHTWING TO SHRUG OFF THE SHADOW OF YOUR MENTOR...
KRAKK
...BUT YOU STILL DO EVERYTHING BATMAN TELLS YOU.
NUUHH!
BUT I'M NOT JUST "THE GUY WITH THE BOW."

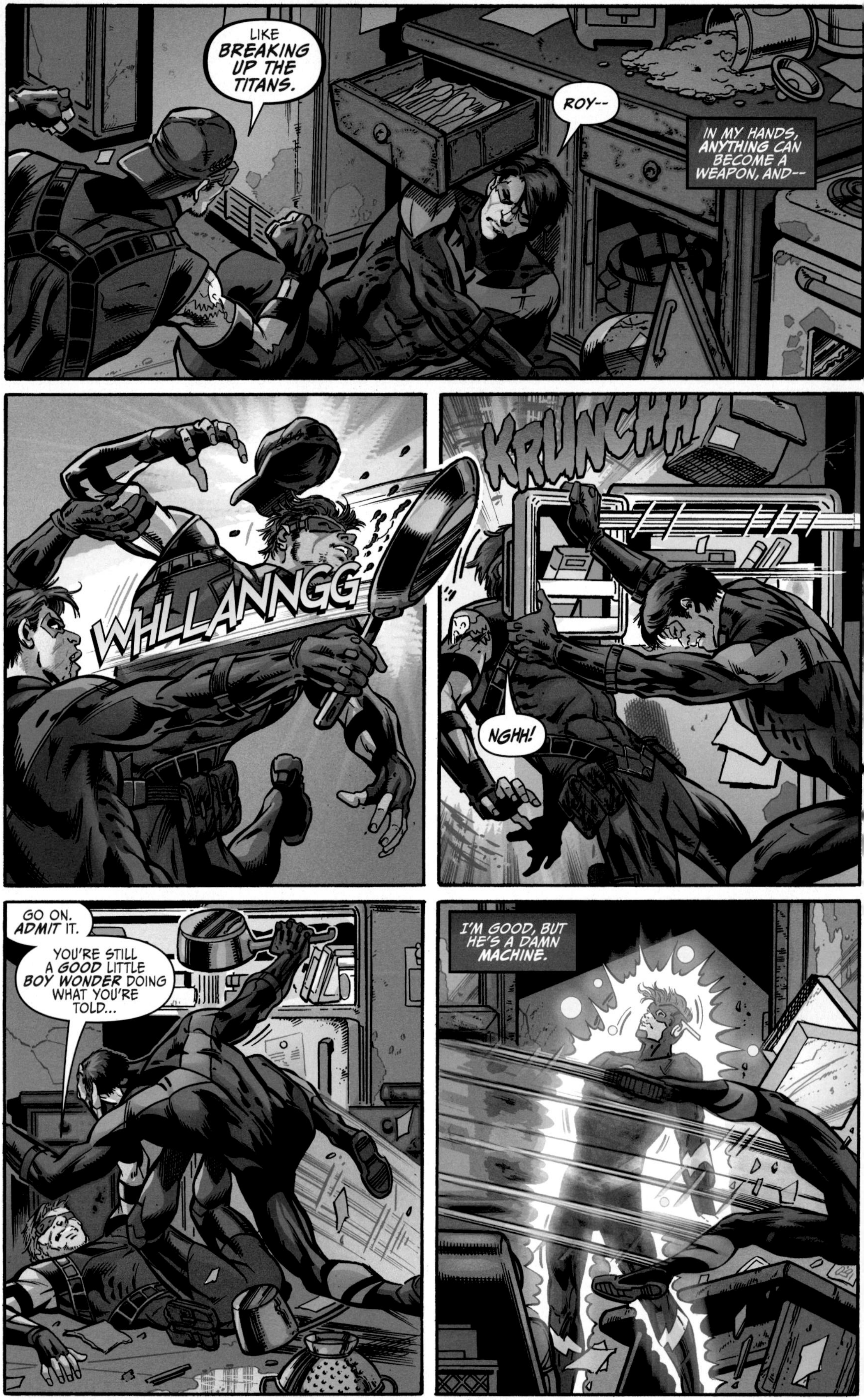
LIKE BREAKING UP THE TITANS.
ROY--
IN MY HANDS, ANYTHING CAN BECOME A WEAPON, AND--
WHLLANNGG
KRUNCHH!
NGHH!
GO ON. ADMIT IT.
YOU'RE STILL A GOOD LITTLE BOY WONDER DOING WHAT YOU'RE TOLD...
I'M GOOD, BUT HE'S A DAMN MACHINE.

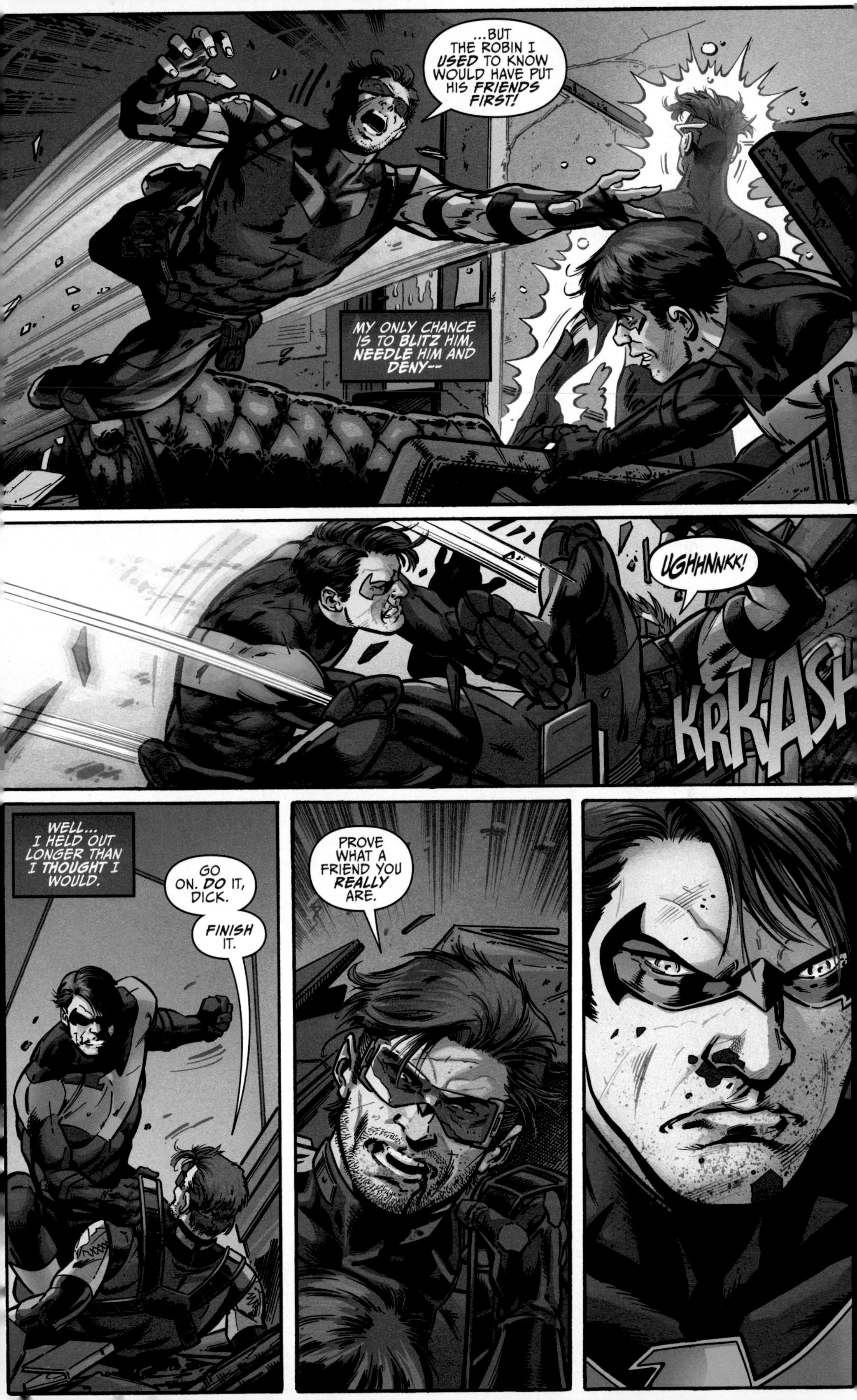
...BUT THE ROBIN I USED TO KNOW WOULD HAVE PUT HIS FRIENDS FIRST!
MY ONLY CHANCE IS TO BLITZ HIM, NEEDLE HIM AND DENY--
UGHHNNKK!
KRKASH
WELL... I HELD OUT LONGER THAN I THOUGHT I WOULD.
GO ON. DO IT, DICK.
FINISH IT.
PROVE WHAT A FRIEND YOU REALLY ARE.

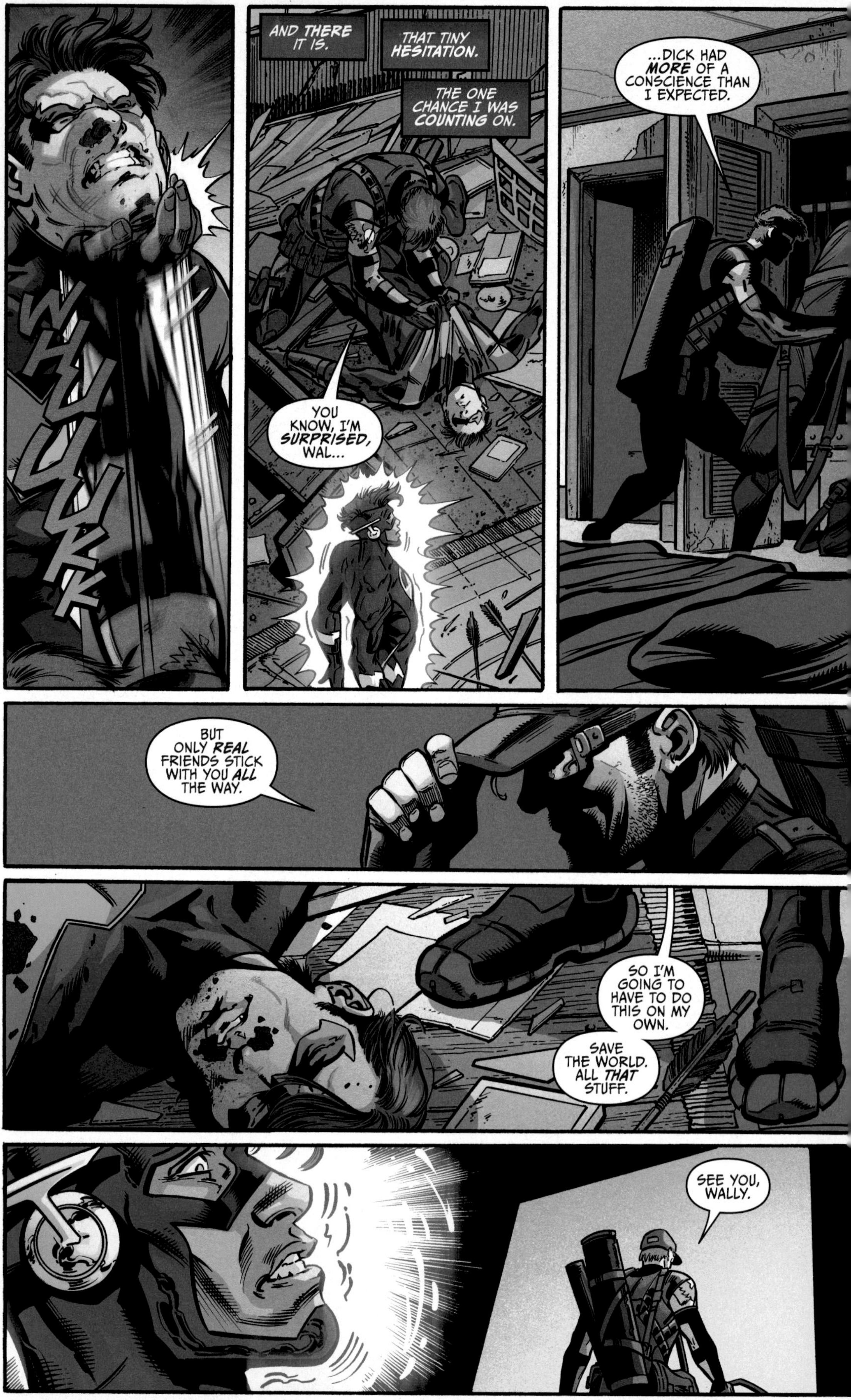
WHUUURK
AND THERE IT IS.
THAT TINY HESITATION.
THE ONE CHANCE I WAS COUNTING ON.
YOU KNOW, I'M SURPRISED, WAL...
...DICK HAD MORE OF A CONSCIENCE THAN I EXPECTED.
BUT ONLY REAL FRIENDS STICK WITH YOU ALL THE WAY.
SO I'M GOING TO HAVE TO DO THIS ON MY OWN.
SAVE THE WORLD. ALL THAT STUFF.
SEE YOU, WALLY.

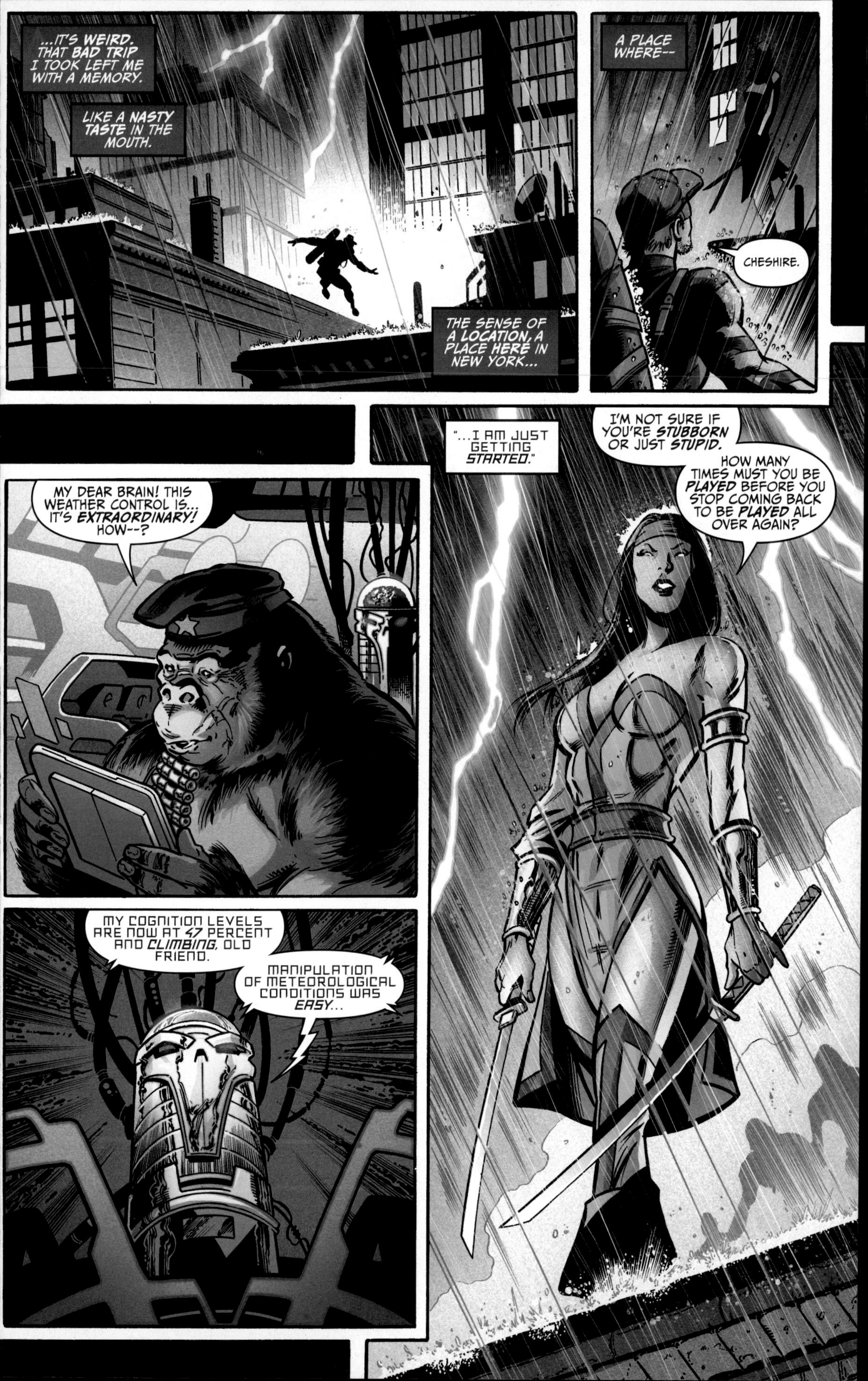

...IT'S WEIRD. THAT BAD TRIP I TOOK LEFT ME WITH A MEMORY.
LIKE A NASTY TASTE IN THE MOUTH.
THE SENSE OF A LOCATION, A PLACE HERE IN NEW YORK...
A PLACE WHERE--
CHESHIRE.
MY DEAR BRAIN! THIS WEATHER CONTROL IS... IT'S EXTRAORDINARY! HOW--?
MY COGNITION LEVELS ARE NOW AT 47 PERCENT AND CLIMBING, OLD FRIEND.
MANIPULATION OF METEOROLOGICAL CONDITIONS WAS EASY...
"...I AM JUST GETTING STARTED."
I'M NOT SURE IF YOU'RE STUBBORN OR JUST STUPID.
HOW MANY TIMES MUST YOU BE PLAYED BEFORE YOU STOP COMING BACK TO BE PLAYED ALL OVER AGAIN?

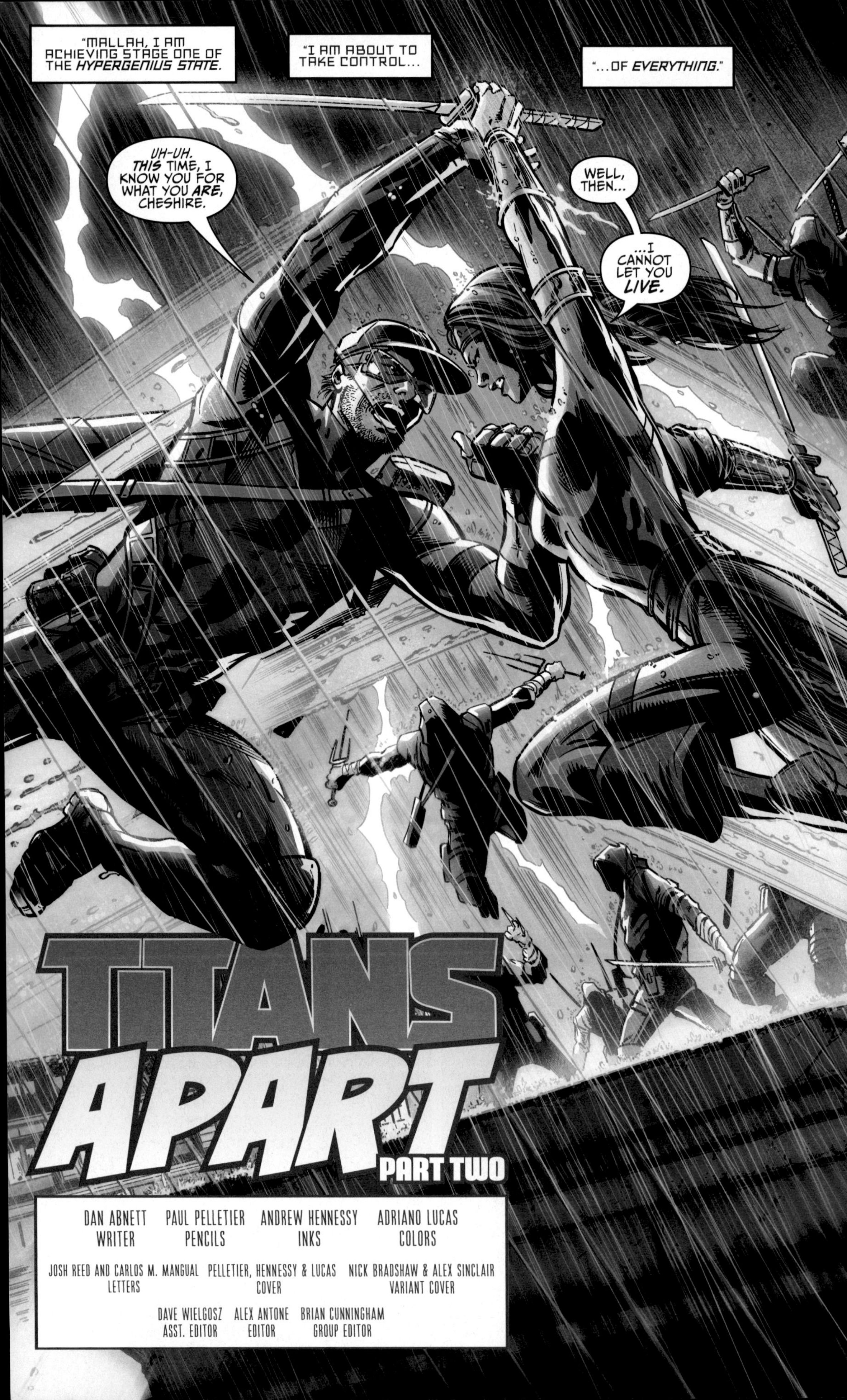
"MALLAH, I AM ACHIEVING STAGE ONE OF THE *HYPERGENIUS STATE*.
"I AM ABOUT TO TAKE CONTROL...
"...OF *EVERYTHING*."
UH-UH. *THIS* TIME, I KNOW YOU FOR WHAT YOU *ARE*, CHESHIRE.
WELL, THEN...
...I CANNOT LET YOU *LIVE*.
TITANS APART
PART TWO
DAN ABNETT WRITER
PAUL PELLETIER PENCILS
ANDREW HENNESSY INKS
ADRIANO LUCAS COLORS
JOSH REED AND CARLOS M. MANGUAL LETTERS
PELLETIER, HENNESSY & LUCAS COVER
NICK BRADSHAW & ALEX SINCLAIR VARIANT COVER
DAVE WIELGOSZ ASST. EDITOR
ALEX ANTONE EDITOR
BRIAN CUNNINGHAM GROUP EDITOR

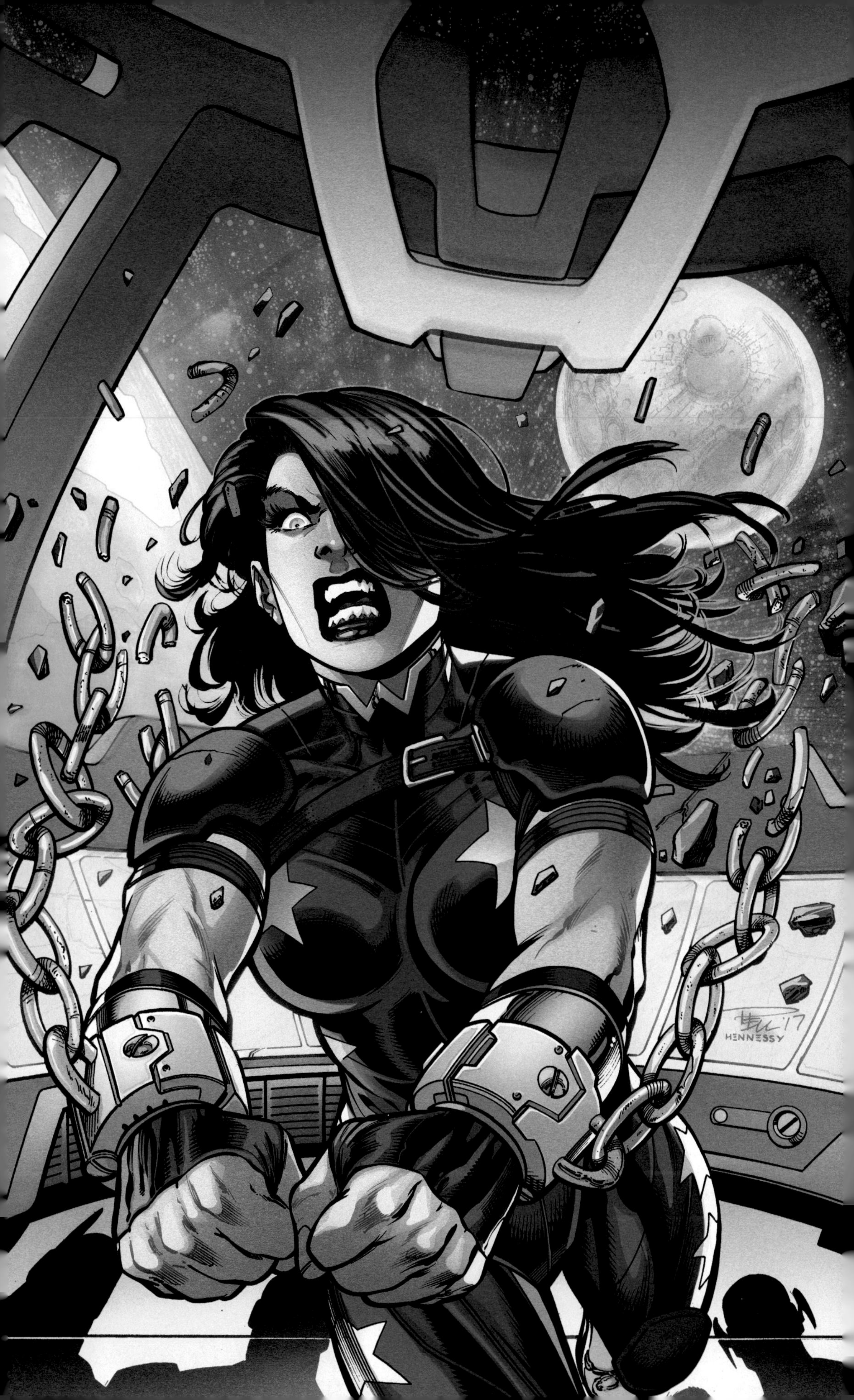
HENNESSY

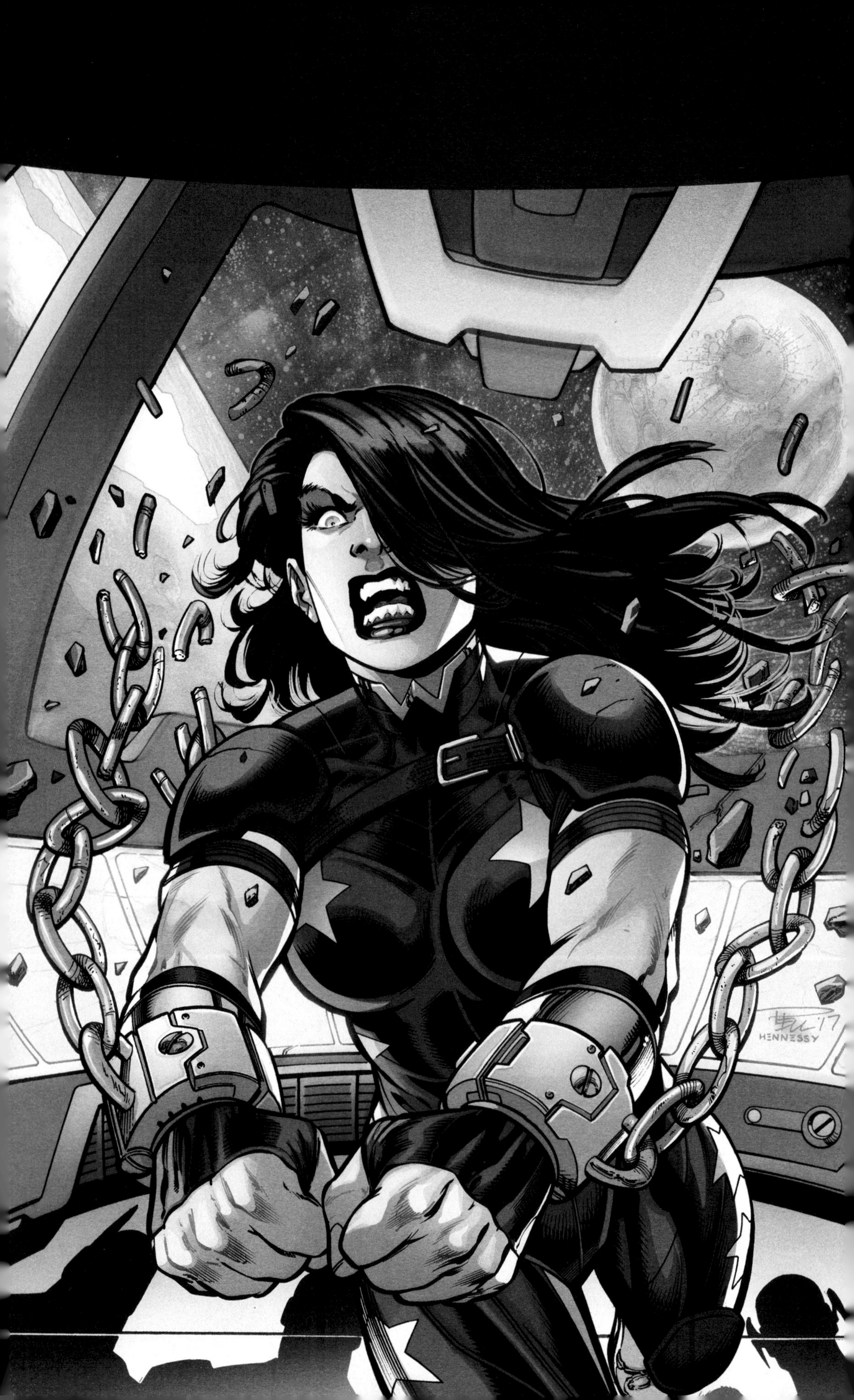
HENNESSY

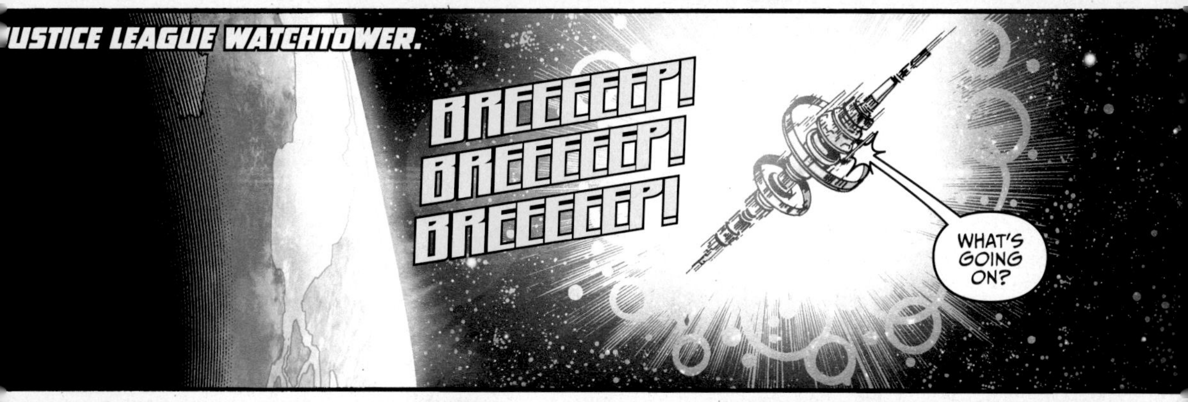
USTICE LEAGUE WATCHTOWER.
BREEEEEP! BREEEEEP! BREEEEEP!
WHAT'S GOING ON?

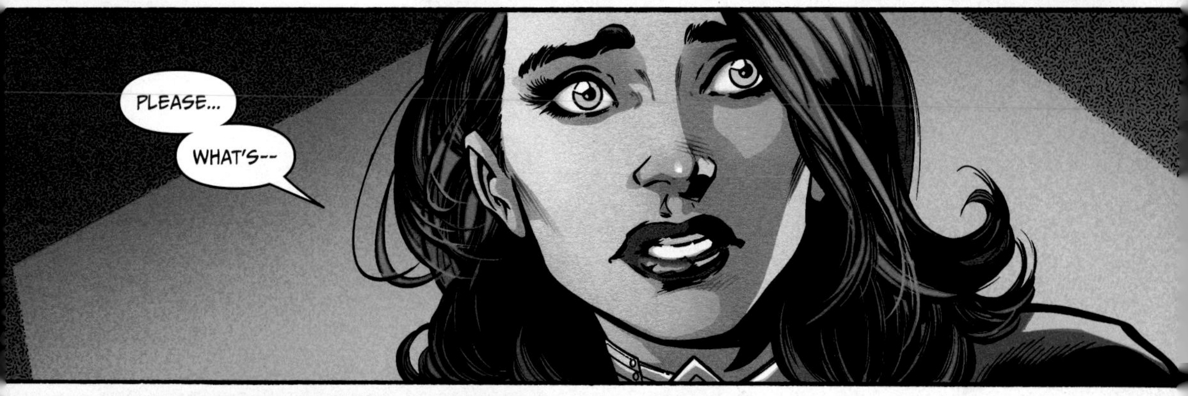
PLEASE...
WHAT'S--

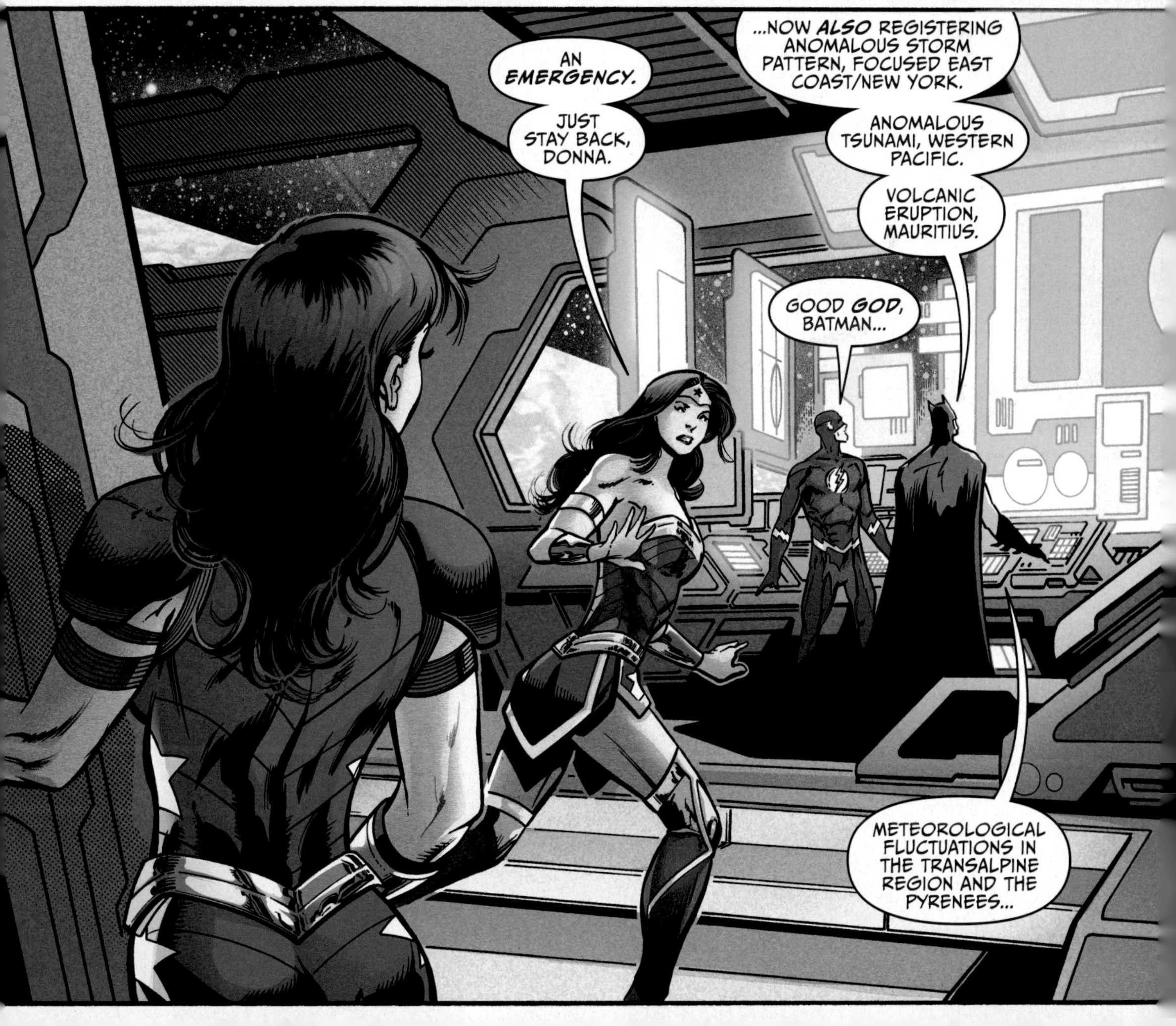
AN *EMERGENCY.*
JUST STAY BACK, DONNA.
...NOW *ALSO* REGISTERING ANOMALOUS STORM PATTERN, FOCUSED EAST COAST/NEW YORK.
ANOMALOUS TSUNAMI, WESTERN PACIFIC.
VOLCANIC ERUPTION, MAURITIUS.
GOOD *GOD,* BATMAN...
METEOROLOGICAL FLUCTUATIONS IN THE TRANSALPINE REGION AND THE PYRENEES...

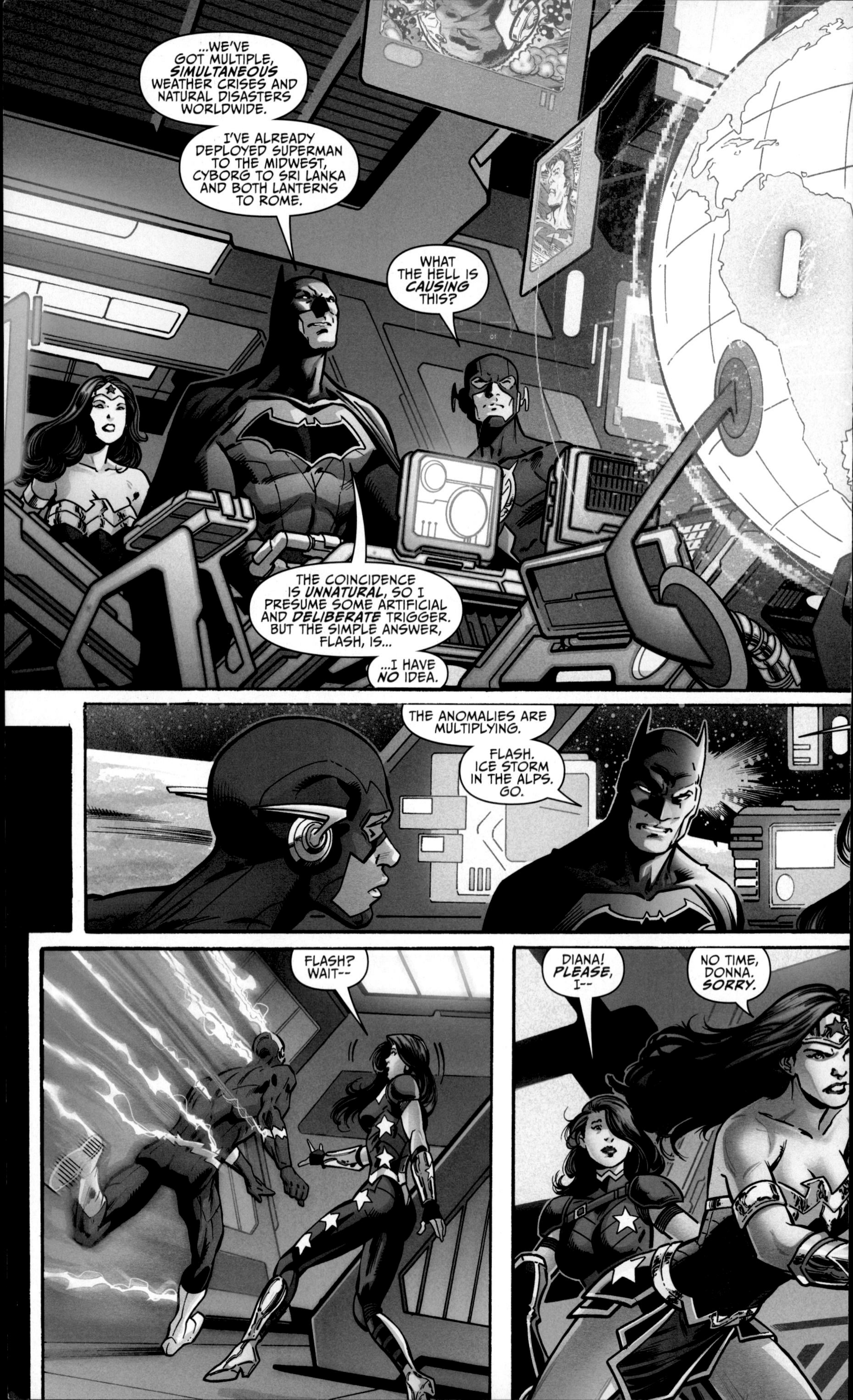
...WE'VE GOT MULTIPLE, SIMULTANEOUS WEATHER CRISES AND NATURAL DISASTERS WORLDWIDE.
I'VE ALREADY DEPLOYED SUPERMAN TO THE MIDWEST, CYBORG TO SRI LANKA AND BOTH LANTERNS TO ROME.
WHAT THE HELL IS CAUSING THIS?
THE COINCIDENCE IS UNNATURAL, SO I PRESUME SOME ARTIFICIAL AND DELIBERATE TRIGGER. BUT THE SIMPLE ANSWER, FLASH, IS...
...I HAVE NO IDEA.
THE ANOMALIES ARE MULTIPLYING.
FLASH. ICE STORM IN THE ALPS. GO.
FLASH? WAIT--
DIANA! PLEASE, I--
NO TIME, DONNA. SORRY.

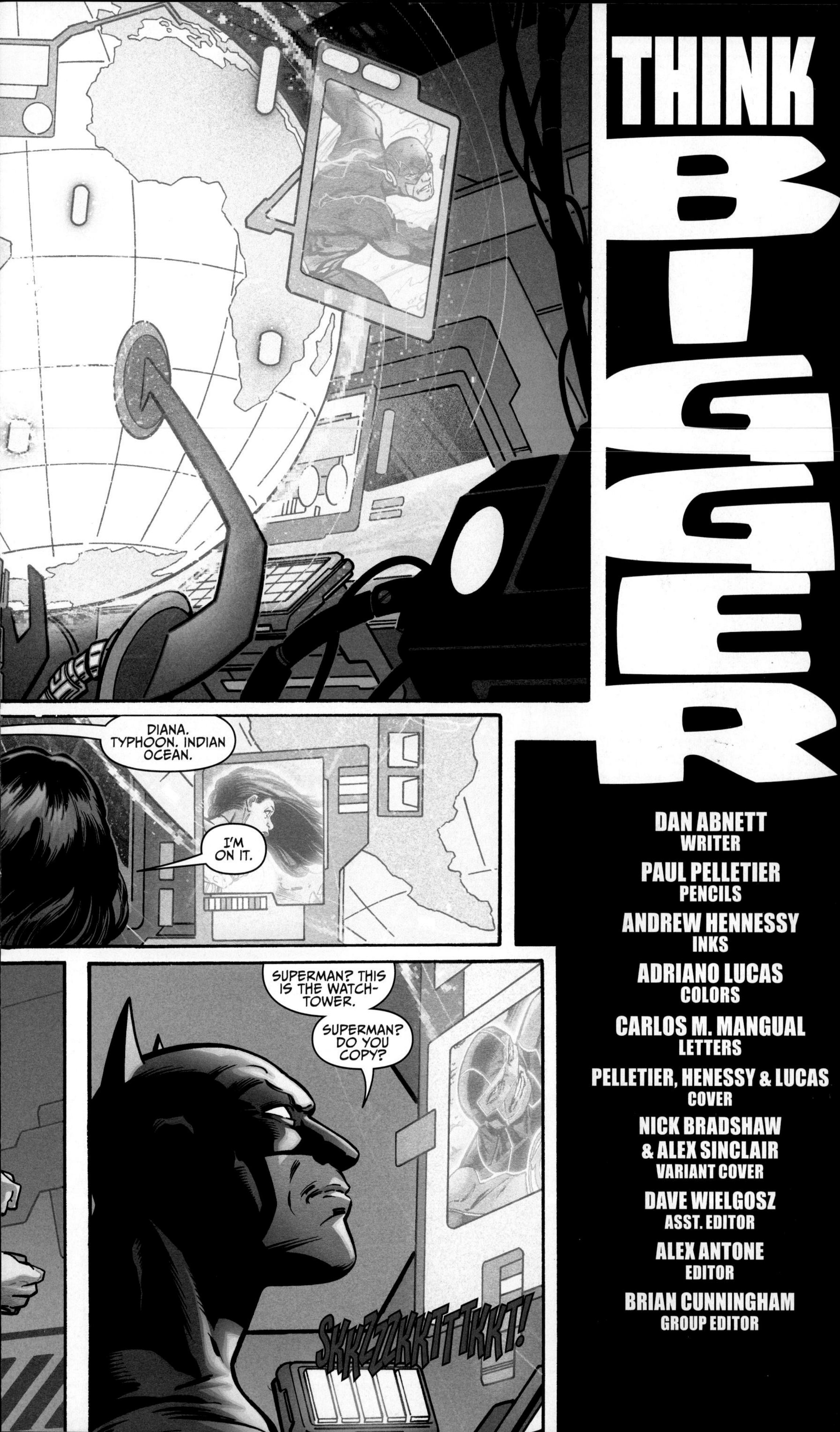
DIANA. TYPHOON. INDIAN OCEAN.
I'M ON IT.
SUPERMAN? THIS IS THE WATCH-TOWER.
SUPERMAN? DO YOU COPY?
SKKZZZKKKTTTKKT!

THINK BIGGER

DAN ABNETT
WRITER

PAUL PELLETIER
PENCILS

ANDREW HENNESSY
INKS

ADRIANO LUCAS
COLORS

CARLOS M. MANGUAL
LETTERS

PELLETIER, HENESSY & LUCAS
COVER

NICK BRADSHAW & ALEX SINCLAIR
VARIANT COVER

DAVE WIELGOSZ
ASST. EDITOR

ALEX ANTONE
EDITOR

BRIAN CUNNINGHAM
GROUP EDITOR

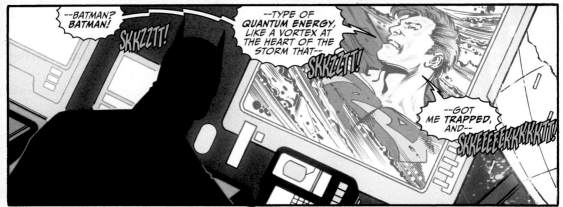

--BATMAN? BATMAN!

SKKZZZT!

--TYPE OF *QUANTUM ENERGY,* LIKE A VORTEX AT THE HEART OF THE STORM THAT--

SKKZZZT!

--GOT ME *TRAPPED,* AND--

SKKEEEEKKKKKT!!

SUPERMAN? *SUPERMAN?*

DO YOU COPY?

PLEASE, THERE'S GOT TO BE SOMETHING I CAN--

JUST GO BACK TO YOUR ROOM.

ROY WARNED ME OF A *THREAT,* SIR. A *MAJOR* THREAT.

SURELY *THIS--*

THERE IS *NO* EVIDENCE OF CORRELATION, MS. TROY.

I CHECKED AND *RECHECKED* FOR INDICATORS OF THE ALLEGED THREAT YOUR FRIEND DESCRIBED, AND FOUND *NOTHING.*

THIS CRISIS IS BEYOND *ANYTHING* ROY HARPER MAY HAVE STUMBLED INTO.

NOW PLEASE. CLEAR THE MONITOR ROOM.

...

AND *CONSOLE* YOURSELF THAT YOUR FRIEND MR. HARPER...

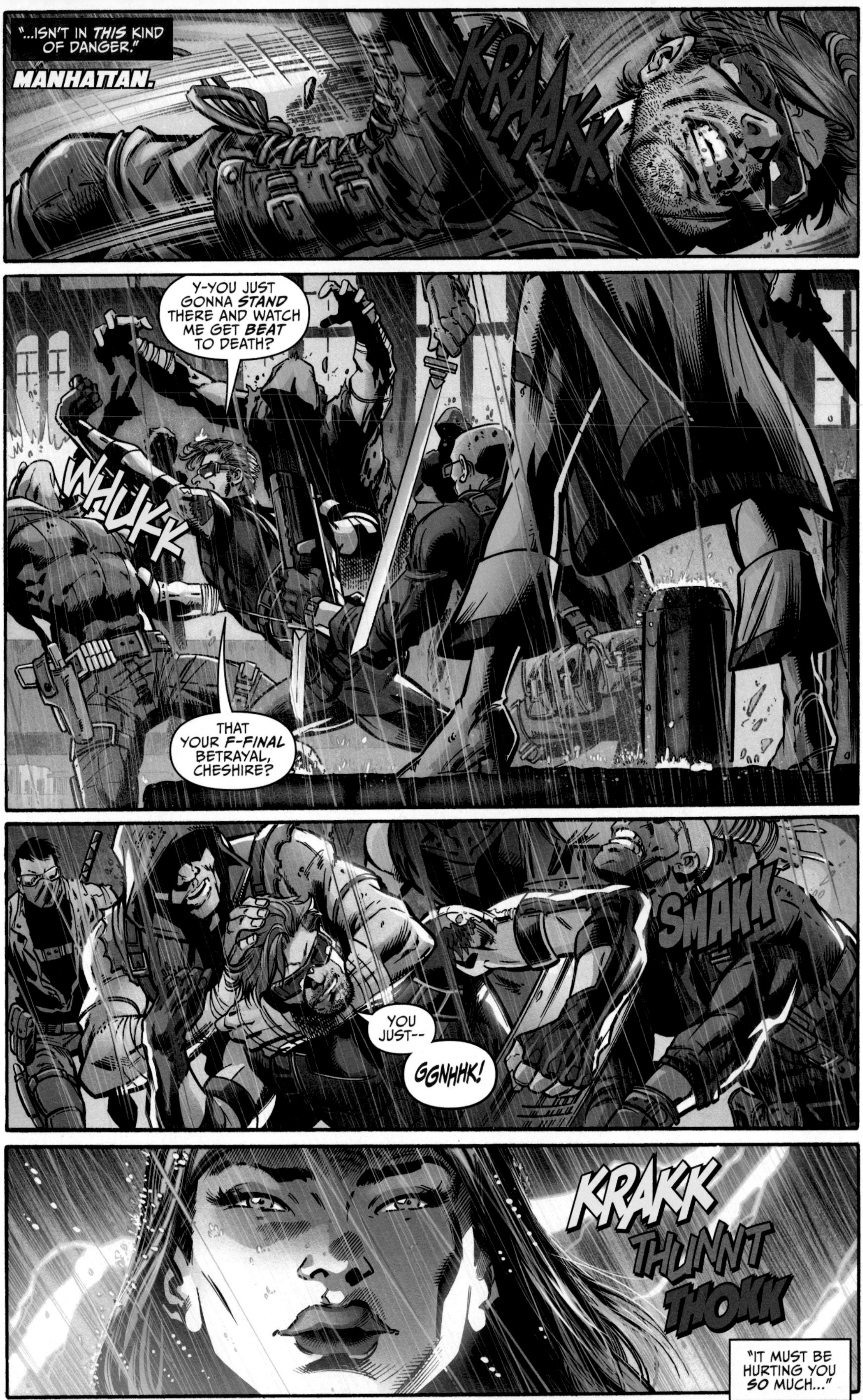

"...ISN'T IN THIS KIND OF DANGER."
MANHATTAN.
KRAAKK
Y-YOU JUST GONNA STAND THERE AND WATCH ME GET BEAT TO DEATH?
WHUKK
THAT YOUR F-FINAL BETRAYAL, CHESHIRE?
SMAKK
YOU JUST--
GGNHHK!
KRAKK
THUNNT
THOKK
"IT MUST BE HURTING YOU SO MUCH..."

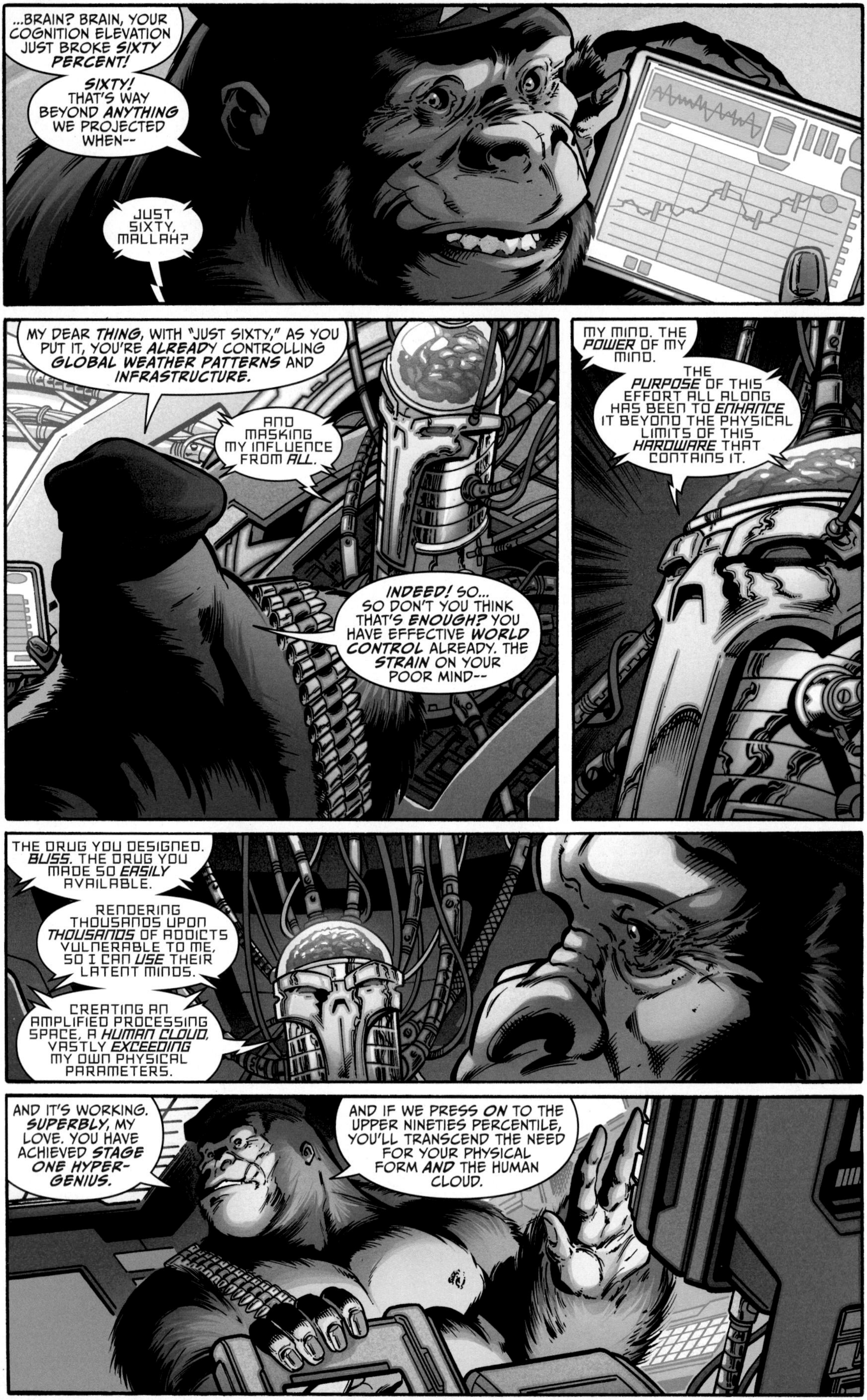
...BRAIN? BRAIN, YOUR COGNITION ELEVATION JUST BROKE SIXTY PERCENT!
SIXTY! THAT'S WAY BEYOND ANYTHING WE PROJECTED WHEN--
JUST SIXTY, MALLAH?
MY DEAR THING, WITH "JUST SIXTY," AS YOU PUT IT, YOU'RE ALREADY CONTROLLING GLOBAL WEATHER PATTERNS AND INFRASTRUCTURE.
AND MASKING MY INFLUENCE FROM ALL.
INDEED! SO... SO DON'T YOU THINK THAT'S ENOUGH? YOU HAVE EFFECTIVE WORLD CONTROL ALREADY. THE STRAIN ON YOUR POOR MIND--
MY MIND. THE POWER OF MY MIND.
THE PURPOSE OF THIS EFFORT ALL ALONG HAS BEEN TO ENHANCE IT BEYOND THE PHYSICAL LIMITS OF THIS HARDWARE THAT CONTAINS IT.
THE DRUG YOU DESIGNED. BLISS. THE DRUG YOU MADE SO EASILY AVAILABLE.
RENDERING THOUSANDS UPON THOUSANDS OF ADDICTS VULNERABLE TO ME, SO I CAN USE THEIR LATENT MINDS.
CREATING AN AMPLIFIED PROCESSING SPACE, A HUMAN CLOUD, VASTLY EXCEEDING MY OWN PHYSICAL PARAMETERS.
AND IT'S WORKING. SUPERBLY, MY LOVE. YOU HAVE ACHIEVED STAGE ONE HYPER-GENIUS.
AND IF WE PRESS ON TO THE UPPER NINETIES PERCENTILE, YOU'LL TRANSCEND THE NEED FOR YOUR PHYSICAL FORM AND THE HUMAN CLOUD.

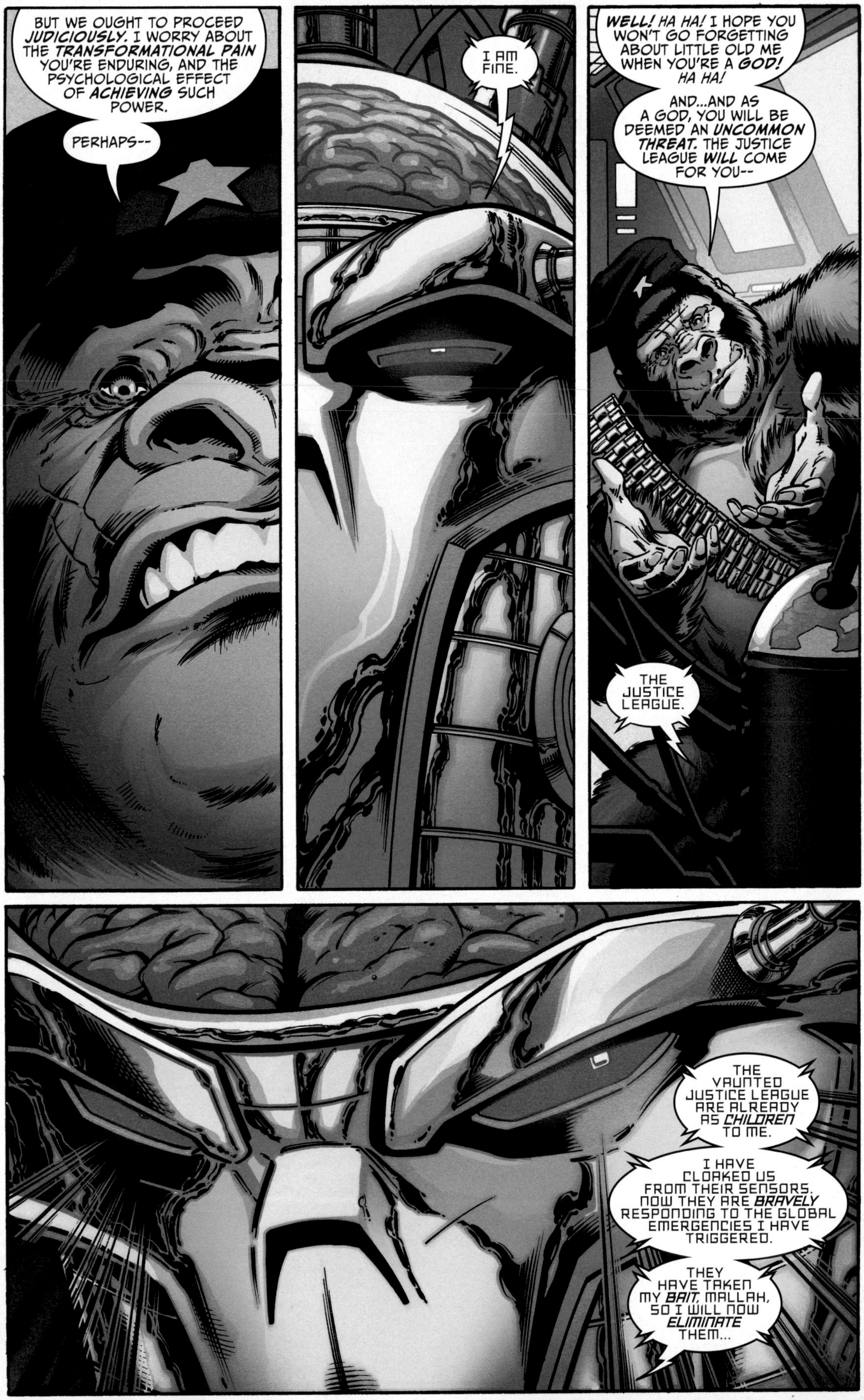
BUT WE OUGHT TO PROCEED JUDICIOUSLY. I WORRY ABOUT THE TRANSFORMATIONAL PAIN YOU'RE ENDURING, AND THE PSYCHOLOGICAL EFFECT OF ACHIEVING SUCH POWER.
PERHAPS--
I AM FINE.
WELL! HA HA! I HOPE YOU WON'T GO FORGETTING ABOUT LITTLE OLD ME WHEN YOU'RE A GOD! HA HA!
AND...AND AS A GOD, YOU WILL BE DEEMED AN UNCOMMON THREAT. THE JUSTICE LEAGUE WILL COME FOR YOU--
THE JUSTICE LEAGUE.
THE VAUNTED JUSTICE LEAGUE ARE ALREADY AS CHILDREN TO ME.
I HAVE CLOAKED US FROM THEIR SENSORS. NOW THEY ARE BRAVELY RESPONDING TO THE GLOBAL EMERGENCIES I HAVE TRIGGERED.
THEY HAVE TAKEN MY BAIT, MALLAH, SO I WILL NOW ELIMINATE THEM...

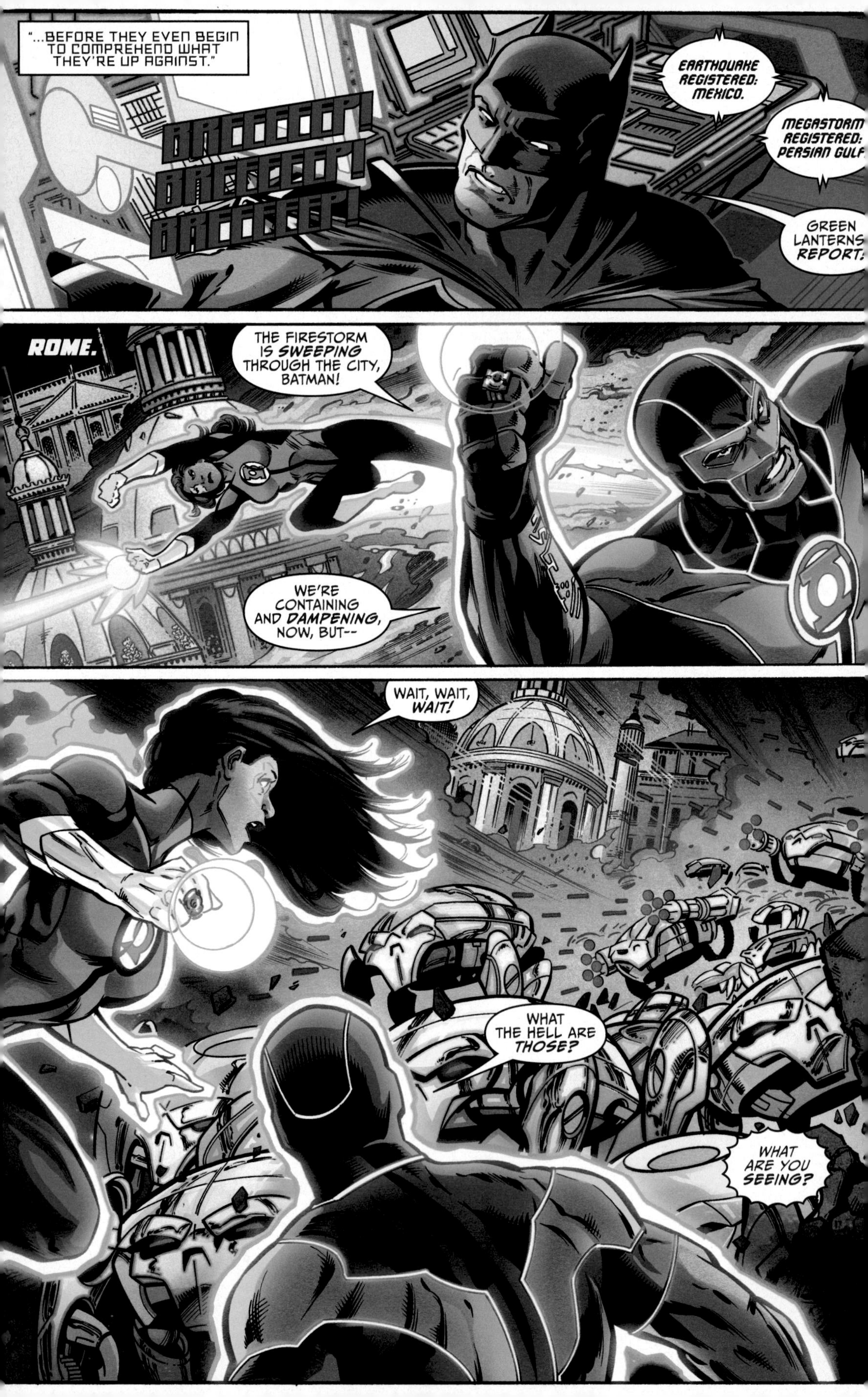
"...BEFORE THEY EVEN BEGIN TO COMPREHEND WHAT THEY'RE UP AGAINST."
BREEEEEP! BREEEEEP! BREEEEEP!
EARTHQUAKE REGISTERED: MEXICO.
MEGASTORM REGISTERED: PERSIAN GULF.
GREEN LANTERNS REPORT:
ROME.
THE FIRESTORM IS SWEEPING THROUGH THE CITY, BATMAN!
WE'RE CONTAINING AND DAMPENING, NOW, BUT--
WAIT, WAIT, WAIT!
WHAT THE HELL ARE THOSE?
WHAT ARE YOU SEEING?

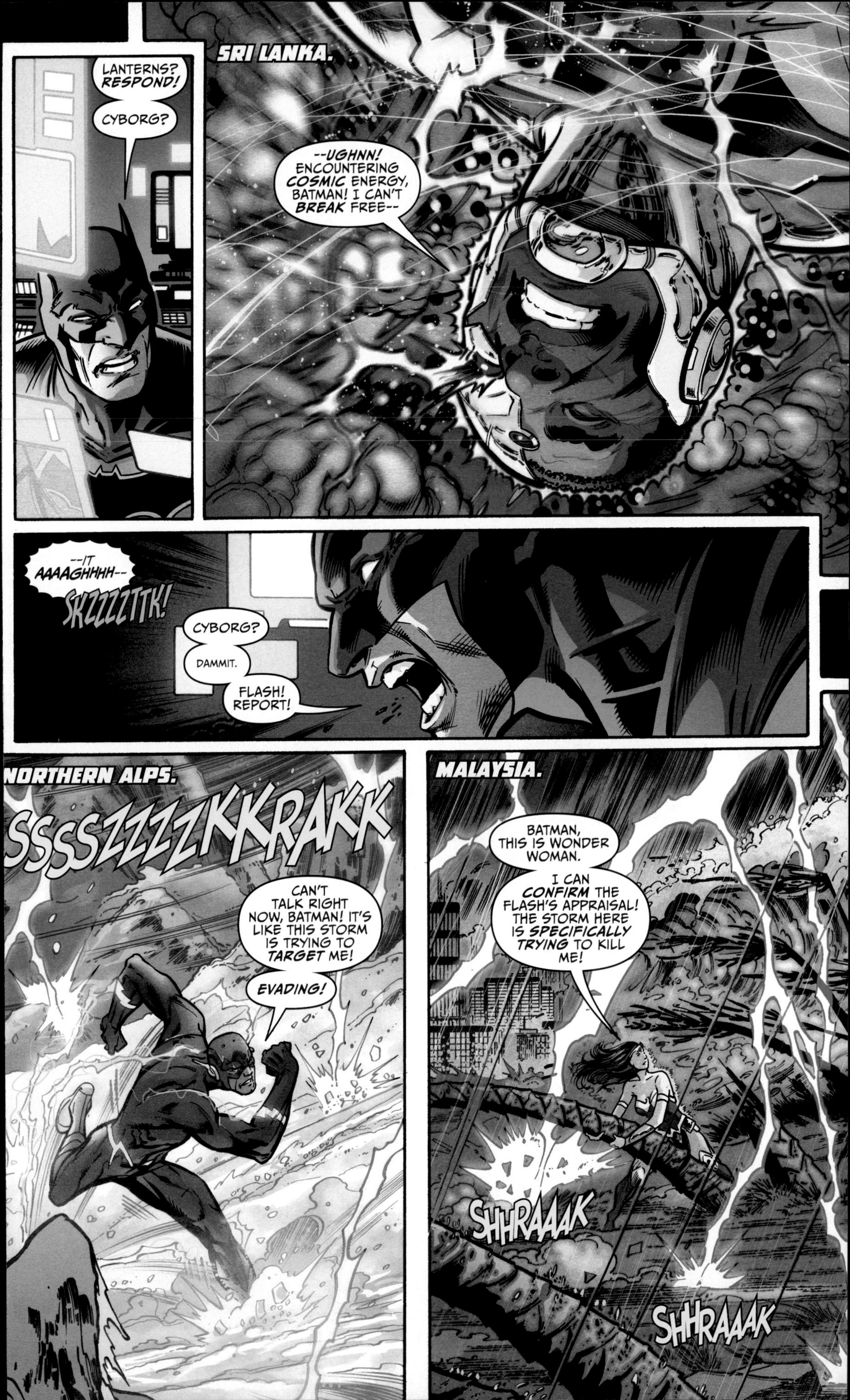

SRI LANKA.
LANTERNS? RESPOND!
CYBORG?
--UGHNN! ENCOUNTERING COSMIC ENERGY, BATMAN! I CAN'T BREAK FREE--
--IT AAAAGHHHH--
SKZZZZTTK!
CYBORG?
DAMMIT.
FLASH! REPORT!
NORTHERN ALPS.
SSSSZZZZKKRAKK
CAN'T TALK RIGHT NOW, BATMAN! IT'S LIKE THIS STORM IS TRYING TO TARGET ME!
EVADING!
MALAYSIA.
BATMAN, THIS IS WONDER WOMAN.
I CAN CONFIRM THE FLASH'S APPRAISAL! THE STORM HERE IS SPECIFICALLY TRYING TO KILL ME!
SHHRAAAK
SHHRAAAK

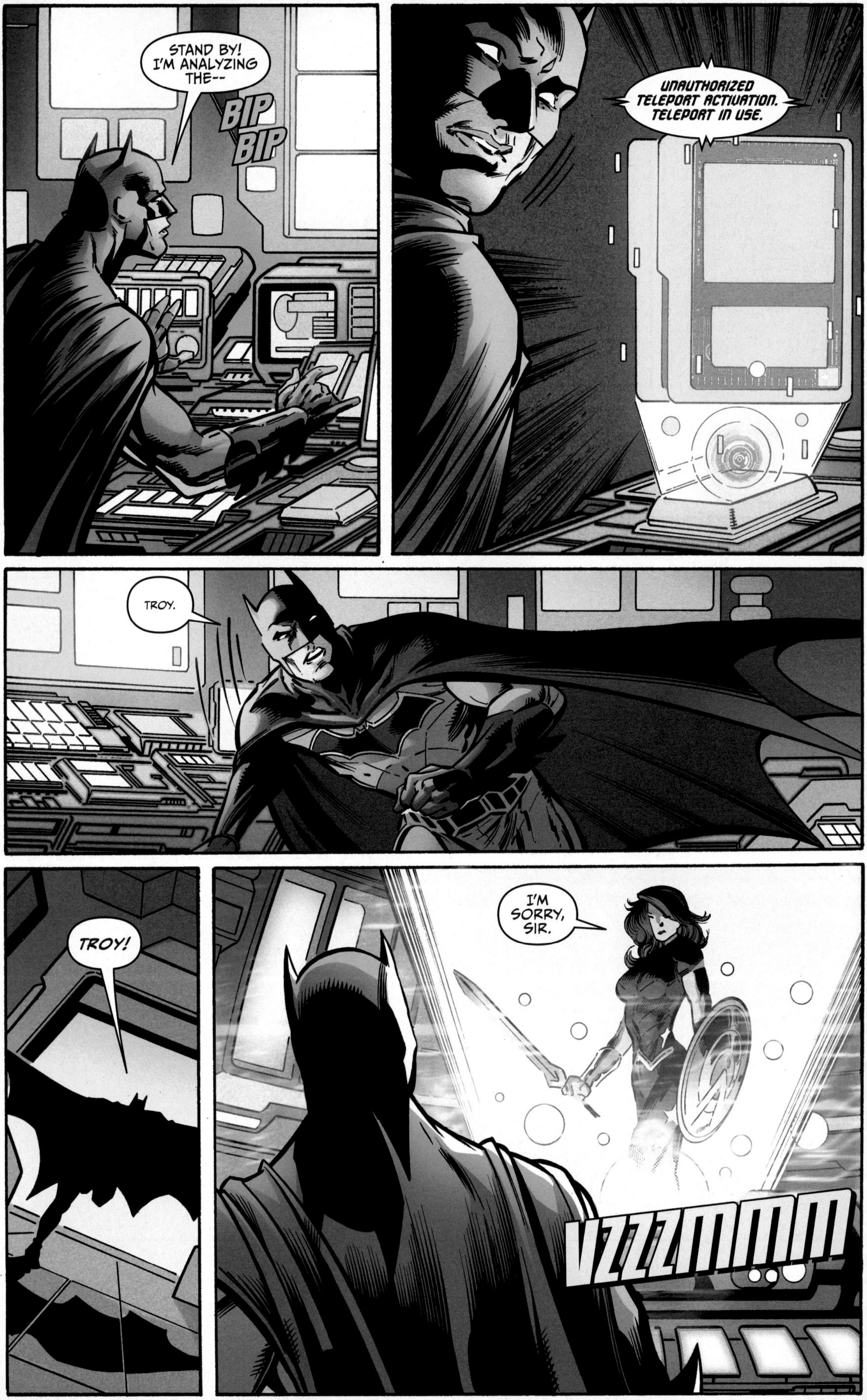
STAND BY! I'M ANALYZING THE--
BIP BIP
UNAUTHORIZED TELEPORT ACTIVATION. TELEPORT IN USE.
TROY.
TROY!
I'M SORRY, SIR.
VZZZMMMM

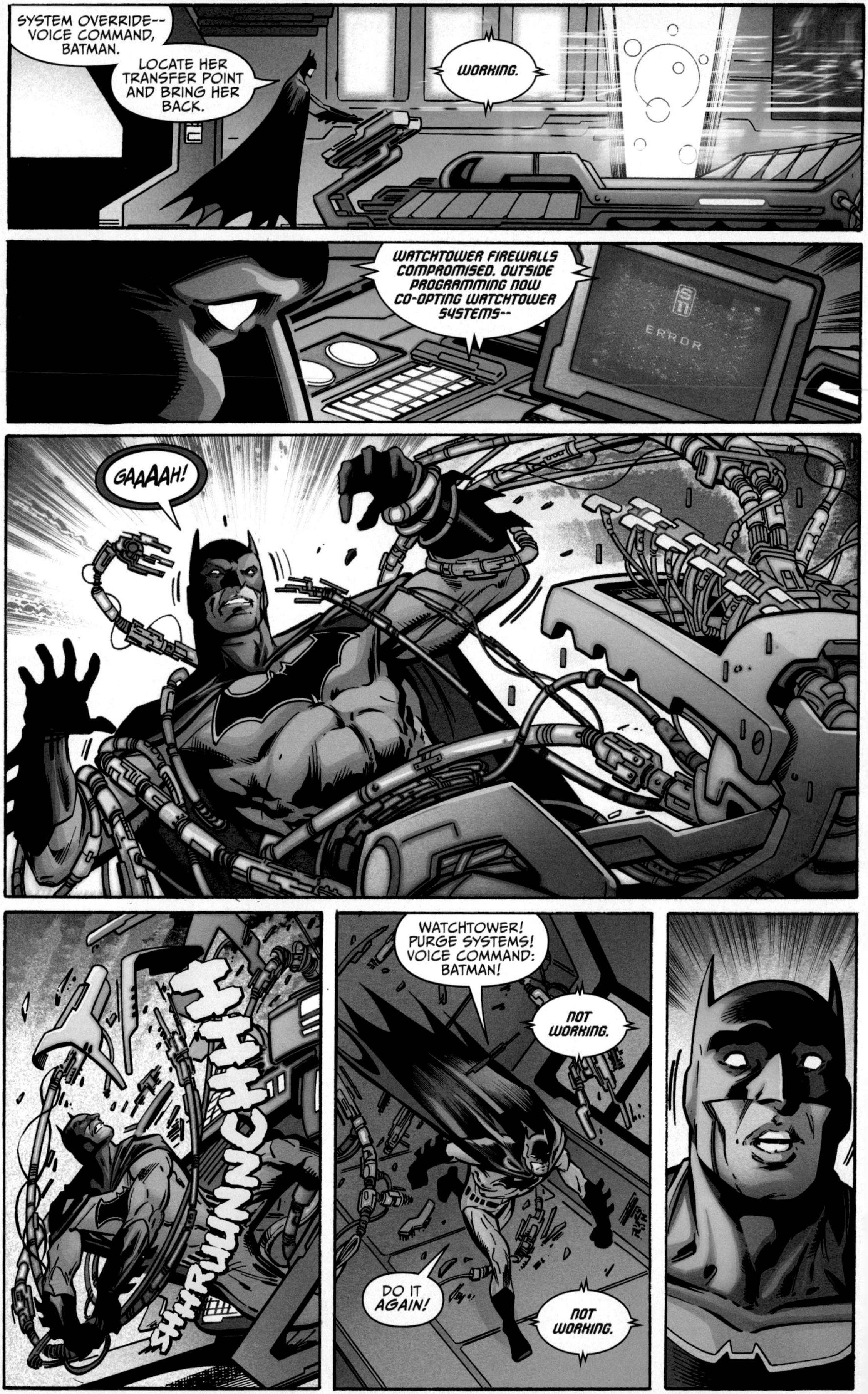
SYSTEM OVERRIDE--VOICE COMMAND, BATMAN.
LOCATE HER TRANSFER POINT AND BRING HER BACK.
WORKING.
WATCHTOWER FIREWALLS COMPROMISED. OUTSIDE PROGRAMMING NOW CO-OPTING WATCHTOWER SYSTEMS--
ERROR
GAAAAH!
SHRUUNNCHHH
WATCHTOWER! PURGE SYSTEMS! VOICE COMMAND: BATMAN!
NOT WORKING.
DO IT AGAIN!
NOT WORKING.

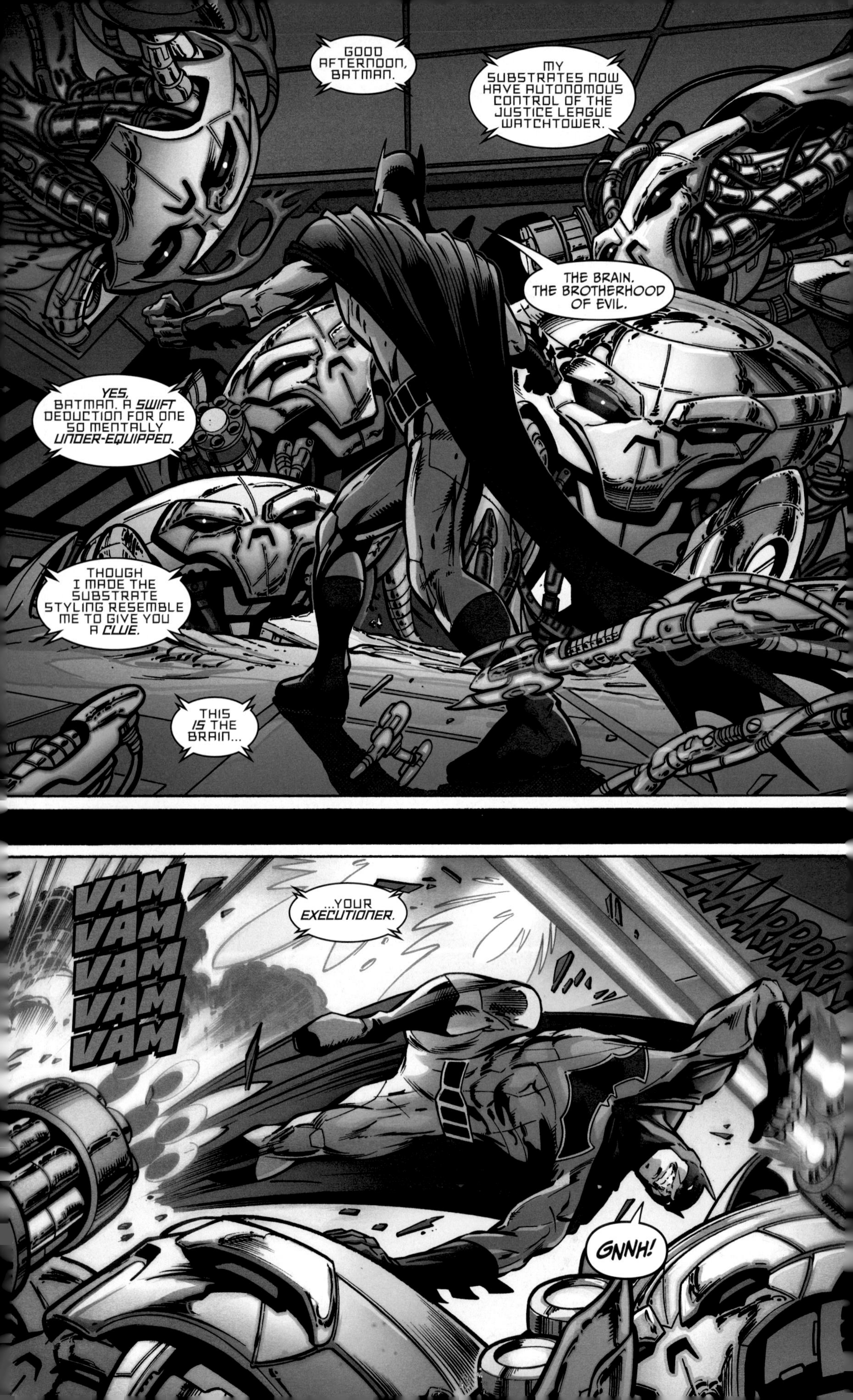
GOOD AFTERNOON, BATMAN.
MY SUBSTRATES NOW HAVE AUTONOMOUS CONTROL OF THE JUSTICE LEAGUE WATCHTOWER.
THE BRAIN. THE BROTHERHOOD OF EVIL.
YES, BATMAN. A SWIFT DEDUCTION FOR ONE SO MENTALLY UNDER-EQUIPPED.
THOUGH I MADE THE SUBSTRATE STYLING RESEMBLE ME TO GIVE YOU A CLUE.
THIS IS THE BRAIN...
VAM VAM VAM VAM VAM
...YOUR EXECUTIONER.
ZAAARRRRR
GNNH!

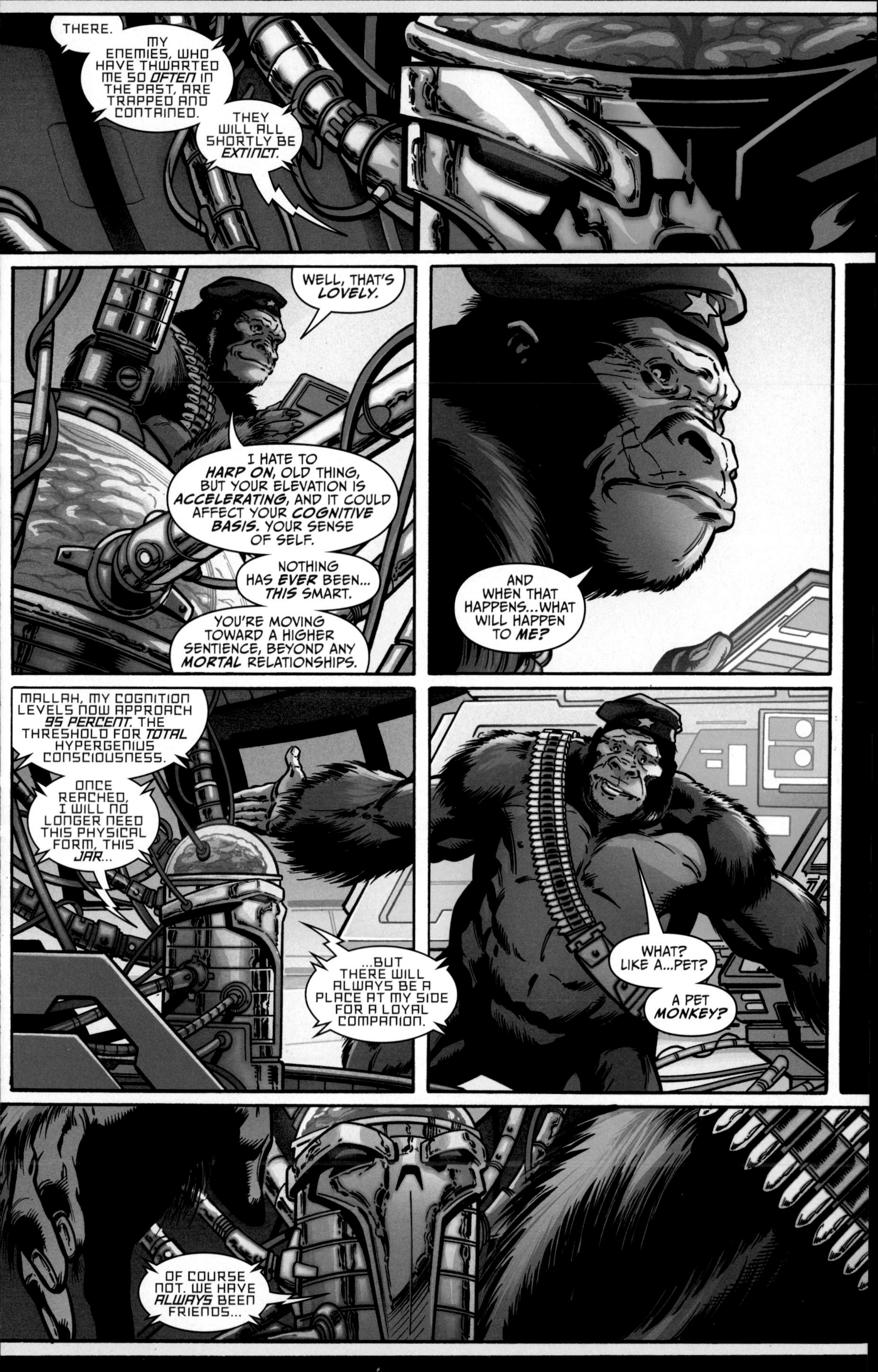
THERE.
MY ENEMIES, WHO HAVE THWARTED ME SO OFTEN IN THE PAST, ARE TRAPPED AND CONTAINED.
THEY WILL ALL SHORTLY BE EXTINCT.
WELL, THAT'S LOVELY.
I HATE TO HARP ON, OLD THING, BUT YOUR ELEVATION IS ACCELERATING, AND IT COULD AFFECT YOUR COGNITIVE BASIS. YOUR SENSE OF SELF.
NOTHING HAS EVER BEEN... THIS SMART.
YOU'RE MOVING TOWARD A HIGHER SENTIENCE, BEYOND ANY MORTAL RELATIONSHIPS.
AND WHEN THAT HAPPENS...WHAT WILL HAPPEN TO ME?
MALLAH, MY COGNITION LEVELS NOW APPROACH 95 PERCENT. THE THRESHOLD FOR TOTAL HYPERGENIUS CONSCIOUSNESS.
ONCE REACHED, I WILL NO LONGER NEED THIS PHYSICAL FORM, THIS JAR...
...BUT THERE WILL ALWAYS BE A PLACE AT MY SIDE FOR A LOYAL COMPANION.
WHAT? LIKE A...PET?
A PET MONKEY?
OF COURSE NOT. WE HAVE ALWAYS BEEN FRIENDS...

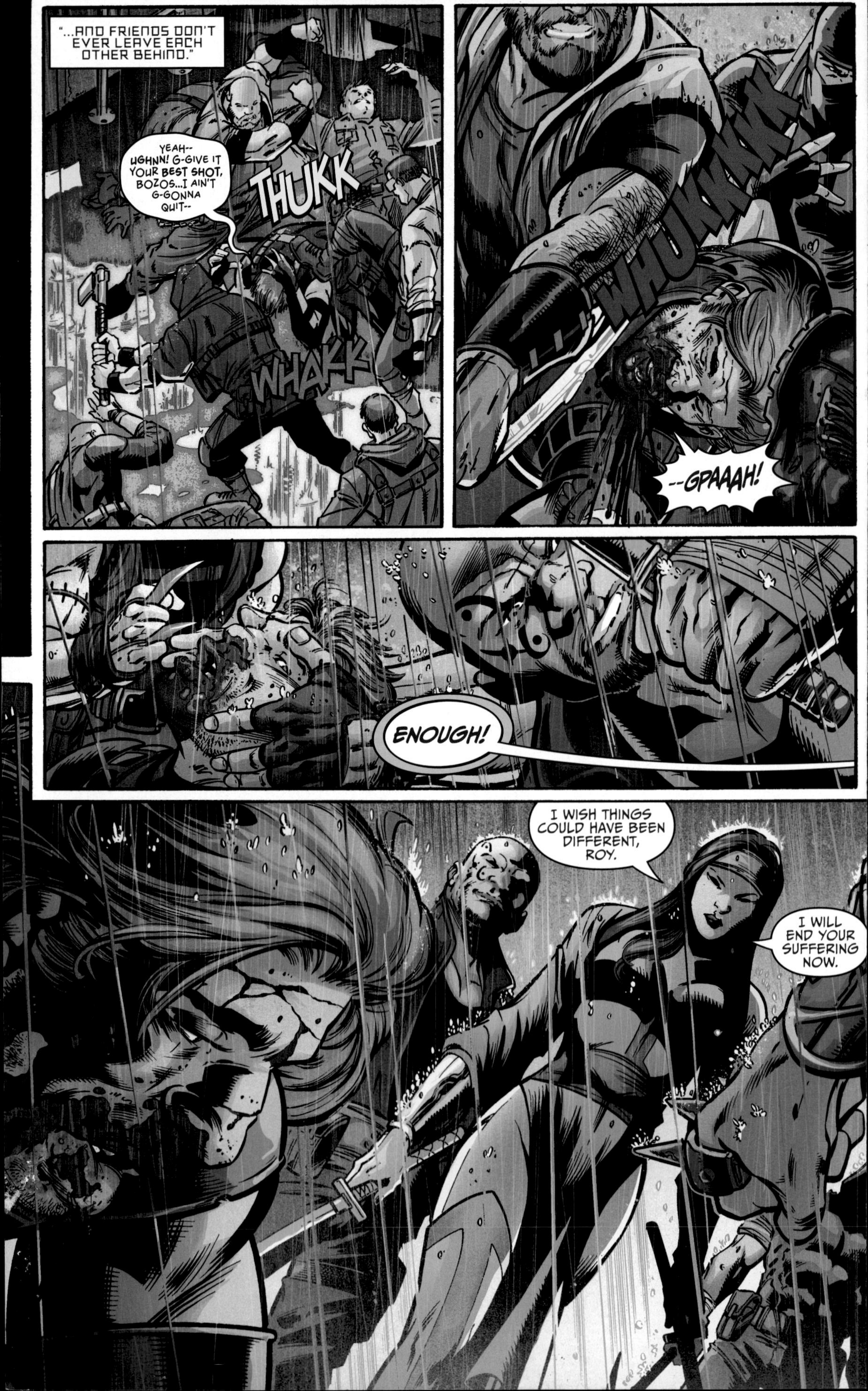
"...AND FRIENDS DON'T EVER LEAVE EACH OTHER BEHIND."
YEAH-- UGHNN! G-GIVE IT YOUR BEST SHOT, BOZOS...I AIN'T G-GONNA QUIT--
THUKK
WHAKK
WHUKKKK
--GPAAAH!
ENOUGH!
I WISH THINGS COULD HAVE BEEN DIFFERENT, ROY.
I WILL END YOUR SUFFERING NOW.

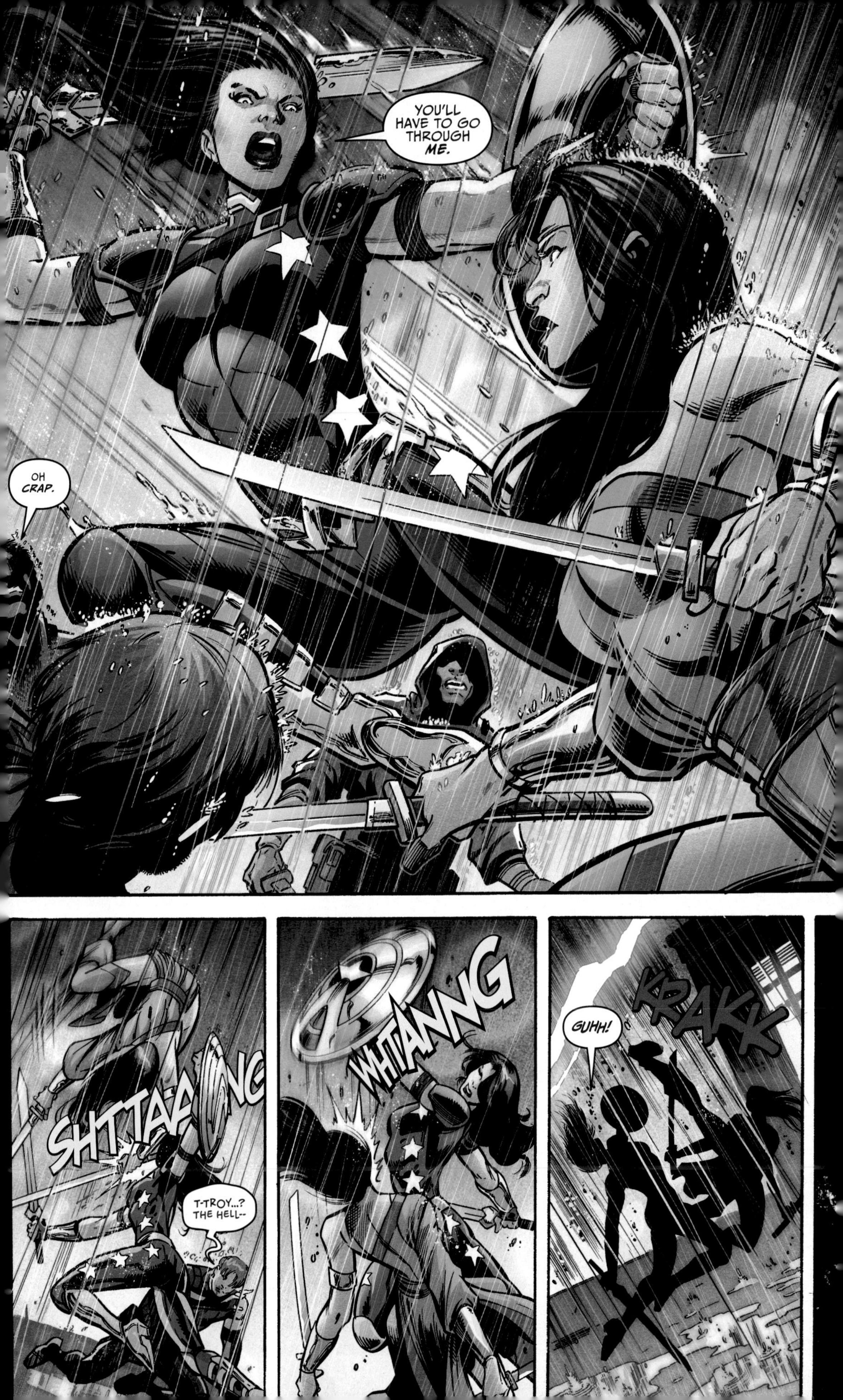
YOU'LL HAVE TO GO THROUGH *ME.*
OH *CRAP.*
SHTTA
T-TROY...? THE HELL--
WHTANNG
KRAKK
GUHH!

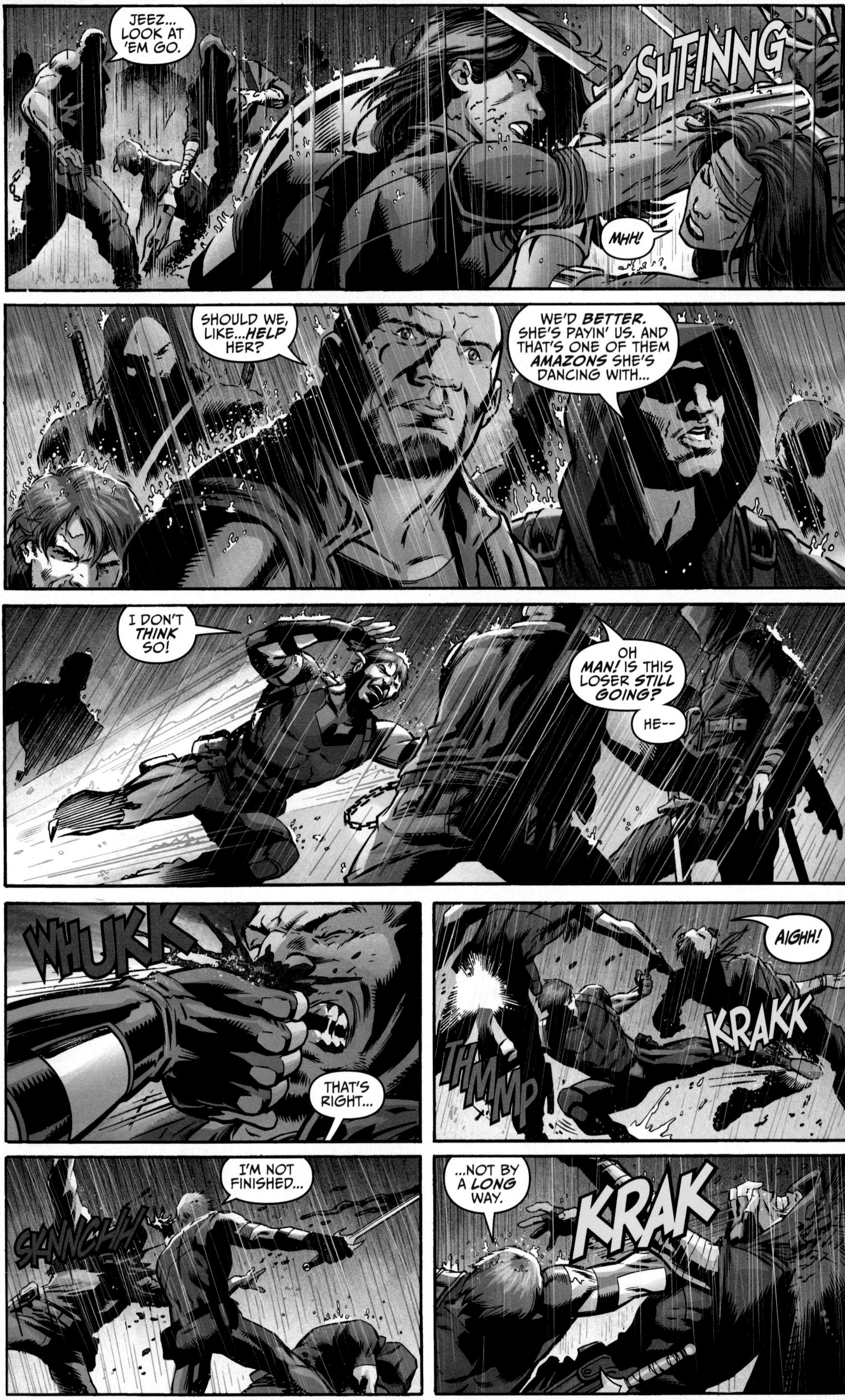
JEEZ... LOOK AT 'EM GO.
SHTINNG
MHH!
SHOULD WE, LIKE...HELP HER?
WE'D BETTER. SHE'S PAYIN' US. AND THAT'S ONE OF THEM AMAZONS SHE'S DANCING WITH...
I DON'T THINK SO!
OH MAN! IS THIS LOSER STILL GOING?
HE--
WHUKK
THAT'S RIGHT...
AIGHH!
KRAKK
THMMP
I'M NOT FINISHED...
SKNNCHH
...NOT BY A LONG WAY.
KRAK

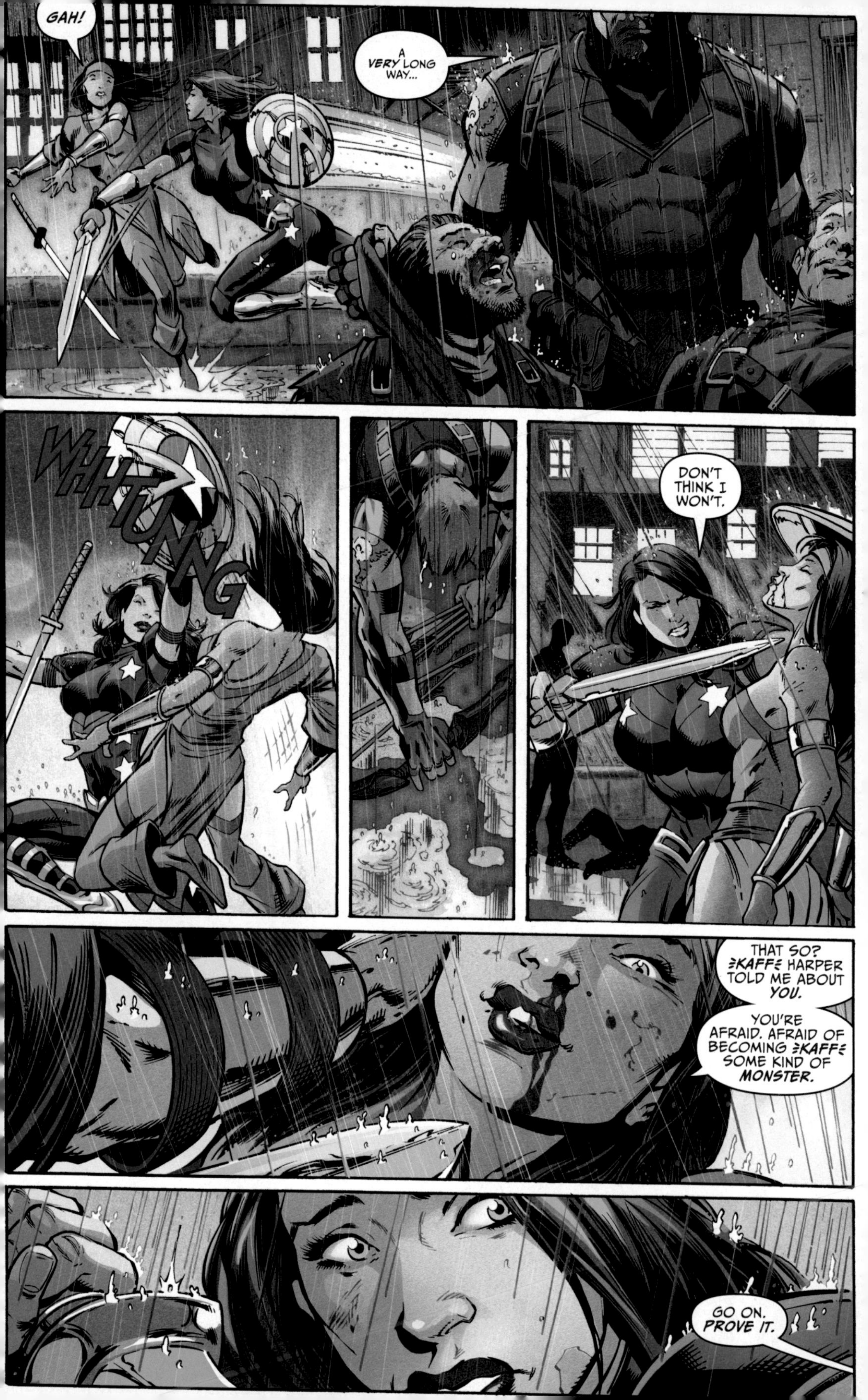
GAH!
A VERY LONG WAY...
WHHTUNNG
DON'T THINK I WON'T.
THAT SO? ≥KAFF≤ HARPER TOLD ME ABOUT YOU.
YOU'RE AFRAID. AFRAID OF BECOMING ≥KAFF≤ SOME KIND OF MONSTER.
GO ON. PROVE IT.

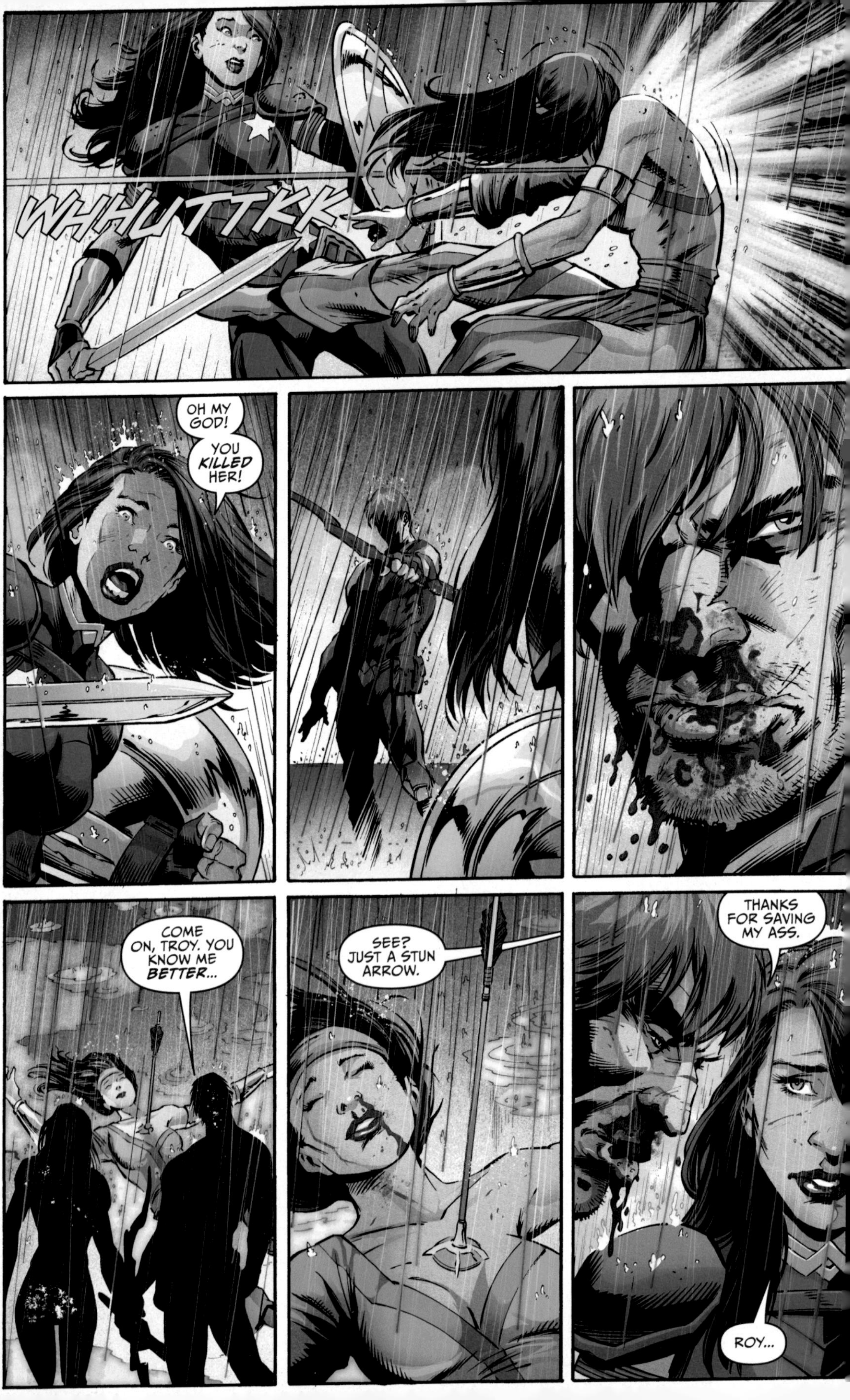
WHHUTTKK
OH MY GOD!
YOU KILLED HER!
COME ON, TROY. YOU KNOW ME BETTER...
SEE? JUST A STUN ARROW.
THANKS FOR SAVING MY ASS.
ROY...

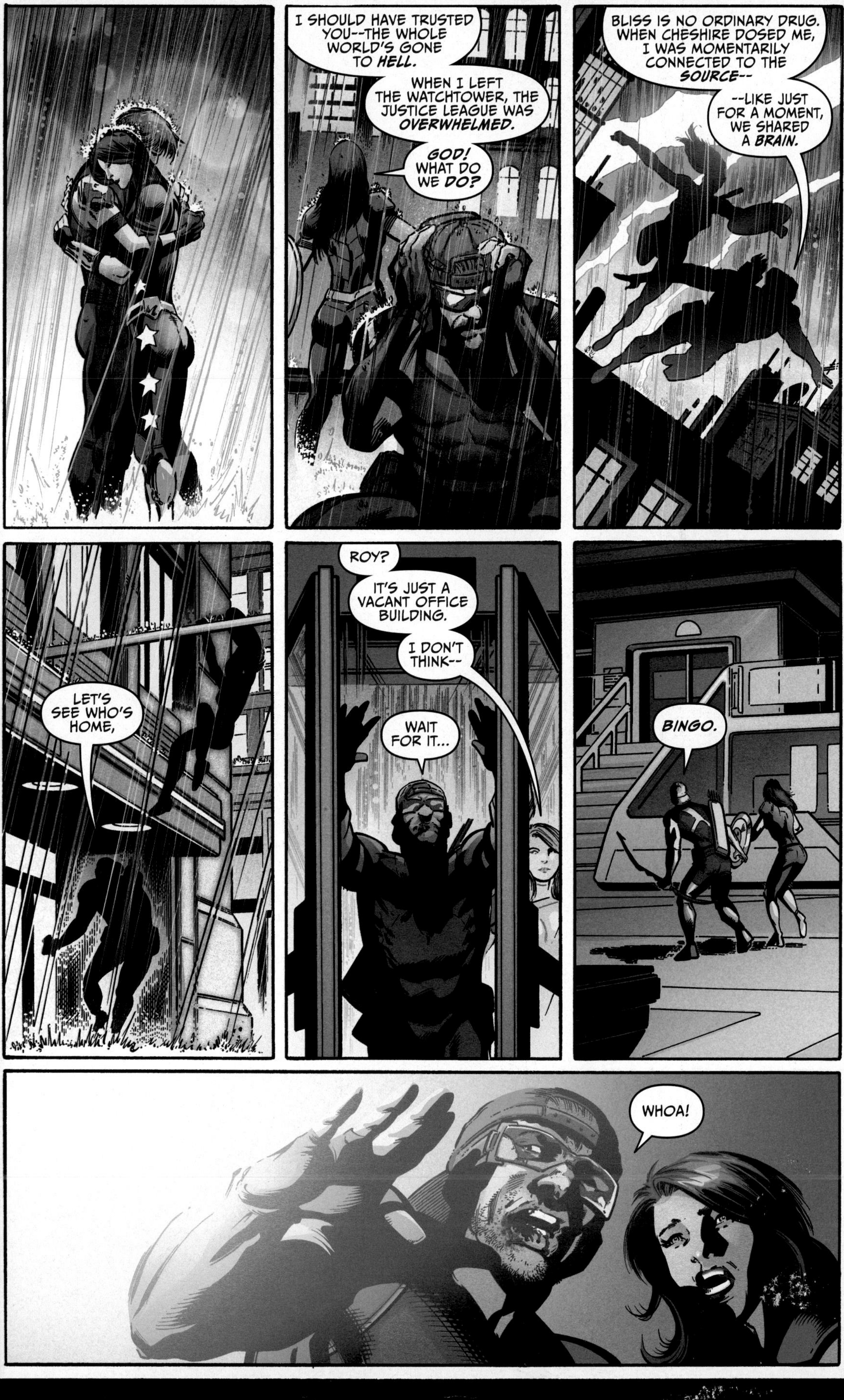

I SHOULD HAVE TRUSTED YOU--THE WHOLE WORLD'S GONE TO *HELL*.
WHEN I LEFT THE WATCHTOWER, THE JUSTICE LEAGUE WAS *OVERWHELMED*.
GOD! WHAT DO WE *DO?*
BLISS IS NO ORDINARY DRUG. WHEN CHESHIRE DOSED ME, I WAS MOMENTARILY CONNECTED TO THE *SOURCE*--
--LIKE JUST FOR A MOMENT, WE SHARED A *BRAIN*.
LET'S SEE WHO'S HOME,
ROY?
IT'S JUST A VACANT OFFICE BUILDING.
I DON'T THINK--
WAIT FOR IT...
BINGO.
WHOA!

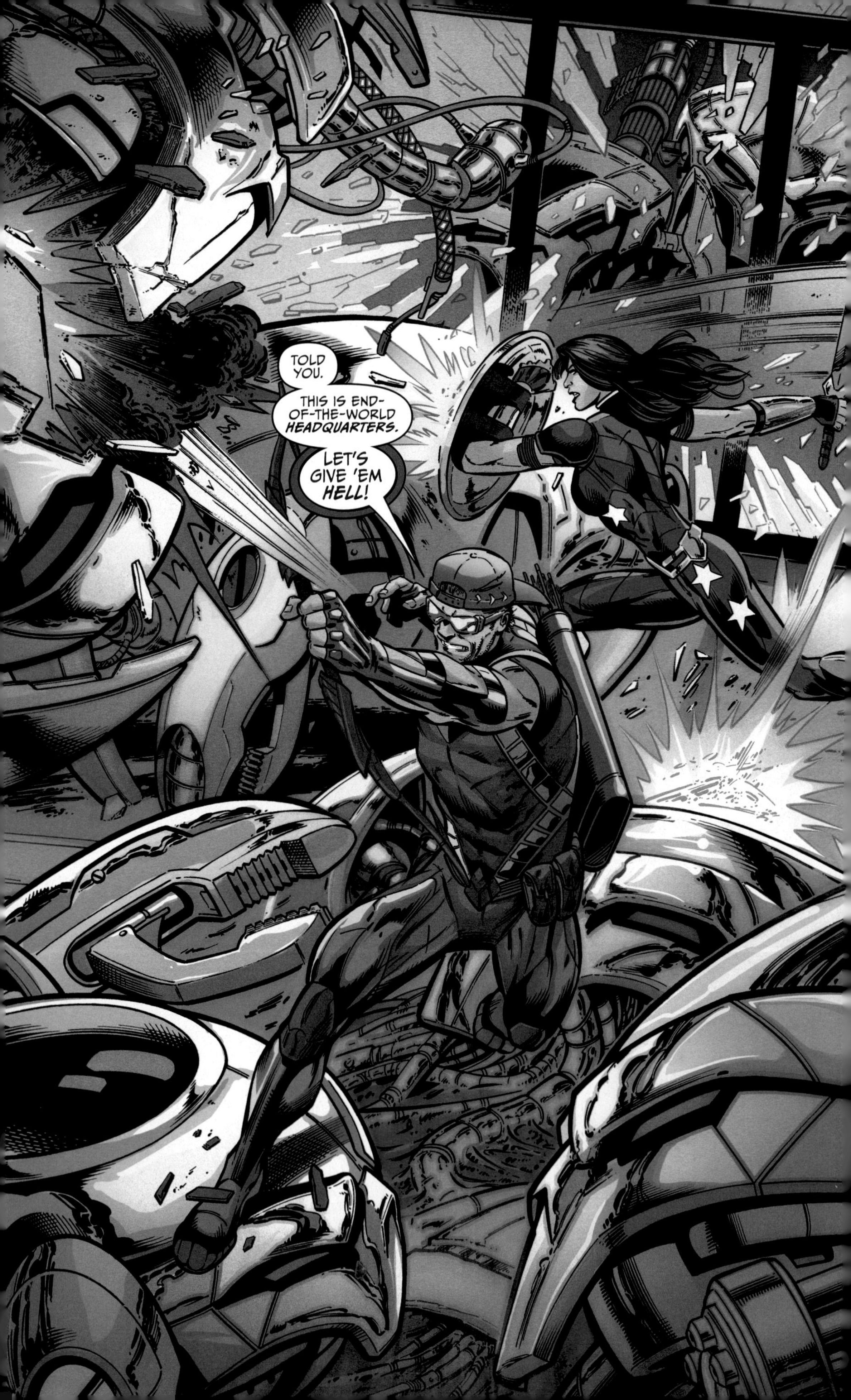
TOLD YOU.
THIS IS END-OF-THE-WORLD HEADQUARTERS.
LET'S GIVE 'EM HELL!

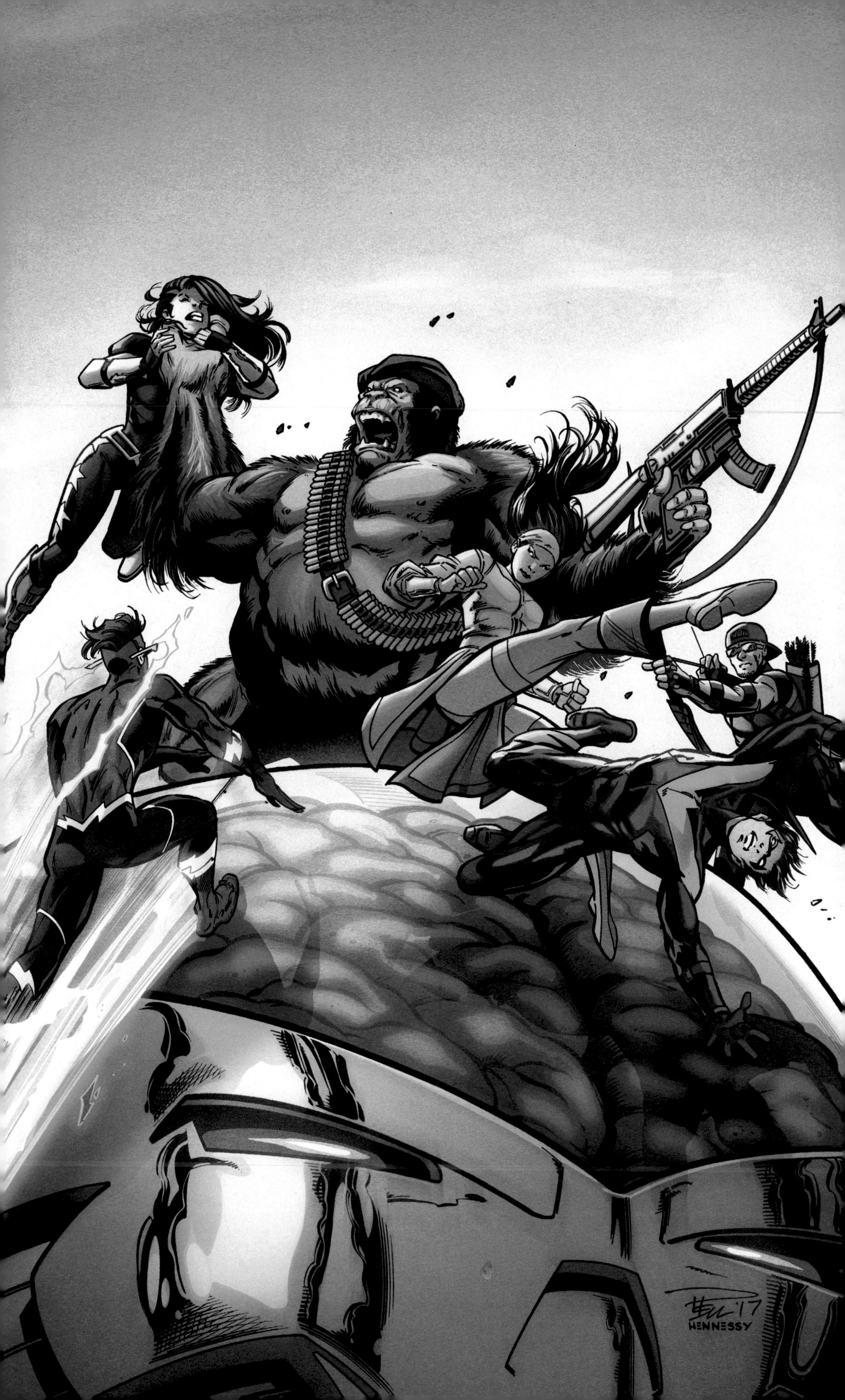
HENNESSY

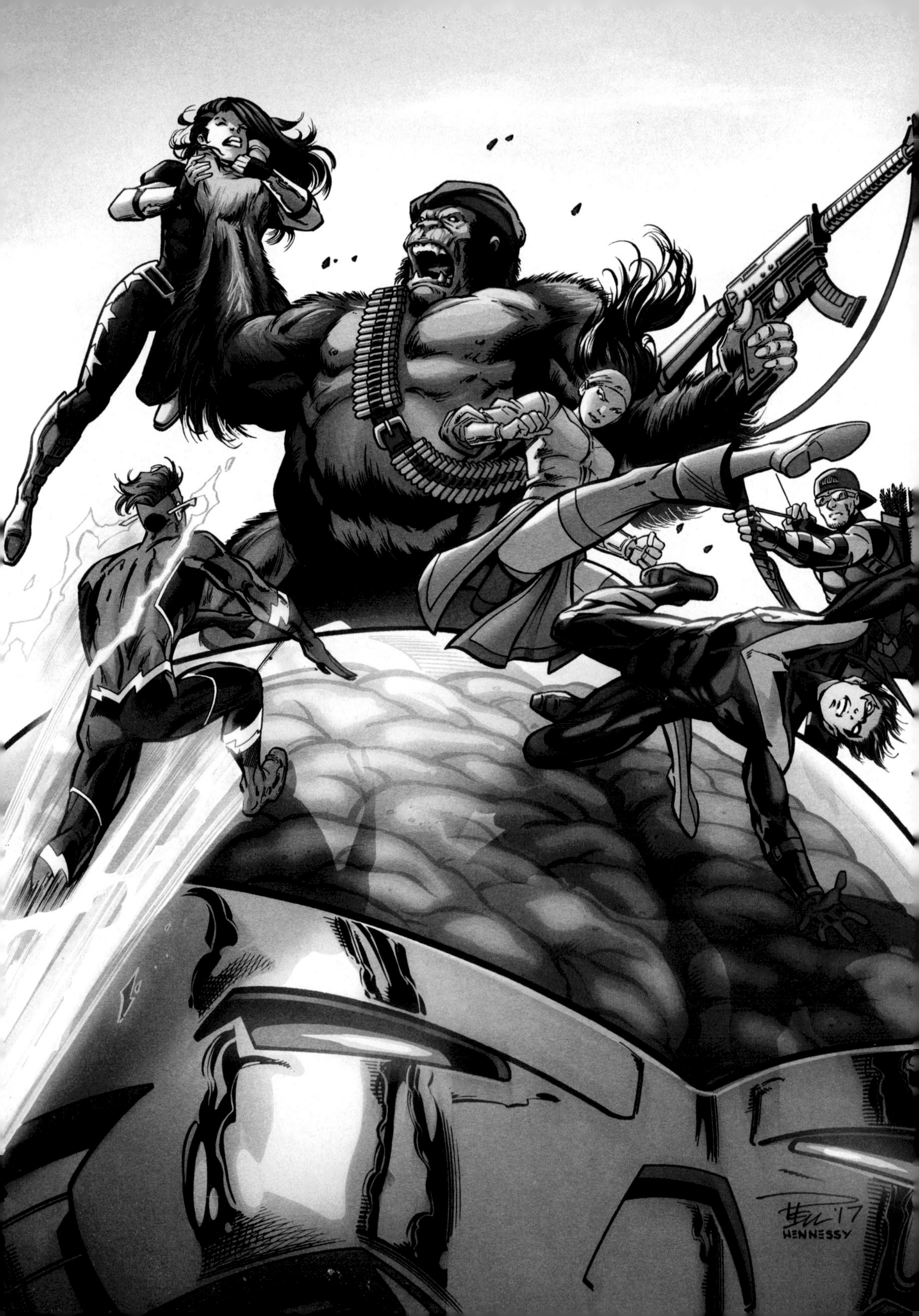
HENNESSY

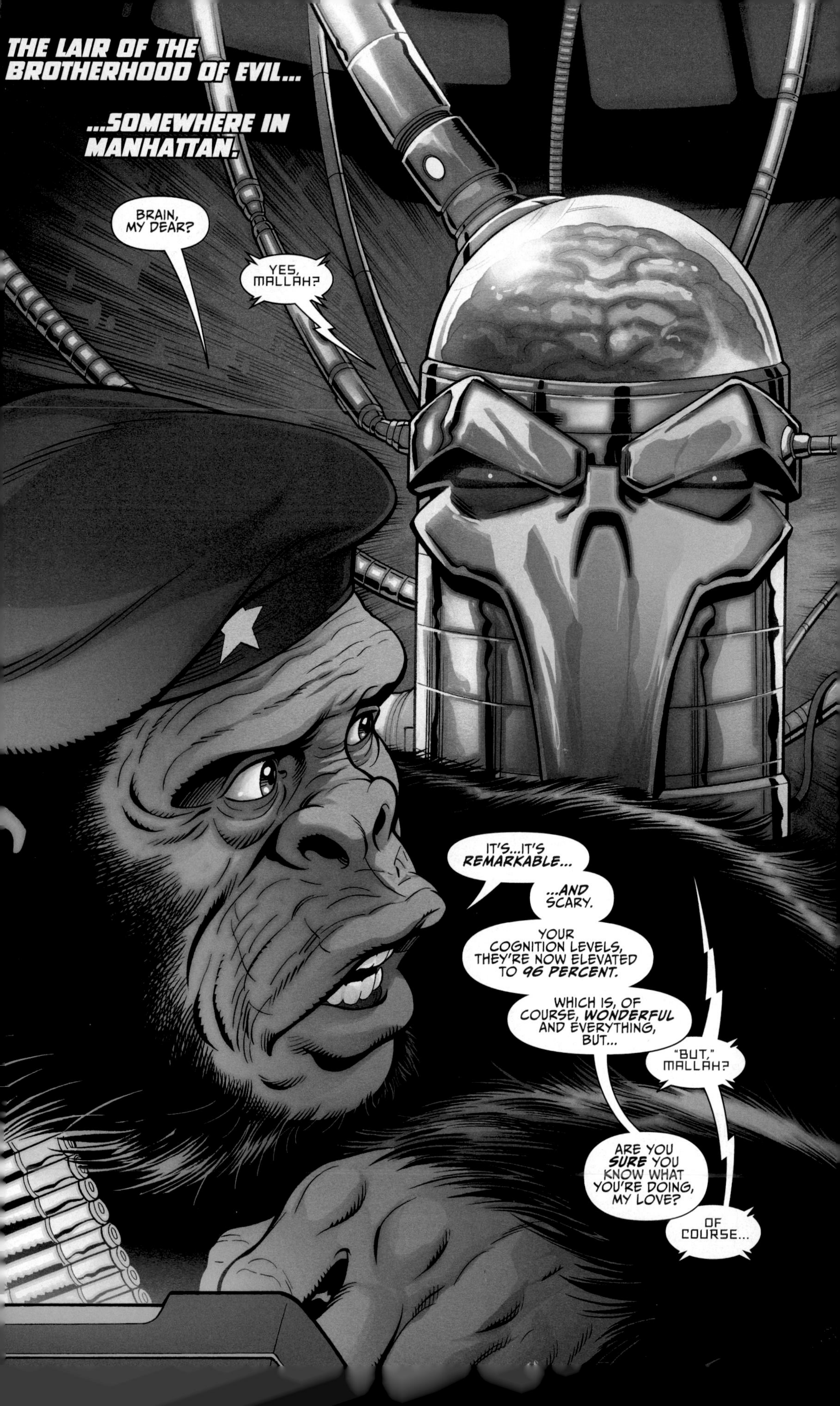
THE LAIR OF THE BROTHERHOOD OF EVIL...
...SOMEWHERE IN MANHATTAN.
BRAIN, MY DEAR?
YES, MALLAH?
IT'S...IT'S REMARKABLE...
...AND SCARY.
YOUR COGNITION LEVELS, THEY'RE NOW ELEVATED TO 96 PERCENT.
WHICH IS, OF COURSE, WONDERFUL AND EVERYTHING, BUT...
"BUT," MALLAH?
ARE YOU SURE YOU KNOW WHAT YOU'RE DOING, MY LOVE?
OF COURSE...

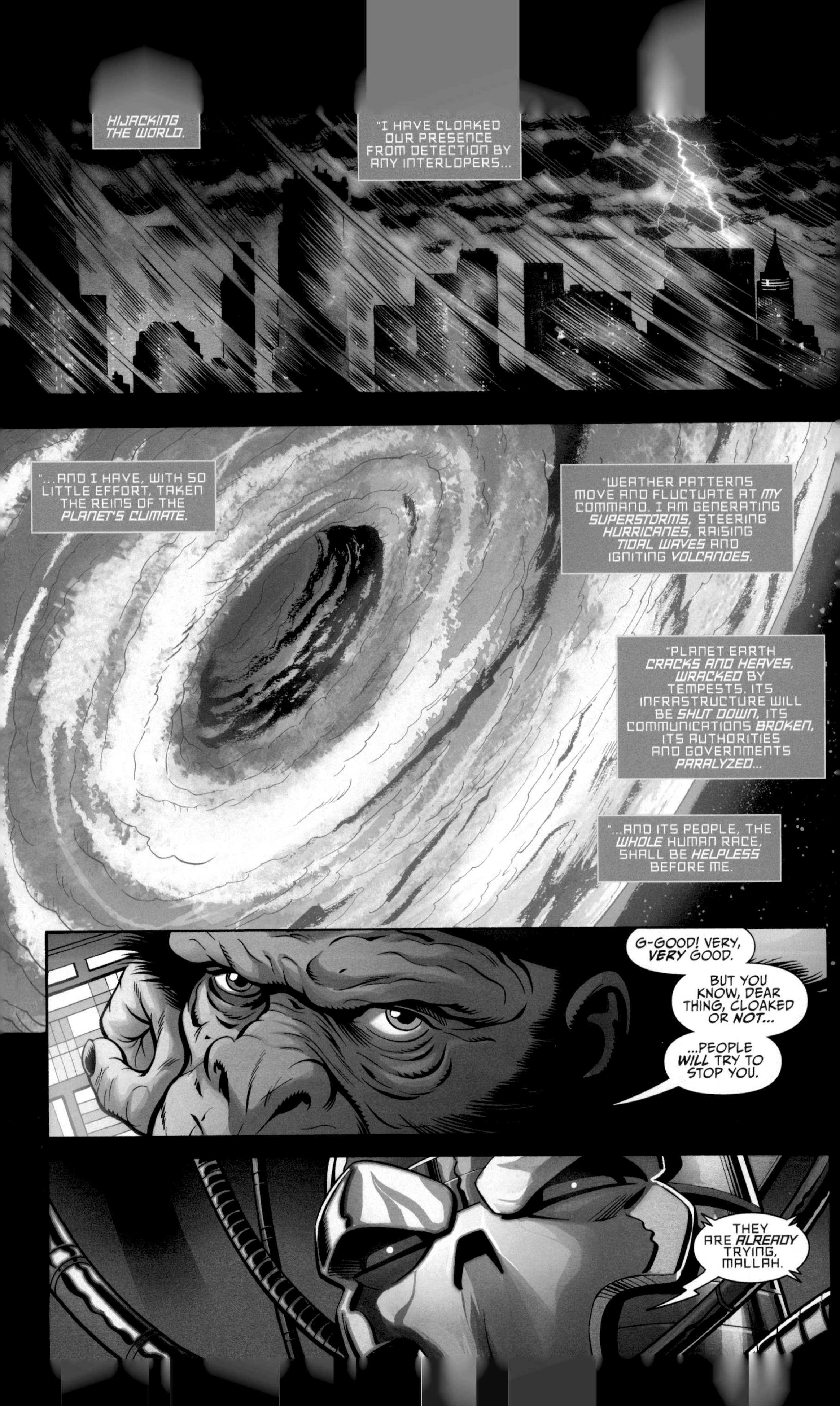
HIJACKING THE WORLD.
"I HAVE CLOAKED OUR PRESENCE FROM DETECTION BY ANY INTERLOPERS...
"...AND I HAVE, WITH SO LITTLE EFFORT, TAKEN THE REINS OF THE PLANET'S CLIMATE.
"WEATHER PATTERNS MOVE AND FLUCTUATE AT MY COMMAND. I AM GENERATING SUPERSTORMS, STEERING HURRICANES, RAISING TIDAL WAVES AND IGNITING VOLCANOES.
"PLANET EARTH CRACKS AND HEAVES, WRACKED BY TEMPESTS. ITS INFRASTRUCTURE WILL BE SHUT DOWN, ITS COMMUNICATIONS BROKEN, ITS AUTHORITIES AND GOVERNMENTS PARALYZED...
"...AND ITS PEOPLE, THE WHOLE HUMAN RACE, SHALL BE HELPLESS BEFORE ME.
G-GOOD! VERY, VERY GOOD.
BUT YOU KNOW, DEAR THING, CLOAKED OR NOT...
...PEOPLE WILL TRY TO STOP YOU.
THEY ARE ALREADY TRYING, MALLAH.

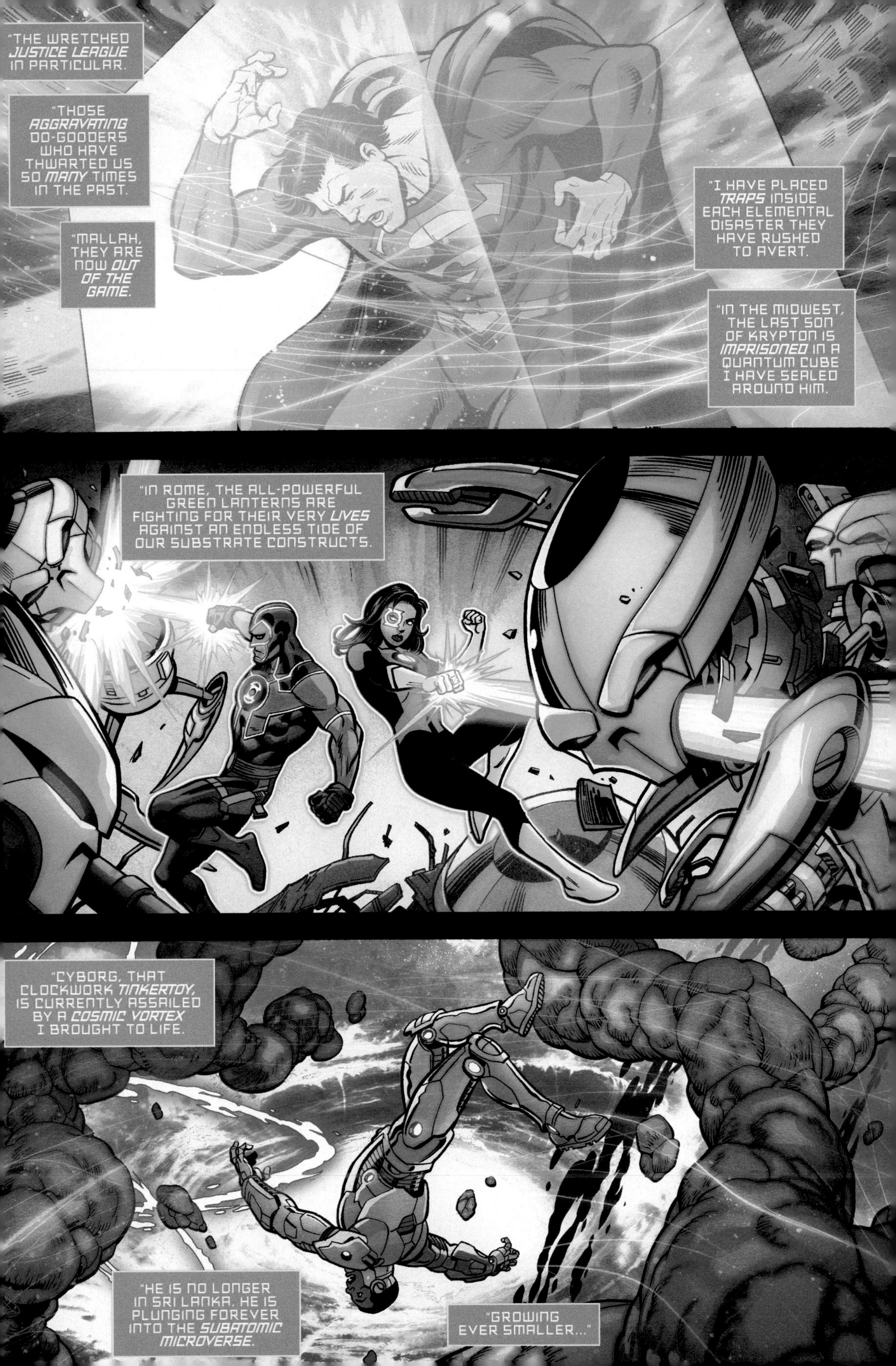
"THE WRETCHED JUSTICE LEAGUE IN PARTICULAR.
"THOSE AGGRAVATING DO-GOODERS WHO HAVE THWARTED US SO MANY TIMES IN THE PAST.
"MALLAH, THEY ARE NOW OUT OF THE GAME.
"I HAVE PLACED TRAPS INSIDE EACH ELEMENTAL DISASTER THEY HAVE RUSHED TO AVERT.
"IN THE MIDWEST, THE LAST SON OF KRYPTON IS IMPRISONED IN A QUANTUM CUBE I HAVE SEALED AROUND HIM.
"IN ROME, THE ALL-POWERFUL GREEN LANTERNS ARE FIGHTING FOR THEIR VERY LIVES AGAINST AN ENDLESS TIDE OF OUR SUBSTRATE CONSTRUCTS.
"CYBORG, THAT CLOCKWORK TINKERTOY, IS CURRENTLY ASSAILED BY A COSMIC VORTEX I BROUGHT TO LIFE.
"HE IS NO LONGER IN SRI LANKA. HE IS PLUNGING FOREVER INTO THE SUBATOMIC MICROVERSE.
"GROWING EVER SMALLER..."

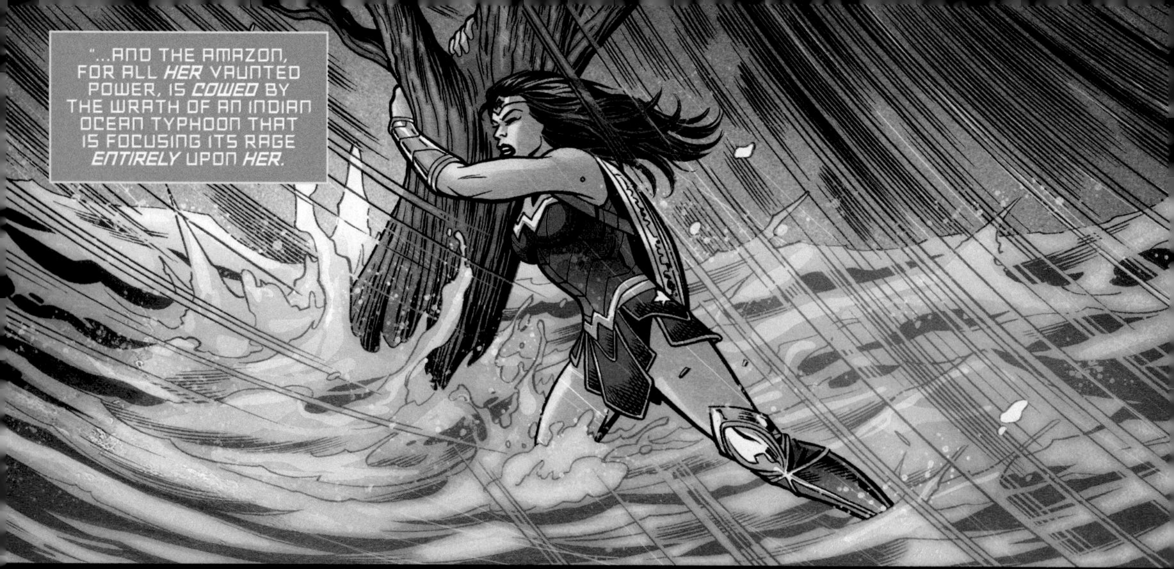
"...AND THE AMAZON, FOR ALL HER VAUNTED POWER, IS COWED BY THE WRATH OF AN INDIAN OCEAN TYPHOON THAT IS FOCUSING ITS RAGE ENTIRELY UPON HER.

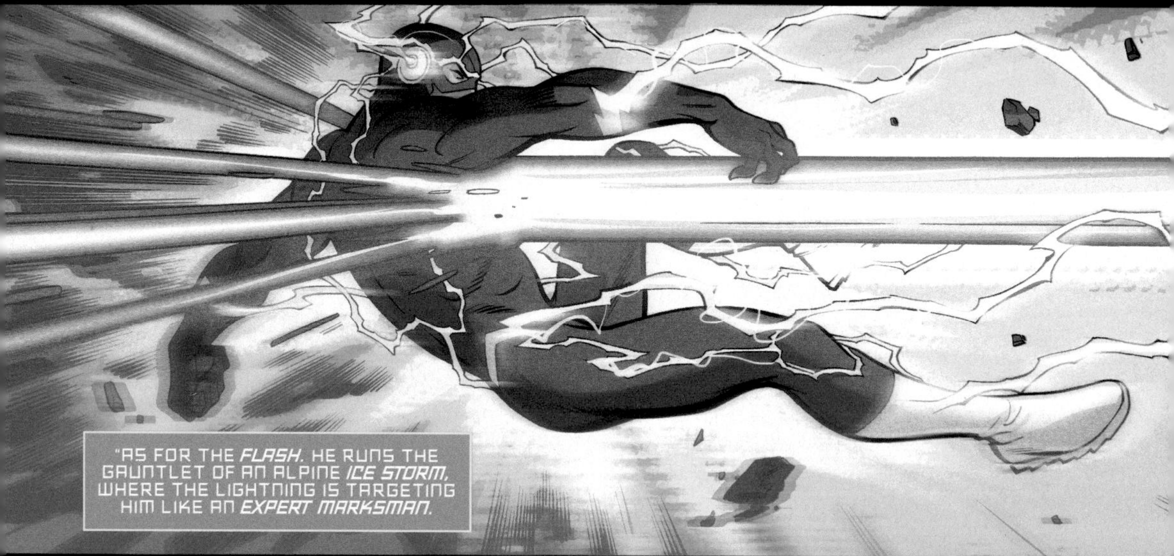
"AS FOR THE FLASH, HE RUNS THE GAUNTLET OF AN ALPINE ICE STORM, WHERE THE LIGHTNING IS TARGETING HIM LIKE AN EXPERT MARKSMAN.

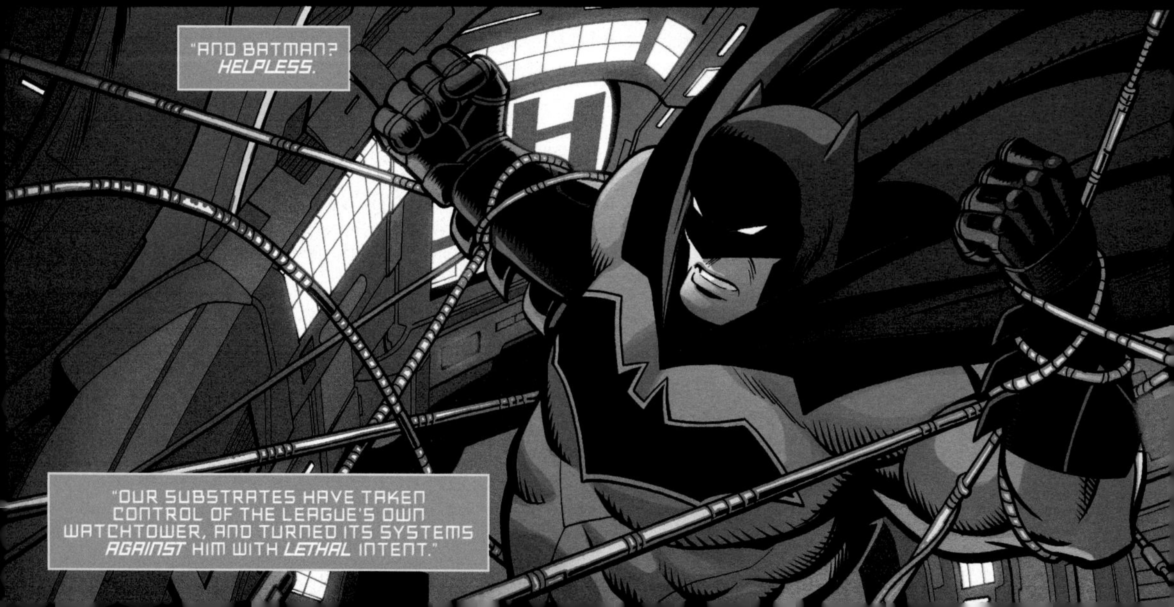
"AND BATMAN? HELPLESS.
"OUR SUBSTRATES HAVE TAKEN CONTROL OF THE LEAGUE'S OWN WATCHTOWER, AND TURNED ITS SYSTEMS AGAINST HIM WITH LETHAL INTENT."

WELL...I SEE YOU'VE GOT IT ALL *COVERED* THEN.

THERE ARE OTHER, *MINOR* THREATS TO US. *TWO* HAVE JUST ENTERED THIS BUILDING.

YOU CAN DEAL WITH THEM EASILY.

WHAT ABOUT *YOU?*

THEY ARE NOT WORTH MY *EFFORT.* MY MIND IS OCCUPIED WITH *HIGHER* THINGS NOW.

DIRECT THE SUBSTRATES, MALLAH. *ERADICATE* THEM.

AM I JUST A SUBSTRATE, *TOO,* BRAIN?

IS THAT ALL I *AM* TO YOU NOW? A *LACKEY?* A *DRONE?*

I THOUGHT WE WERE IN THIS *TOGETHER.*

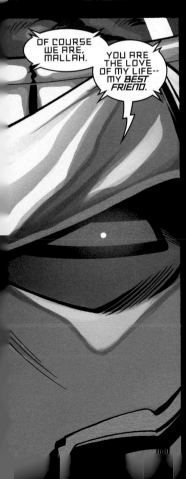

OF COURSE WE ARE, MALLAH.

YOU ARE THE LOVE OF MY LIFE-- MY *BEST FRIEND.*

YOU'RE NOT *ACTING* LIKE IT.

THE HIGHER LEVELS OF CONSCIOUSNESS YOU'RE ACHIEVING SEEM TO BE... *DIVORCING* YOU FROM SIMPLE *PERSONAL* INTERACTIONS.

YOU STAND SO...*APART.*

EVERYTHING SEEMS *BENEATH* YOU NOW.

JUST DEAL WITH THE PROBLEM, PLEASE.

I HAVE A *WORLD* TO OPERATE.

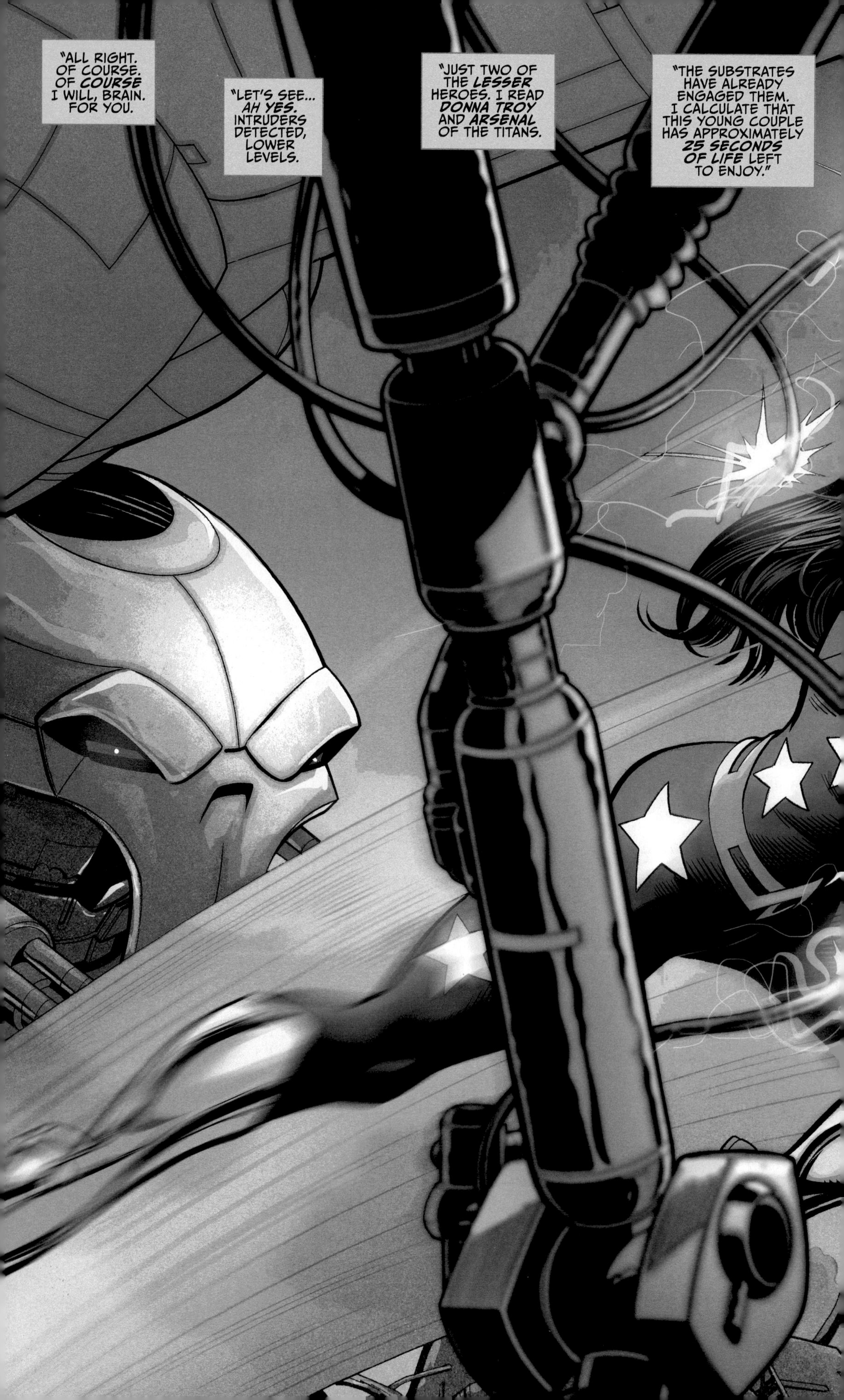
"ALL RIGHT. OF COURSE. OF COURSE I WILL, BRAIN. FOR YOU.
"LET'S SEE... AH YES. INTRUDERS DETECTED, LOWER LEVELS.
"JUST TWO OF THE LESSER HEROES. I READ DONNA TROY AND ARSENAL OF THE TITANS.
"THE SUBSTRATES HAVE ALREADY ENGAGED THEM. I CALCULATE THAT THIS YOUNG COUPLE HAS APPROXIMATELY 25 SECONDS OF LIFE LEFT TO ENJOY."

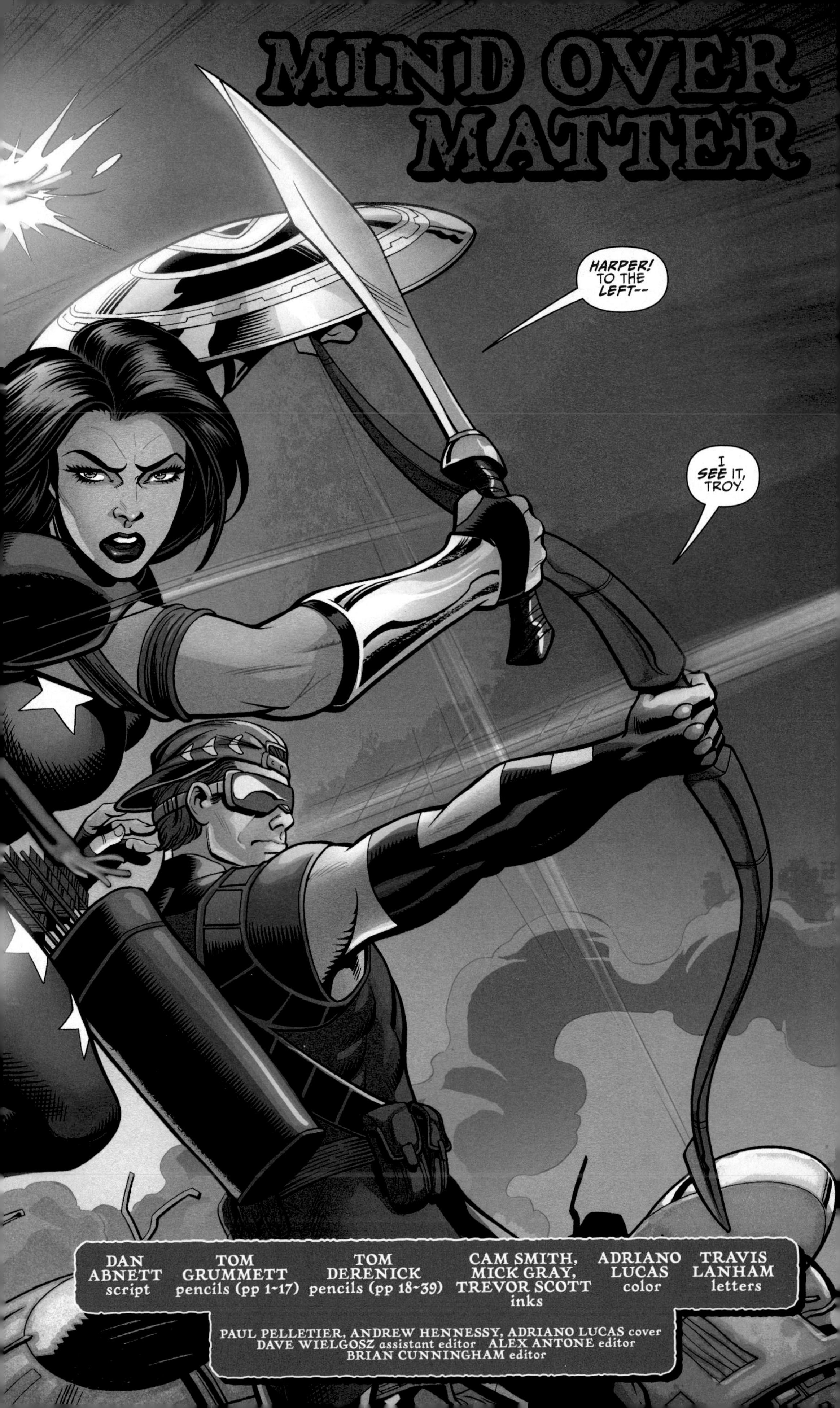

MIND OVER MATTER
HARPER! TO THE LEFT--
I SEE IT, TROY.
DAN ABNETT script
TOM GRUMMETT pencils (pp 1-17)
TOM DERENICK pencils (pp 18-39)
CAM SMITH, MICK GRAY, TREVOR SCOTT inks
ADRIANO LUCAS color
TRAVIS LANHAM letters
PAUL PELLETIER, ANDREW HENNESSY, ADRIANO LUCAS cover
DAVE WIELGOSZ assistant editor ALEX ANTONE editor
BRIAN CUNNINGHAM editor

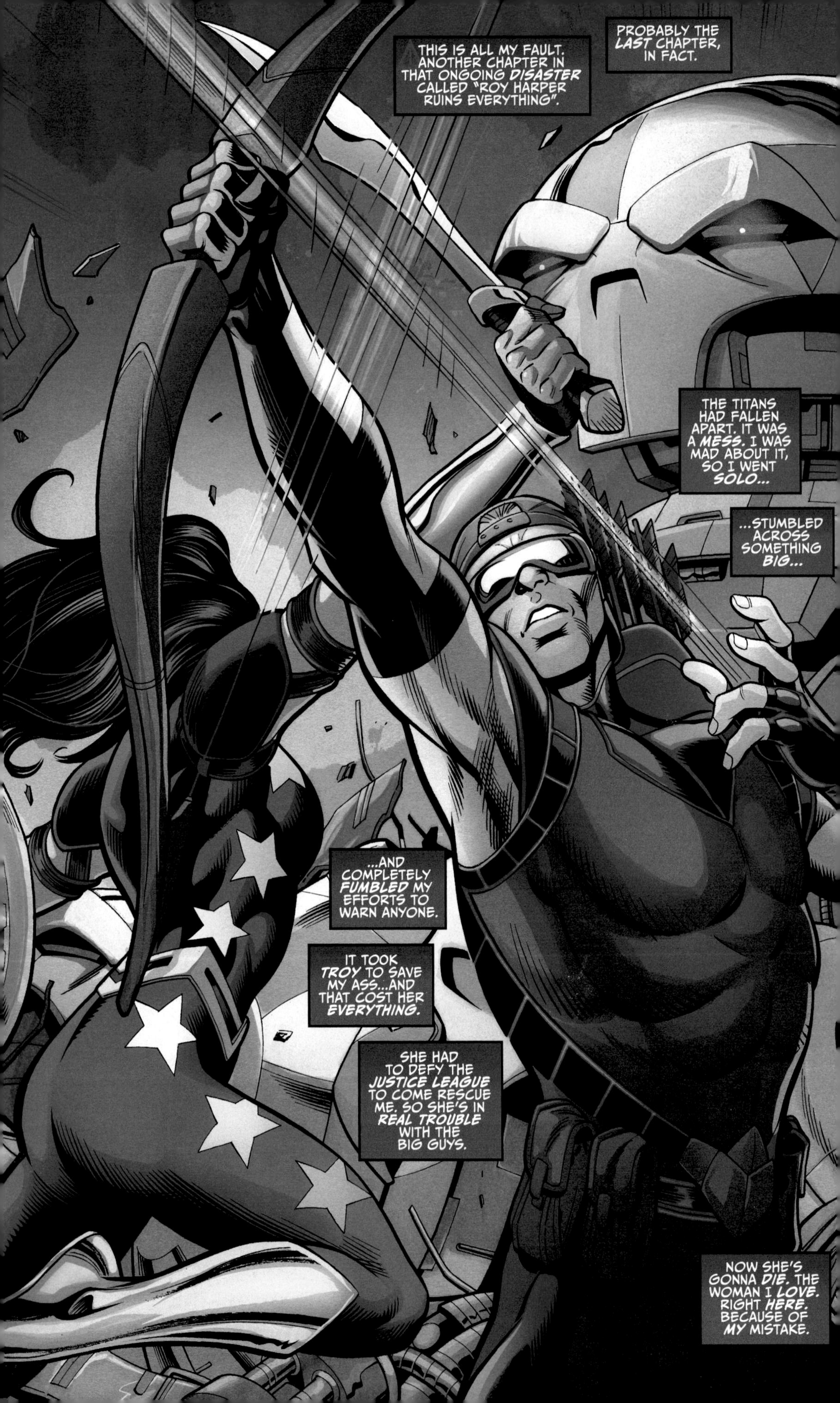
THIS IS ALL MY FAULT. ANOTHER CHAPTER IN THAT ONGOING DISASTER CALLED "ROY HARPER RUINS EVERYTHING".
PROBABLY THE LAST CHAPTER, IN FACT.
THE TITANS HAD FALLEN APART. IT WAS A MESS. I WAS MAD ABOUT IT, SO I WENT SOLO...
...STUMBLED ACROSS SOMETHING BIG...
...AND COMPLETELY FUMBLED MY EFFORTS TO WARN ANYONE.
IT TOOK TROY TO SAVE MY ASS...AND THAT COST HER EVERYTHING.
SHE HAD TO DEFY THE JUSTICE LEAGUE TO COME RESCUE ME. SO SHE'S IN REAL TROUBLE WITH THE BIG GUYS.
NOW SHE'S GONNA DIE. THE WOMAN I LOVE. RIGHT HERE. BECAUSE OF MY MISTAKE.

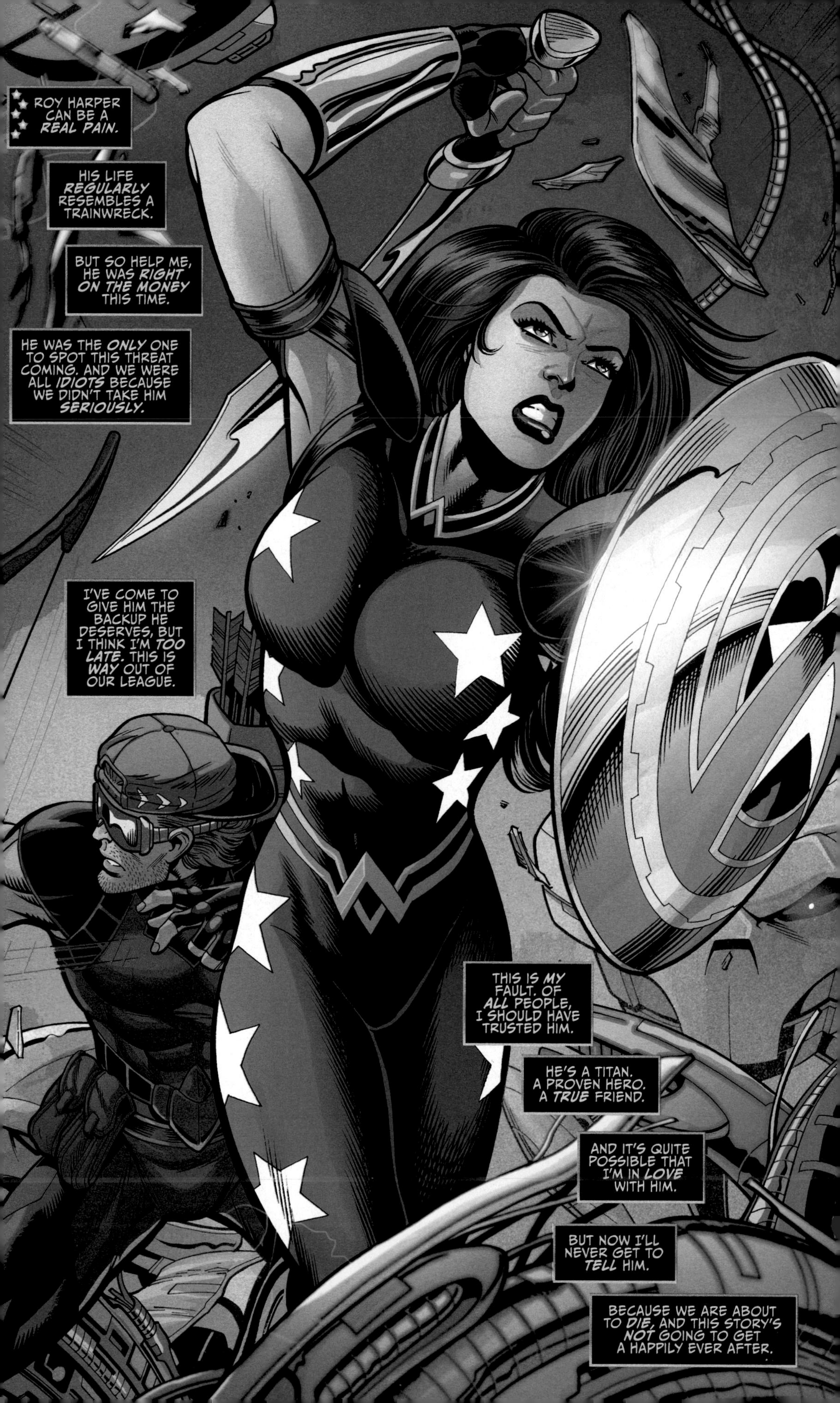
ROY HARPER CAN BE A REAL PAIN.
HIS LIFE REGULARLY RESEMBLES A TRAINWRECK.
BUT SO HELP ME, HE WAS RIGHT ON THE MONEY THIS TIME.
HE WAS THE ONLY ONE TO SPOT THIS THREAT COMING. AND WE WERE ALL IDIOTS BECAUSE WE DIDN'T TAKE HIM SERIOUSLY.
I'VE COME TO GIVE HIM THE BACKUP HE DESERVES, BUT I THINK I'M TOO LATE. THIS IS WAY OUT OF OUR LEAGUE.
THIS IS MY FAULT. OF ALL PEOPLE, I SHOULD HAVE TRUSTED HIM.
HE'S A TITAN. A PROVEN HERO. A TRUE FRIEND.
AND IT'S QUITE POSSIBLE THAT I'M IN LOVE WITH HIM.
BUT NOW I'LL NEVER GET TO TELL HIM.
BECAUSE WE ARE ABOUT TO DIE, AND THIS STORY'S NOT GOING TO GET A HAPPILY EVER AFTER.

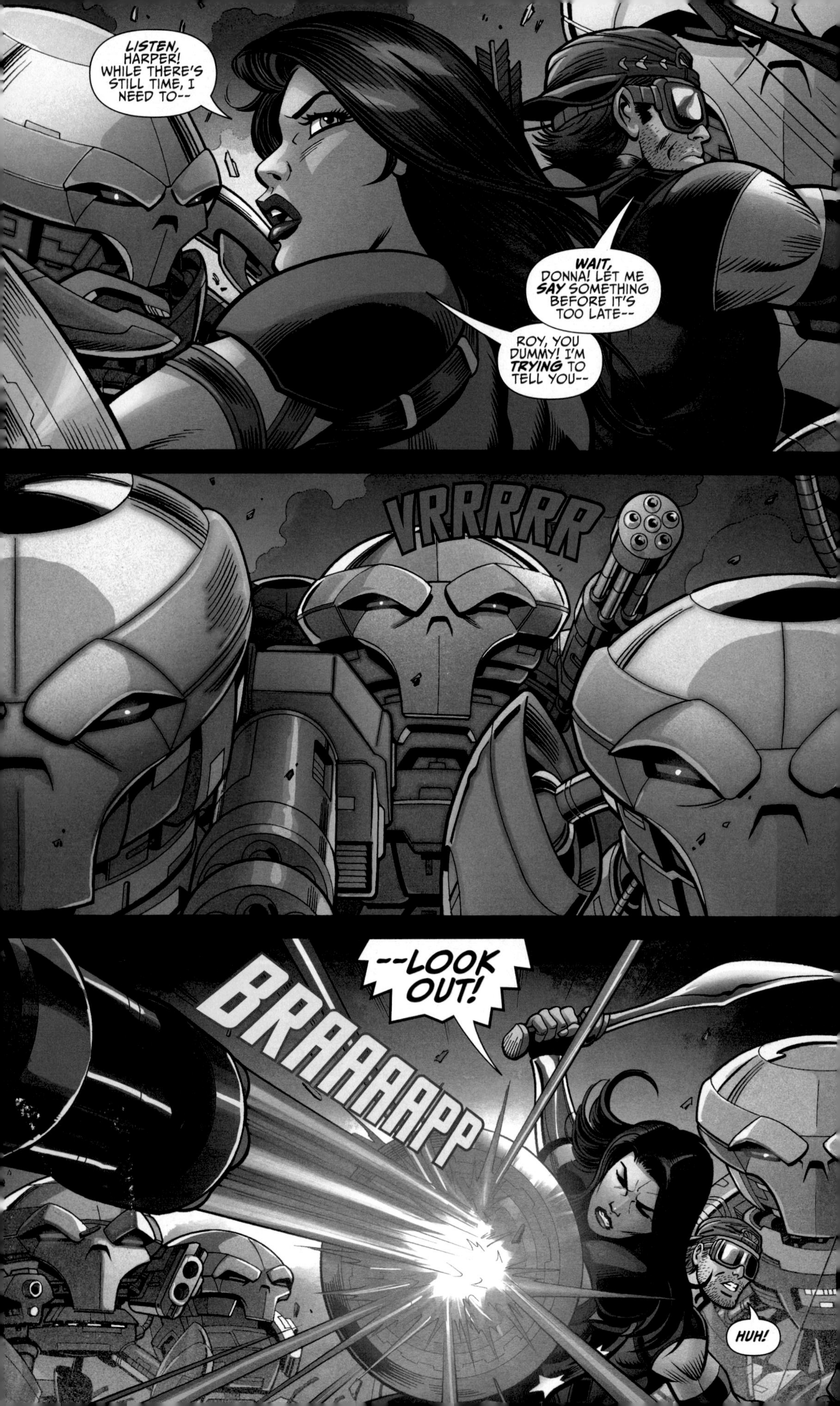
LISTEN, HARPER! WHILE THERE'S STILL TIME, I NEED TO--
WAIT, DONNA! LET ME SAY SOMETHING BEFORE IT'S TOO LATE--
ROY, YOU DUMMY! I'M TRYING TO TELL YOU--
VRRRRR
BRAAAAAPP
--LOOK OUT!
HUH!

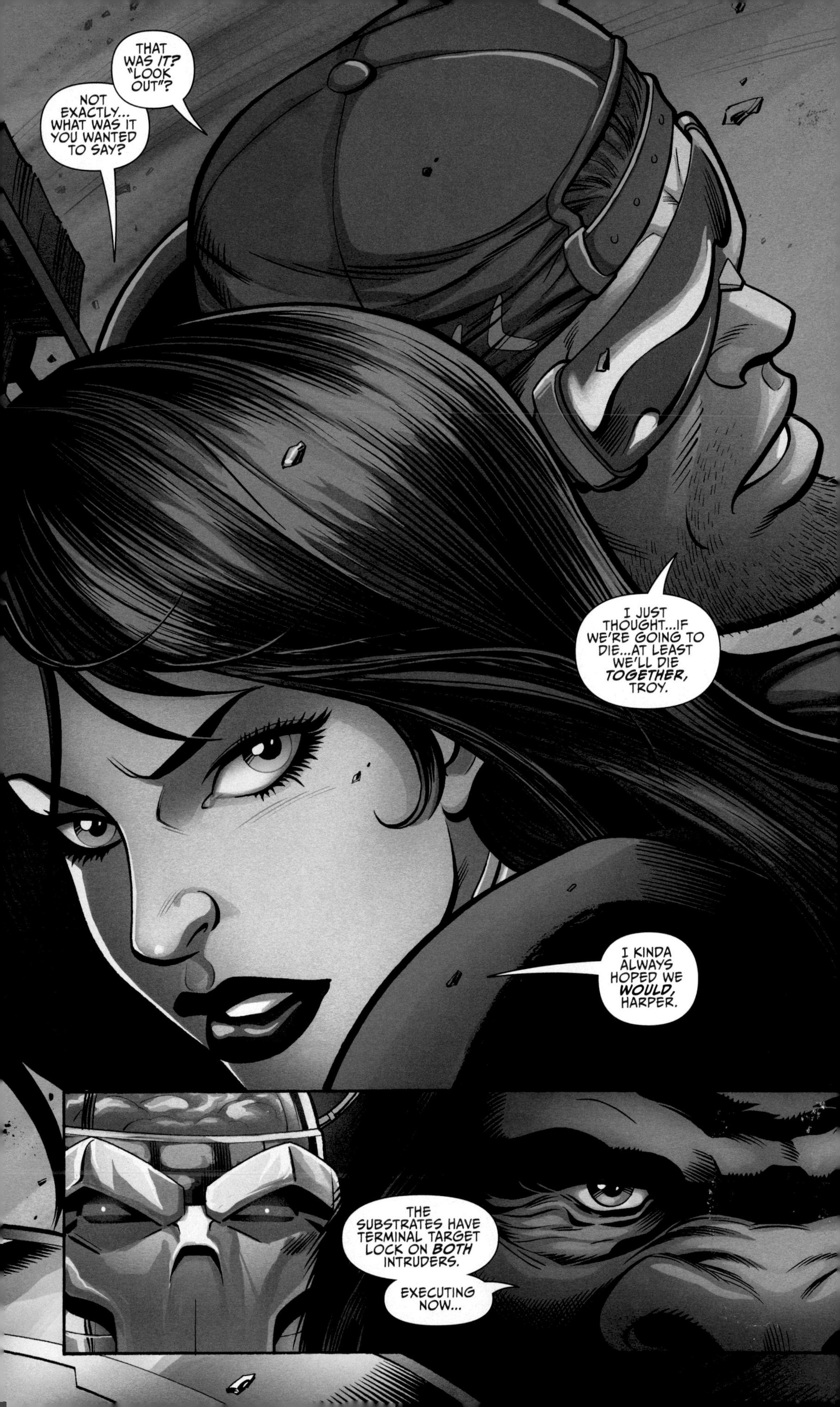
THAT WAS *IT?* "LOOK OUT"?
NOT EXACTLY... WHAT WAS IT YOU WANTED TO SAY?
I JUST THOUGHT...IF WE'RE GOING TO DIE...AT LEAST WE'LL DIE *TOGETHER,* TROY.
I KINDA ALWAYS HOPED WE *WOULD,* HARPER.
THE SUBSTRATES HAVE TERMINAL TARGET LOCK ON *BOTH* INTRUDERS.
EXECUTING NOW...

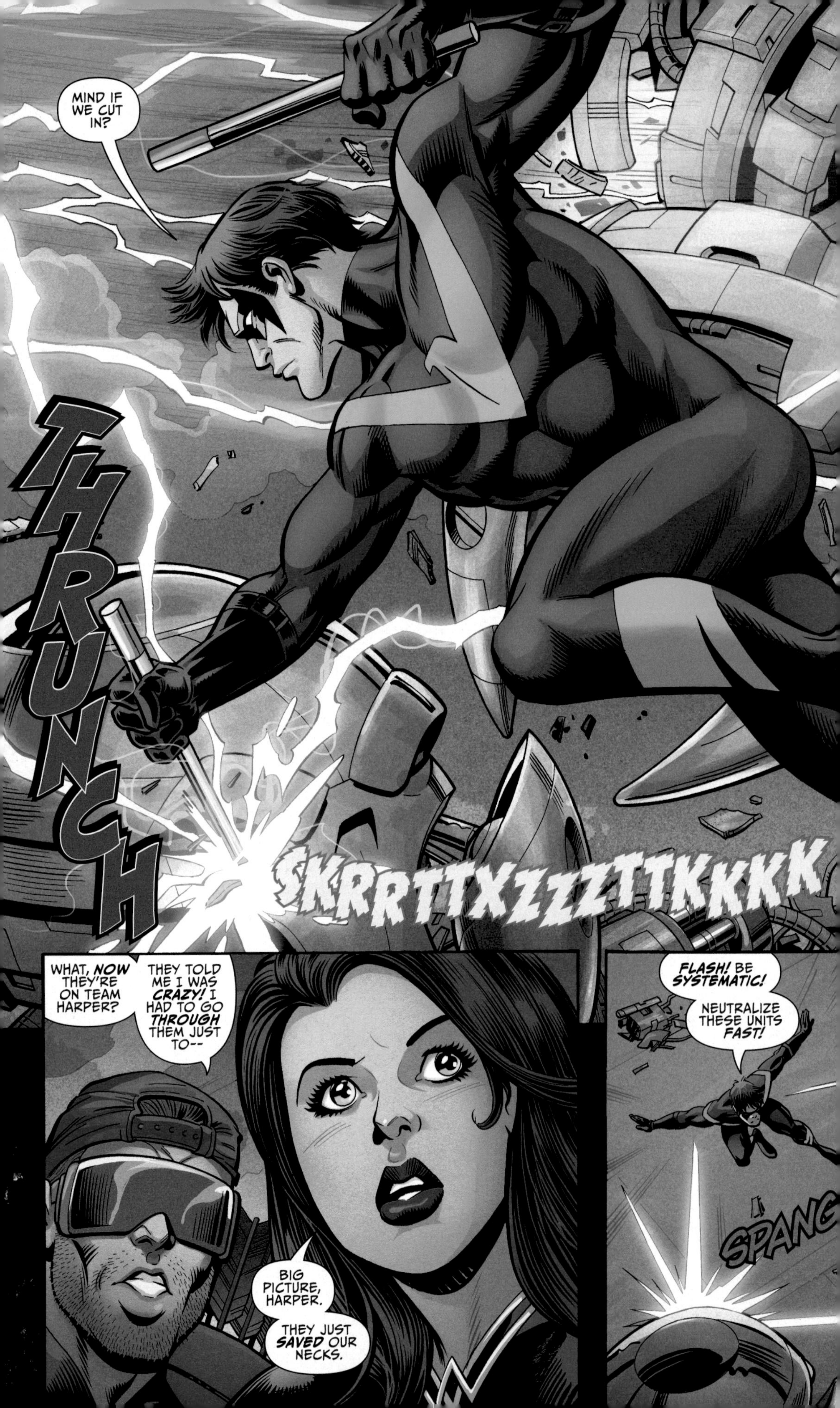

MIND IF WE CUT IN?
THRUNCH
SKRRTTXZZZZTTKKKK
WHAT, NOW THEY'RE ON TEAM HARPER?
THEY TOLD ME I WAS CRAZY! I HAD TO GO THROUGH THEM JUST TO--
BIG PICTURE, HARPER.
THEY JUST SAVED OUR NECKS.
FLASH! BE SYSTEMATIC!
NEUTRALIZE THESE UNITS FAST!
SPANG

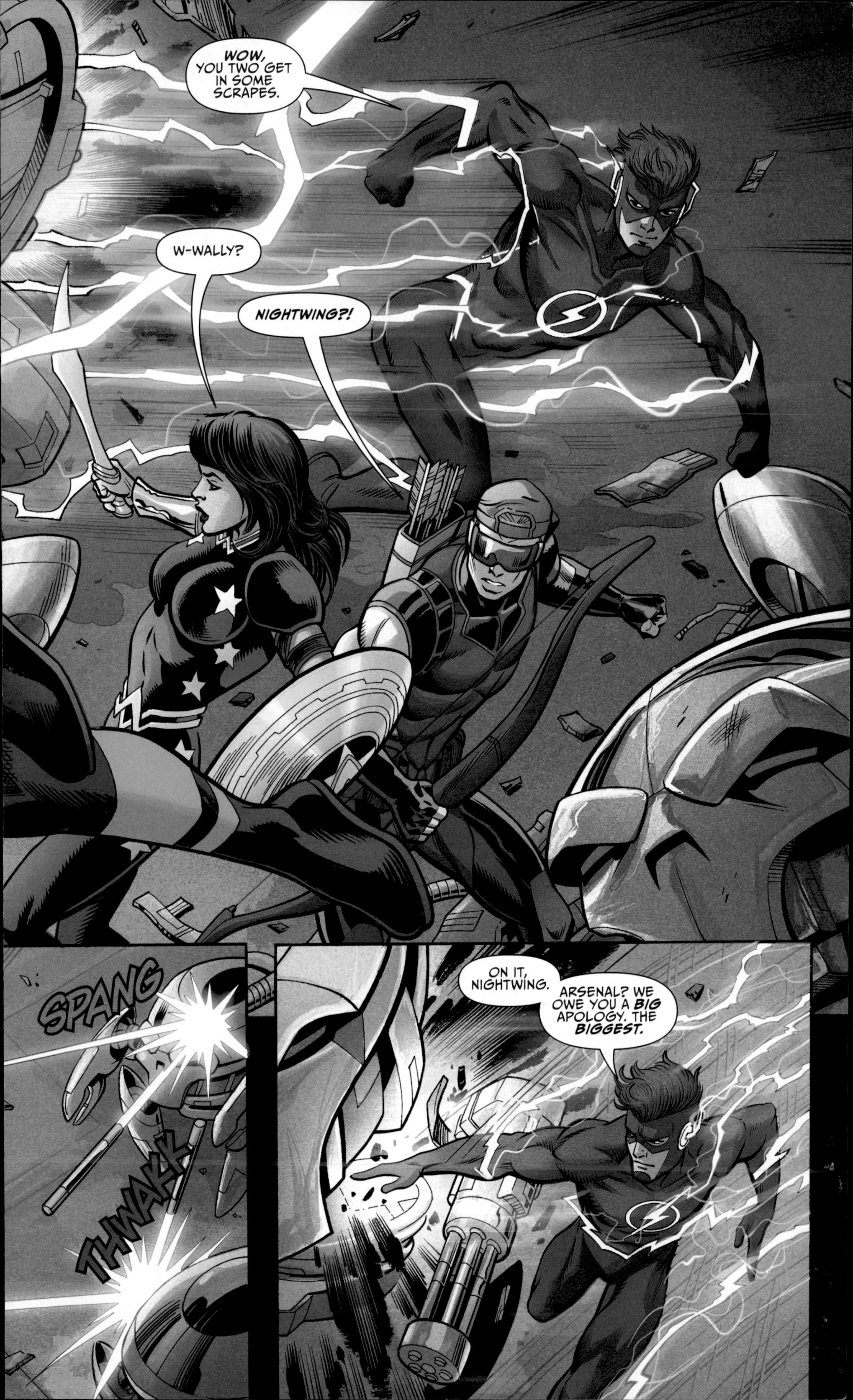
WOW, YOU TWO GET IN SOME SCRAPES.
W-WALLY?
NIGHTWING?!
SPANG
THWAKK
ON IT, NIGHTWING.
ARSENAL? WE OWE YOU A BIG APOLOGY. THE BIGGEST.

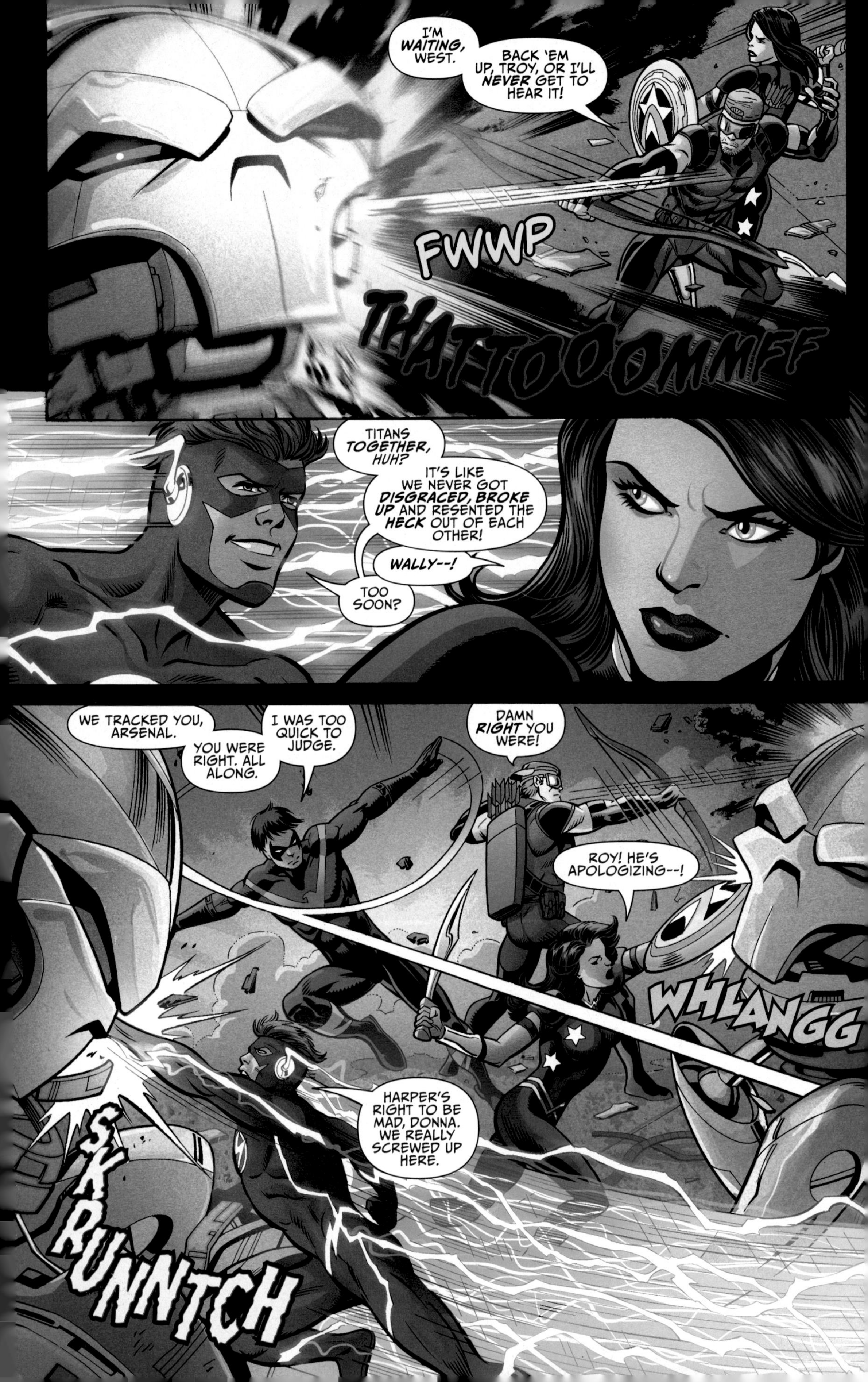
I'M WAITING, WEST.
BACK 'EM UP, TROY, OR I'LL NEVER GET TO HEAR IT!
FWWP
THATTOOOMMFF
TITANS TOGETHER, HUH?
IT'S LIKE WE NEVER GOT DISGRACED, BROKE UP AND RESENTED THE HECK OUT OF EACH OTHER!
WALLY--!
TOO SOON?
WE TRACKED YOU, ARSENAL.
YOU WERE RIGHT. ALL ALONG.
I WAS TOO QUICK TO JUDGE.
DAMN RIGHT YOU WERE!
ROY! HE'S APOLOGIZING--!
WHLANGG
HARPER'S RIGHT TO BE MAD, DONNA. WE REALLY SCREWED UP HERE.
SKRUNNTCH

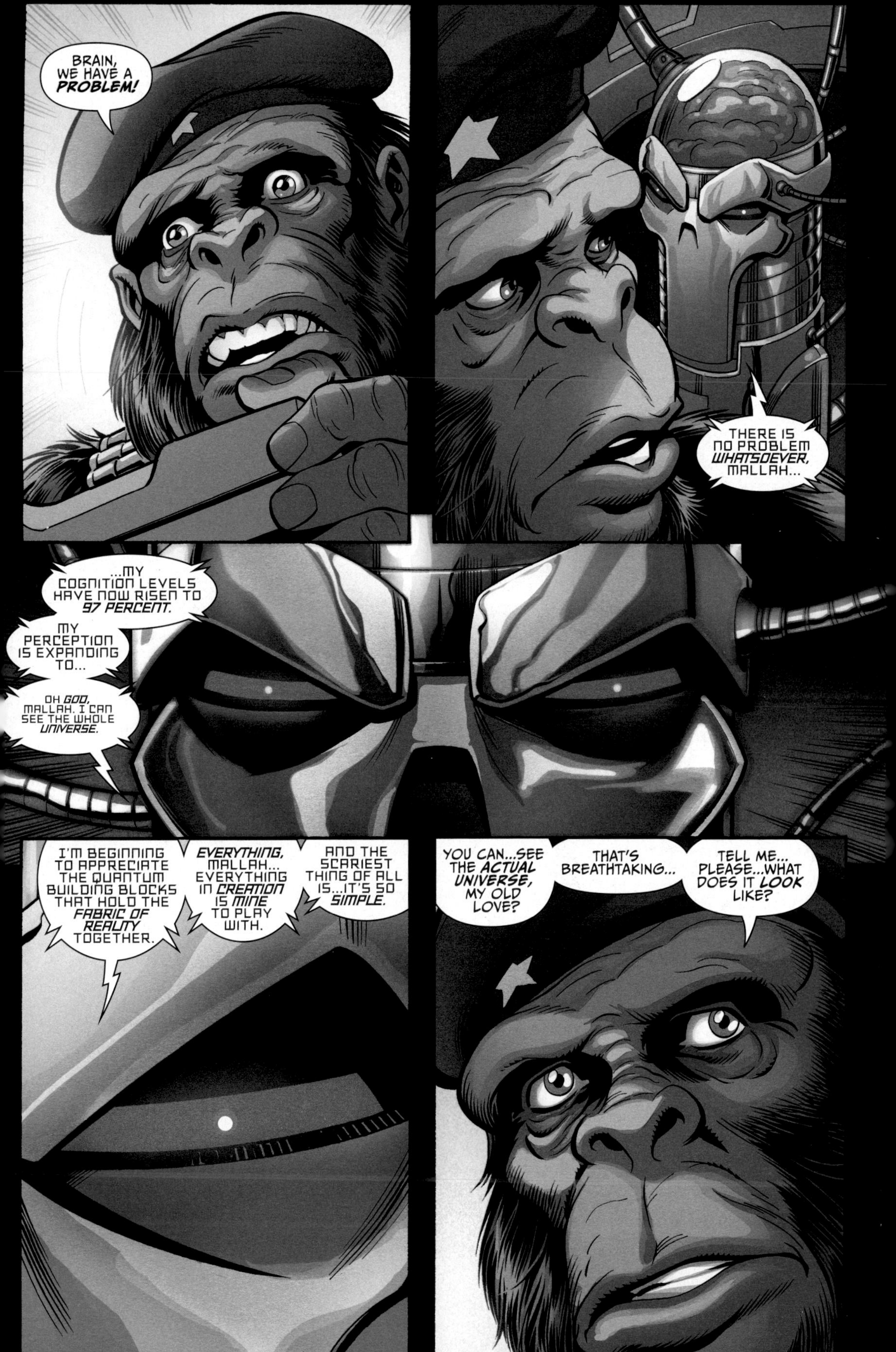
BRAIN, WE HAVE A PROBLEM!
THERE IS NO PROBLEM WHATSOEVER, MALLAH...
...MY COGNITION LEVELS HAVE NOW RISEN TO 97 PERCENT.
MY PERCEPTION IS EXPANDING TO...
OH GOD, MALLAH. I CAN SEE THE WHOLE UNIVERSE.
I'M BEGINNING TO APPRECIATE THE QUANTUM BUILDING BLOCKS THAT HOLD THE FABRIC OF REALITY TOGETHER.
EVERYTHING, MALLAH... EVERYTHING IN CREATION IS MINE TO PLAY WITH.
AND THE SCARIEST THING OF ALL IS...IT'S SO SIMPLE.
YOU CAN...SEE THE ACTUAL UNIVERSE, MY OLD LOVE?
THAT'S BREATHTAKING...
TELL ME... PLEASE...WHAT DOES IT LOOK LIKE?

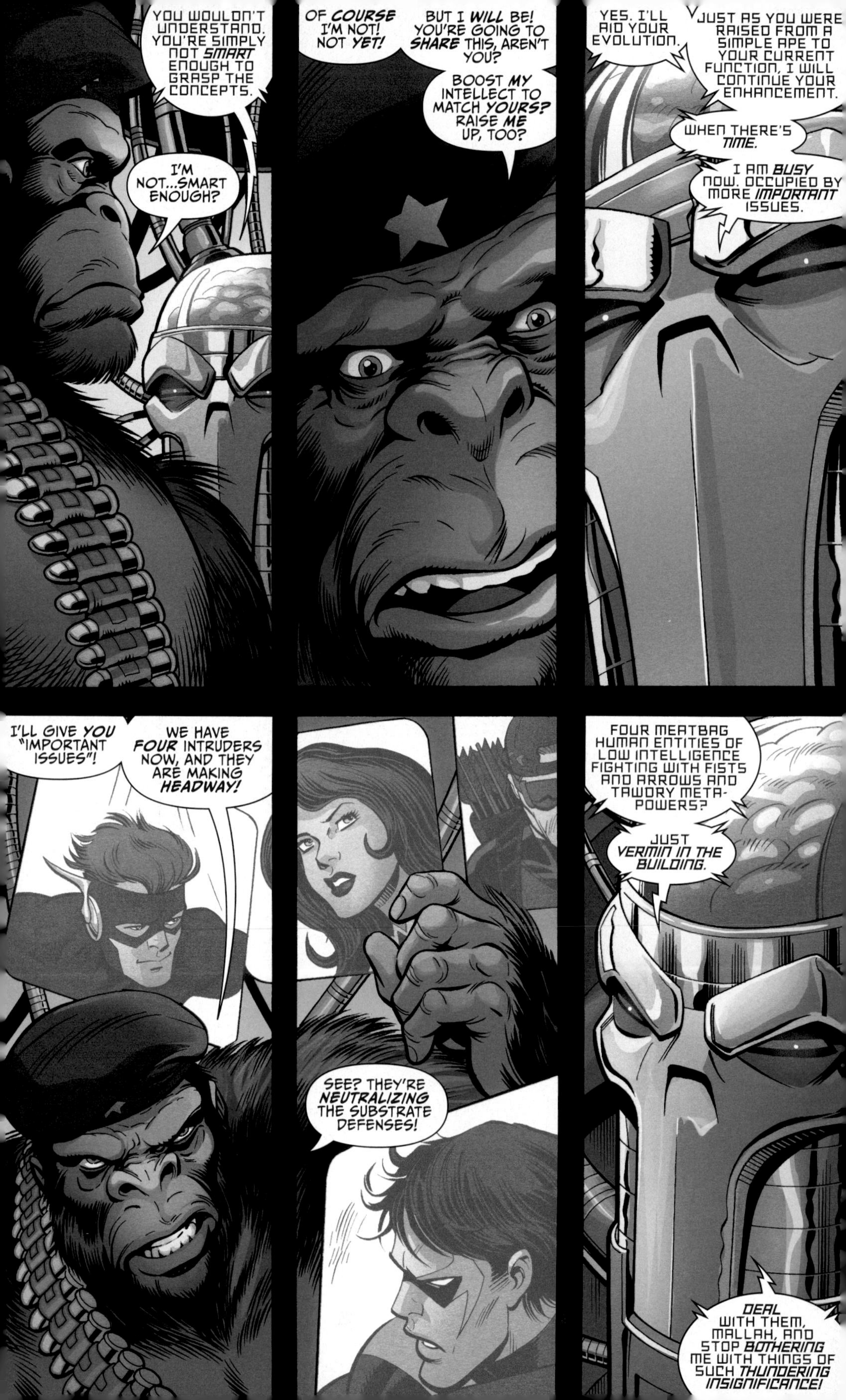
YOU WOULDN'T UNDERSTAND. YOU'RE SIMPLY NOT SMART ENOUGH TO GRASP THE CONCEPTS.
I'M NOT...SMART ENOUGH?
OF COURSE I'M NOT! NOT YET!
BUT I WILL BE! YOU'RE GOING TO SHARE THIS, AREN'T YOU?
BOOST MY INTELLECT TO MATCH YOURS? RAISE ME UP, TOO?
YES. I'LL AID YOUR EVOLUTION.
JUST AS YOU WERE RAISED FROM A SIMPLE APE TO YOUR CURRENT FUNCTION, I WILL CONTINUE YOUR ENHANCEMENT.
WHEN THERE'S TIME.
I AM BUSY NOW. OCCUPIED BY MORE IMPORTANT ISSUES.
I'LL GIVE YOU "IMPORTANT ISSUES"!
WE HAVE FOUR INTRUDERS NOW, AND THEY ARE MAKING HEADWAY!
SEE? THEY'RE NEUTRALIZING THE SUBSTRATE DEFENSES!
FOUR MEATBAG HUMAN ENTITIES OF LOW INTELLIGENCE FIGHTING WITH FISTS AND ARROWS AND TAWDRY META-POWERS?
JUST VERMIN IN THE BUILDING.
DEAL WITH THEM, MALLAH, AND STOP BOTHERING ME WITH THINGS OF SUCH THUNDERING INSIGNIFICANCE!

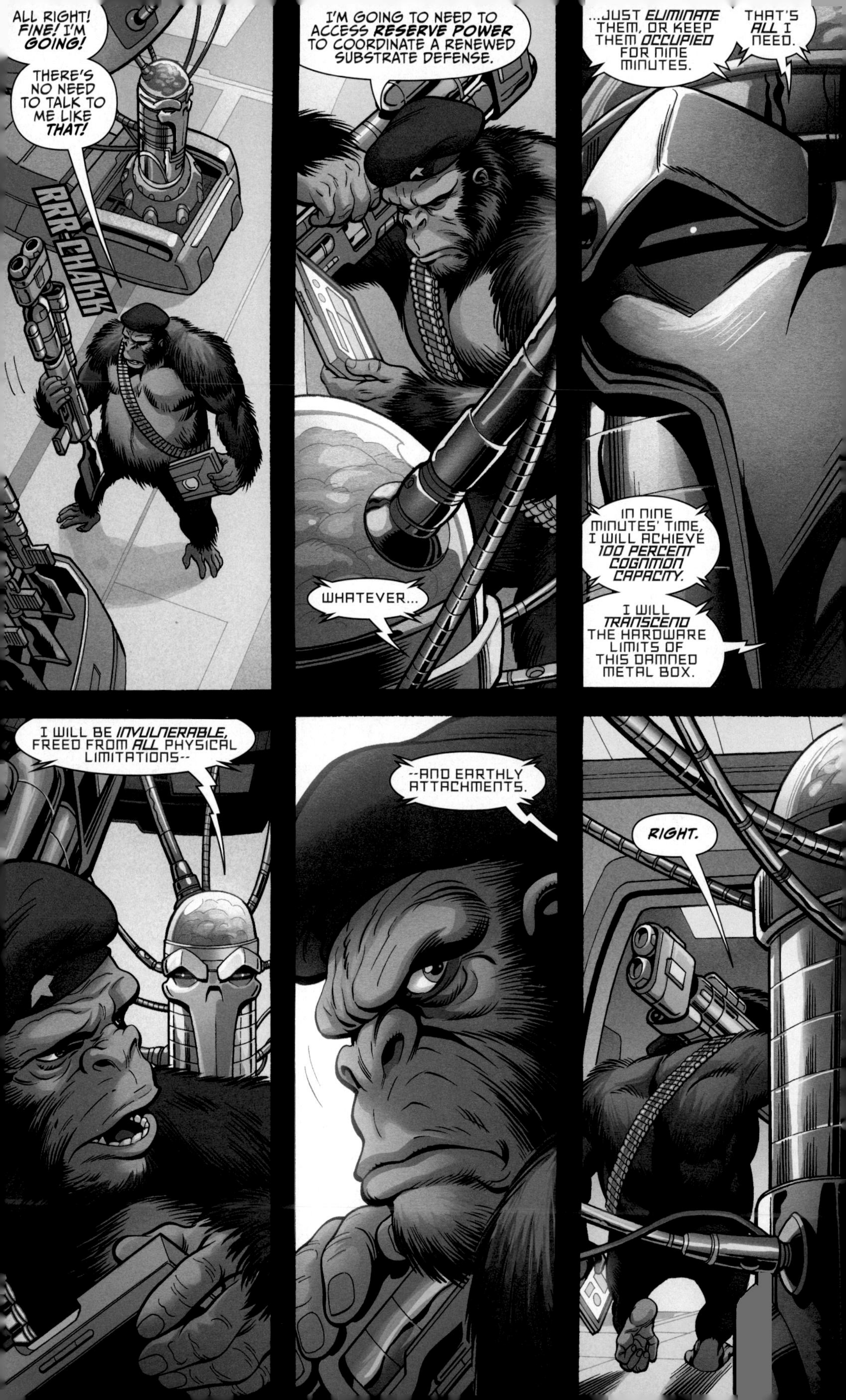
ALL RIGHT! FINE! I'M GOING!
THERE'S NO NEED TO TALK TO ME LIKE THAT!
RRR-CHAKK
I'M GOING TO NEED TO ACCESS RESERVE POWER TO COORDINATE A RENEWED SUBSTRATE DEFENSE.
WHATEVER...
...JUST ELIMINATE THEM, OR KEEP THEM OCCUPIED FOR NINE MINUTES.
THAT'S ALL I NEED.
IN NINE MINUTES' TIME, I WILL ACHIEVE 100 PERCENT COGNMON CAPACITY.
I WILL TRANSCEND THE HARDWARE LIMITS OF THIS DAMNED METAL BOX.
I WILL BE INVULNERABLE, FREED FROM ALL PHYSICAL LIMITATIONS--
--AND EARTHLY ATTACHMENTS.
RIGHT.

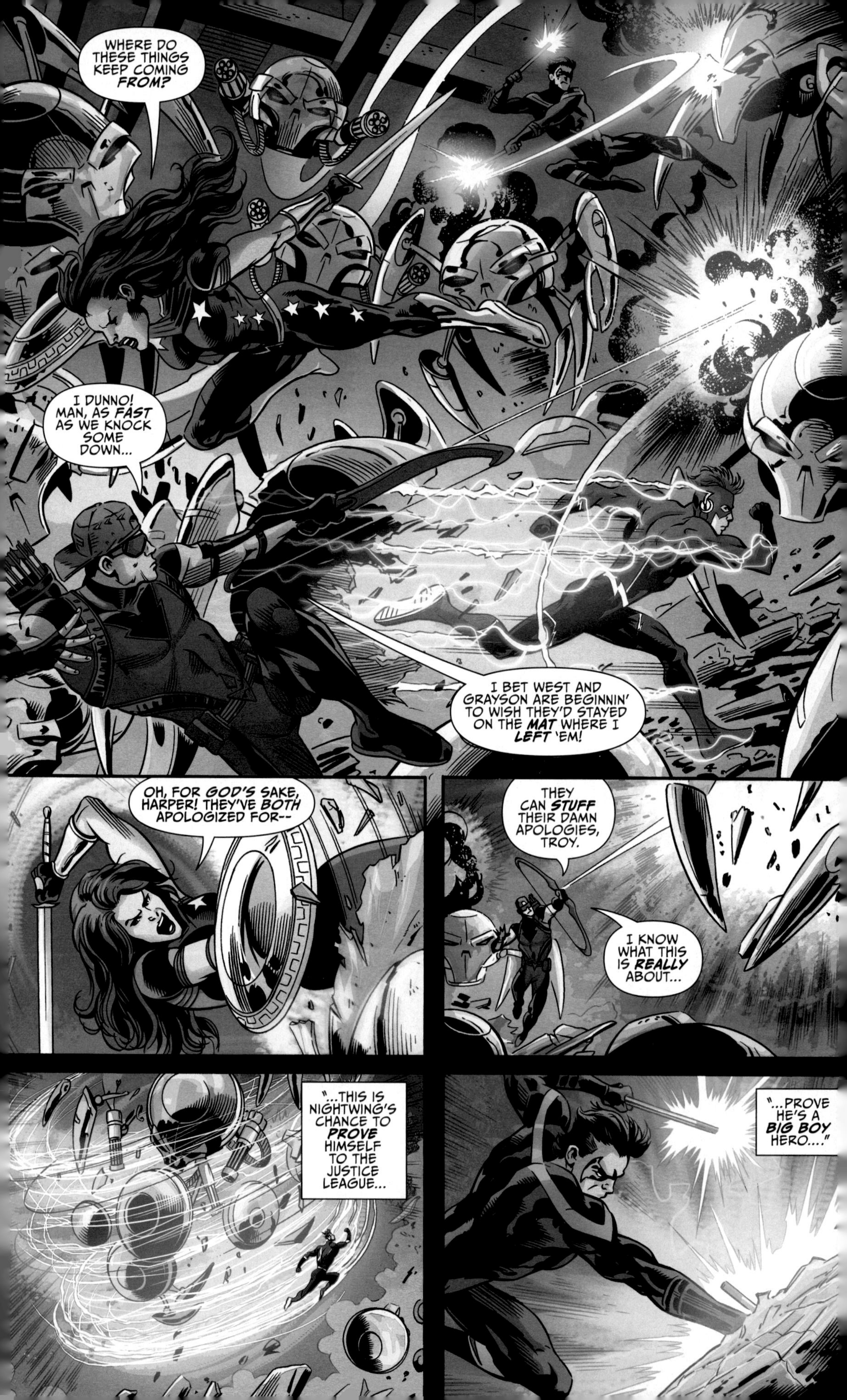
WHERE DO THESE THINGS KEEP COMING FROM?
I DUNNO! MAN, AS FAST AS WE KNOCK SOME DOWN...
I BET WEST AND GRAYSON ARE BEGINNIN' TO WISH THEY'D STAYED ON THE MAT WHERE I LEFT 'EM!
OH, FOR GOD'S SAKE, HARPER! THEY'VE BOTH APOLOGIZED FOR--
THEY CAN STUFF THEIR DAMN APOLOGIES, TROY.
I KNOW WHAT THIS IS REALLY ABOUT...
"...THIS IS NIGHTWING'S CHANCE TO PROVE HIMSELF TO THE JUSTICE LEAGUE...
"...PROVE HE'S A BIG BOY HERO...."

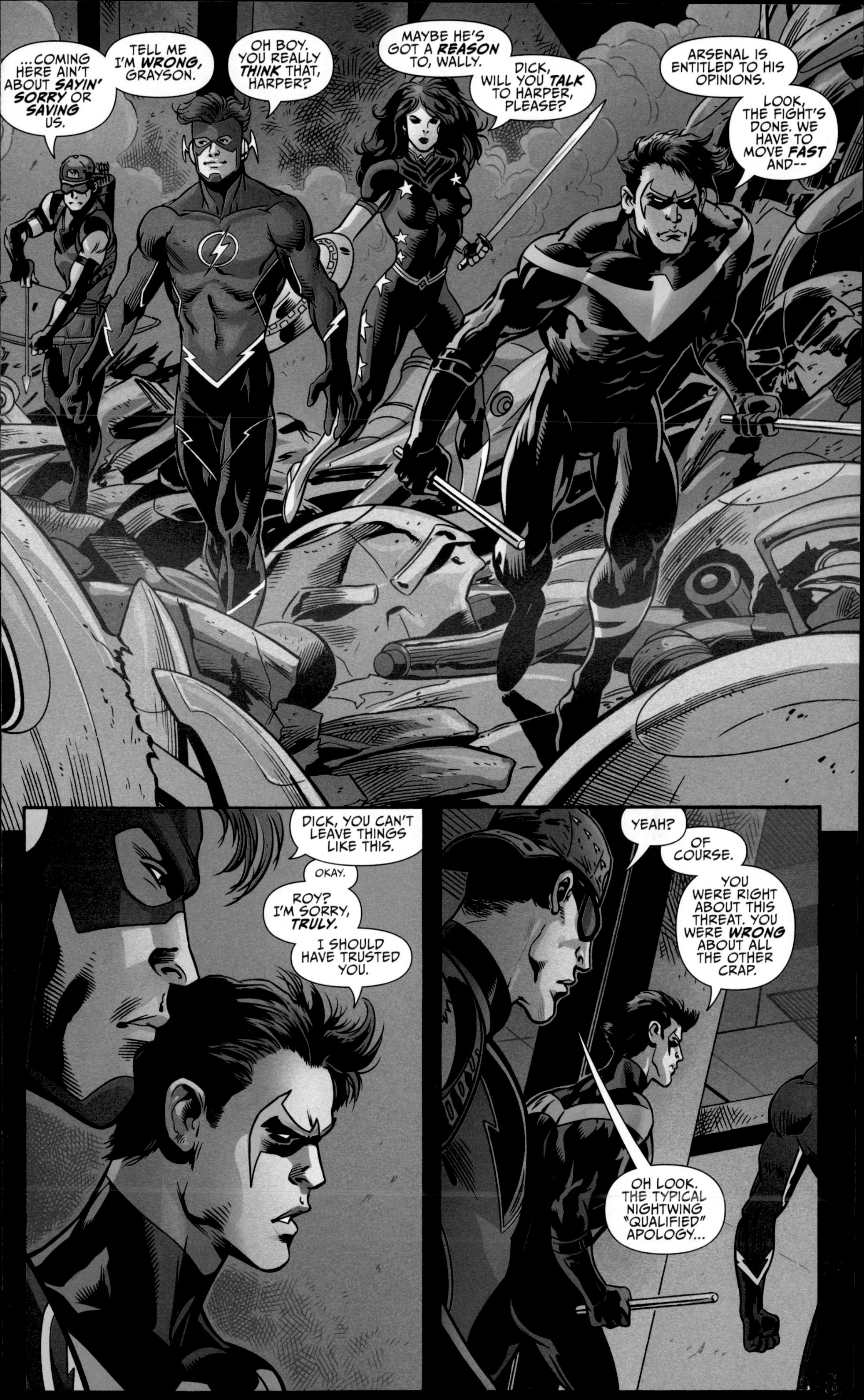
...COMING HERE AIN'T ABOUT **SAYIN' SORRY** OR **SAVING** US.
TELL ME I'M **WRONG**, GRAYSON.
OH BOY. YOU REALLY **THINK** THAT, HARPER?
MAYBE HE'S GOT A **REASON** TO, WALLY.
DICK, WILL YOU **TALK** TO HARPER, PLEASE?
ARSENAL IS ENTITLED TO HIS OPINIONS.
LOOK, THE FIGHT'S DONE. WE HAVE TO MOVE **FAST** AND--
DICK, YOU CAN'T LEAVE THINGS LIKE THIS.
OKAY.
ROY? I'M SORRY, **TRULY.**
I SHOULD HAVE TRUSTED YOU.
YEAH?
OF COURSE.
YOU WERE RIGHT ABOUT THIS THREAT. YOU WERE **WRONG** ABOUT ALL THE OTHER CRAP.
OH LOOK. THE TYPICAL NIGHTWING "QUALIFIED" APOLOGY...

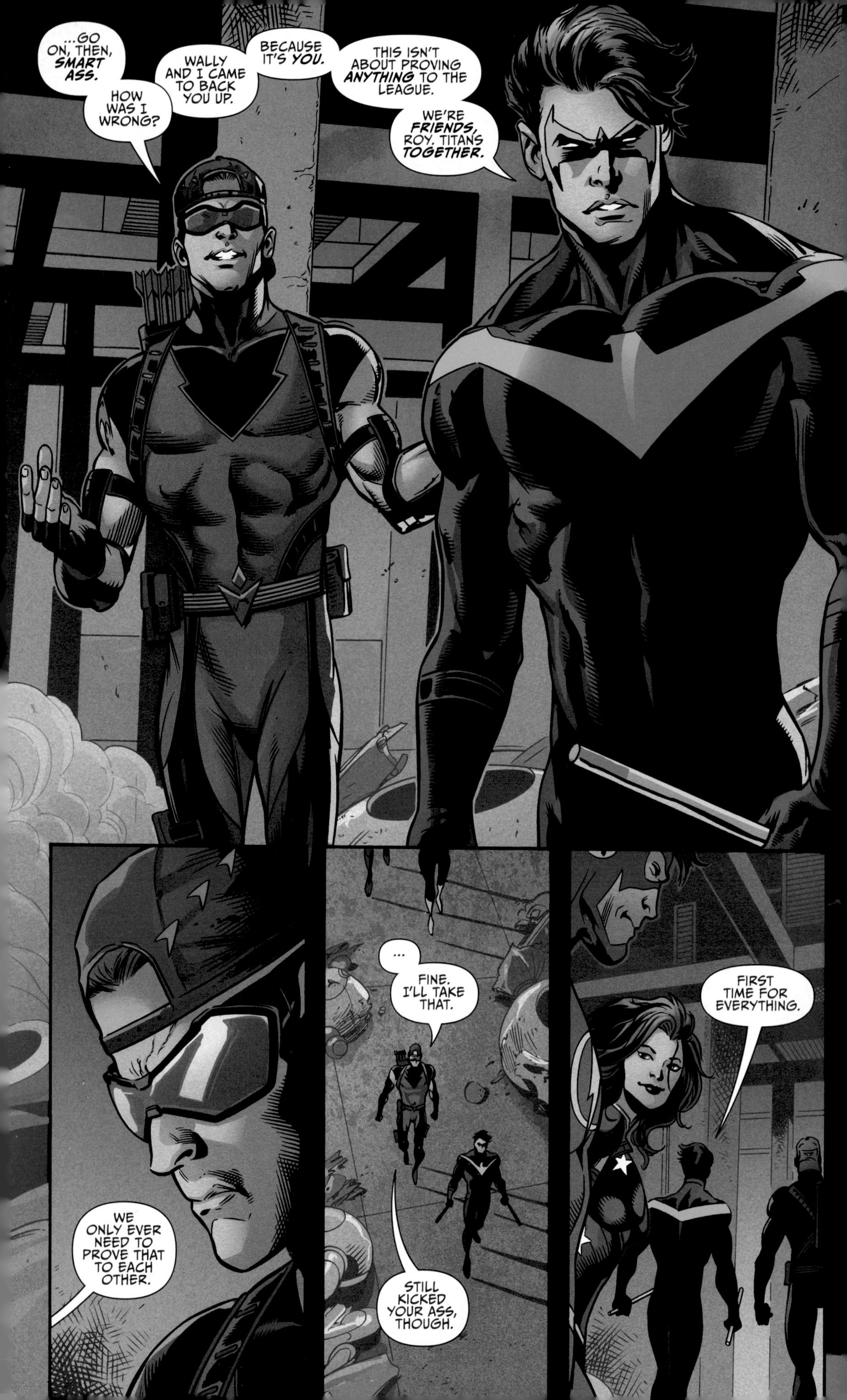
...GO ON, THEN, SMART ASS.
HOW WAS I WRONG?
WALLY AND I CAME TO BACK YOU UP.
BECAUSE IT'S YOU.
THIS ISN'T ABOUT PROVING ANYTHING TO THE LEAGUE.
WE'RE FRIENDS, ROY. TITANS TOGETHER.
WE ONLY EVER NEED TO PROVE THAT TO EACH OTHER.
...
FINE. I'LL TAKE THAT.
STILL KICKED YOUR ASS, THOUGH.
FIRST TIME FOR EVERYTHING.

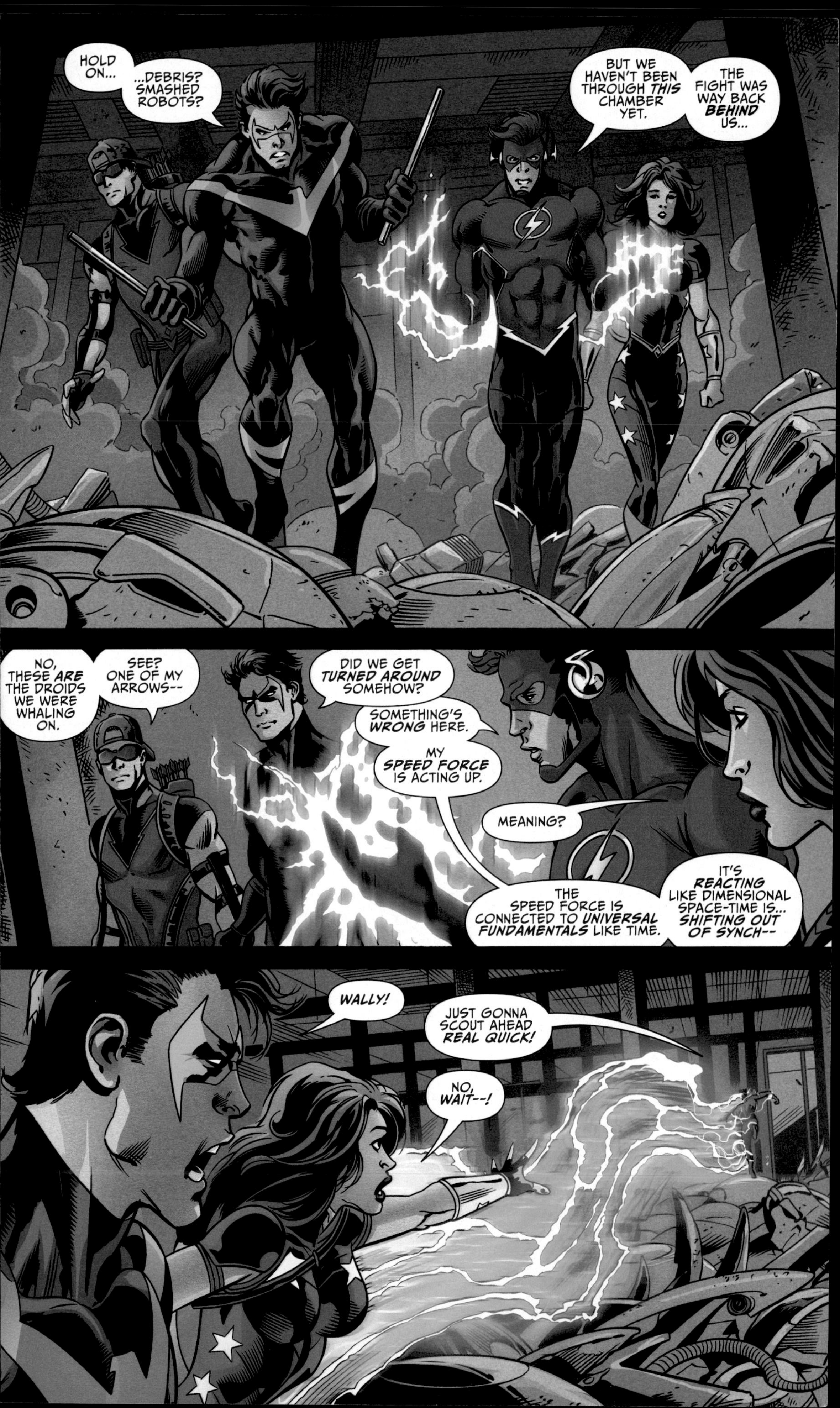
HOLD ON...
...DEBRIS? SMASHED ROBOTS?
BUT WE HAVEN'T BEEN THROUGH THIS CHAMBER YET.
THE FIGHT WAS WAY BACK BEHIND US...
NO, THESE ARE THE DROIDS WE WERE WHALING ON.
SEE? ONE OF MY ARROWS--
DID WE GET TURNED AROUND SOMEHOW?
SOMETHING'S WRONG HERE.
MY SPEED FORCE IS ACTING UP.
MEANING?
THE SPEED FORCE IS CONNECTED TO UNIVERSAL FUNDAMENTALS LIKE TIME.
IT'S REACTING LIKE DIMENSIONAL SPACE-TIME IS... SHIFTING OUT OF SYNCH--
WALLY!
JUST GONNA SCOUT AHEAD REAL QUICK!
NO, WAIT--!

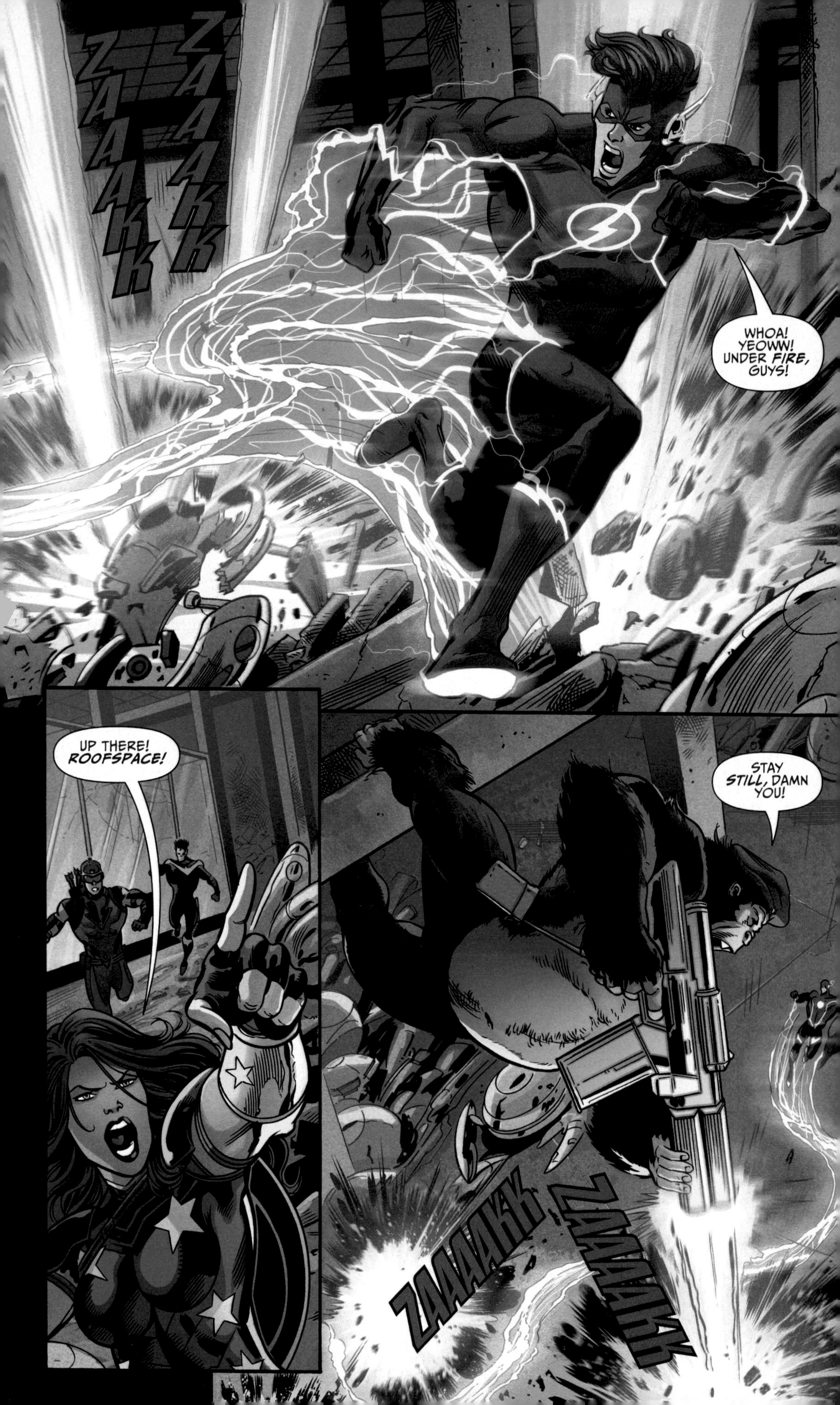
ZAAAKK
ZAAAKK
WHOA! YEOWW! UNDER FIRE, GUYS!
UP THERE! ROOFSPACE!
STAY STILL, DAMN YOU!
ZAAAAKK
ZAAAAKK

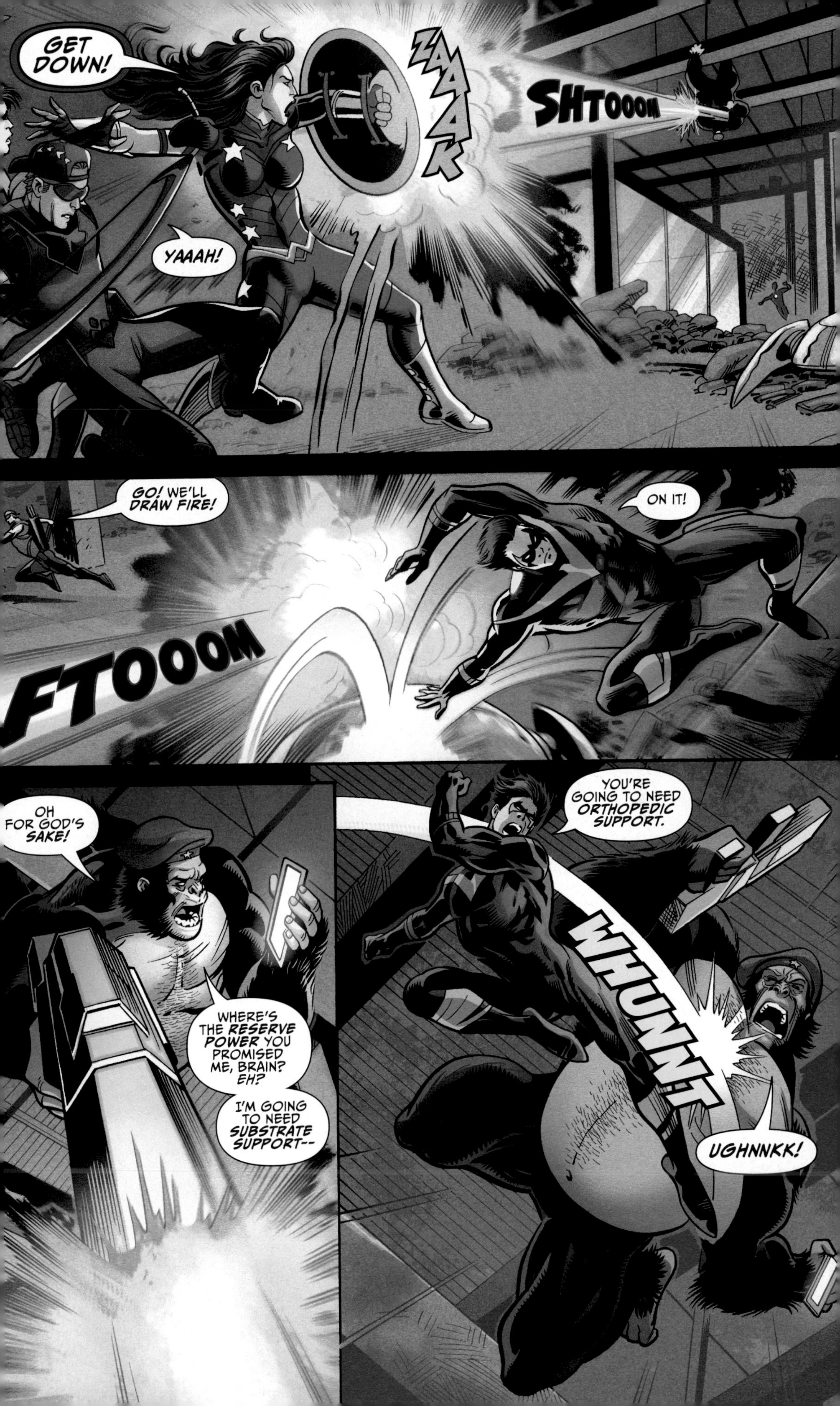
GET DOWN!
ZAAAK
SHTOOOM
YAAAH!
GO! WE'LL DRAW FIRE!
ON IT!
FTOOOM
OH FOR GOD'S SAKE!
WHERE'S THE RESERVE POWER YOU PROMISED ME, BRAIN? EH?
I'M GOING TO NEED SUBSTRATE SUPPORT--
YOU'RE GOING TO NEED ORTHOPEDIC SUPPORT.
WHUNNT
UGHNNKK!

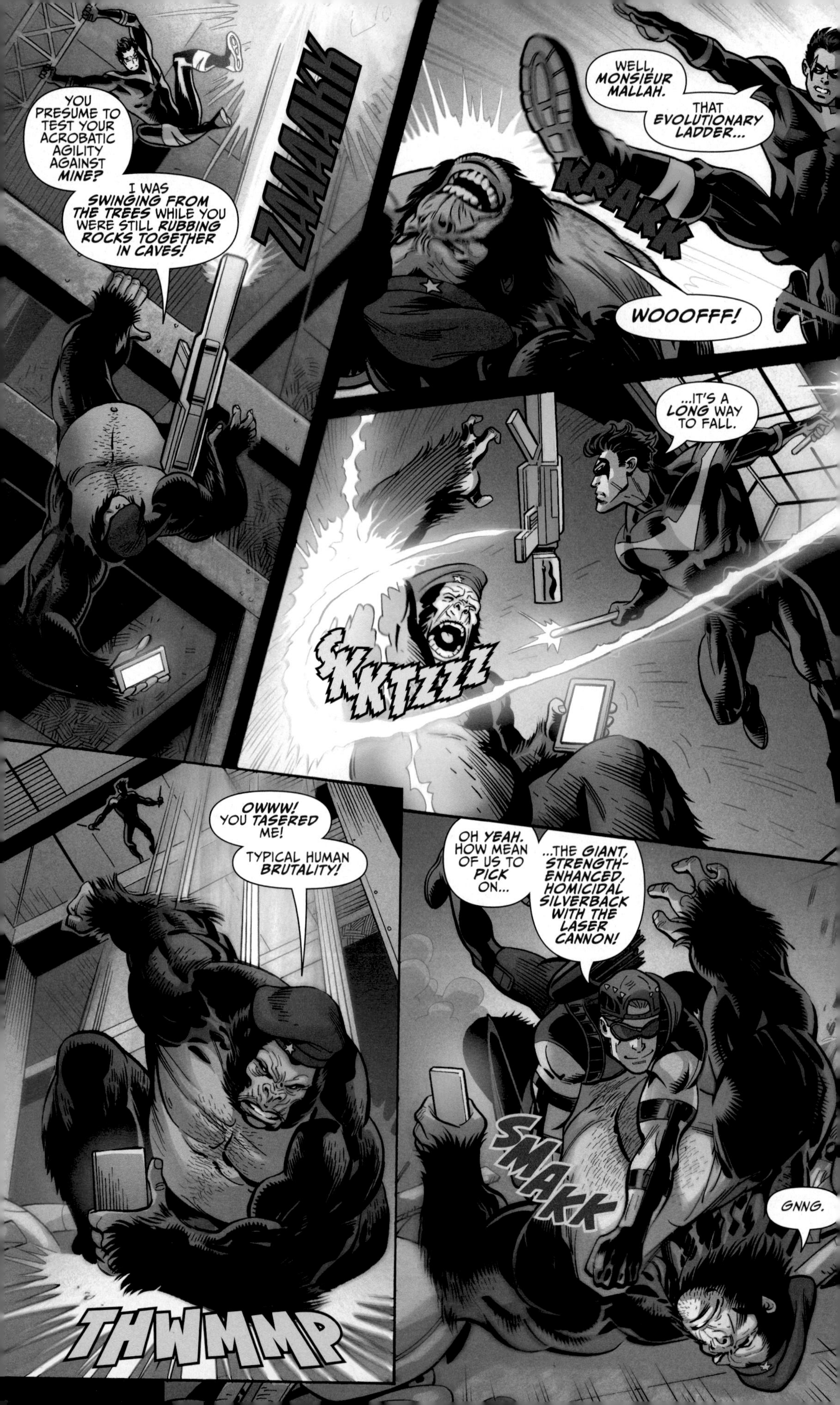
YOU PRESUME TO TEST YOUR ACROBATIC AGILITY AGAINST MINE?
I WAS SWINGING FROM THE TREES WHILE YOU WERE STILL RUBBING ROCKS TOGETHER IN CAVES!
ZAAAAKK
WELL, MONSIEUR MALLAH.
THAT EVOLUTIONARY LADDER...
KRAKK
WOOOFFF!
...IT'S A LONG WAY TO FALL.
SKKTZZZZ
OWWW! YOU TASERED ME!
TYPICAL HUMAN BRUTALITY!
THWMMP
OH YEAH. HOW MEAN OF US TO PICK ON...
...THE GIANT, STRENGTH-ENHANCED, HOMICIDAL SILVERBACK WITH THE LASER CANNON!
SMAKK
GNNG.

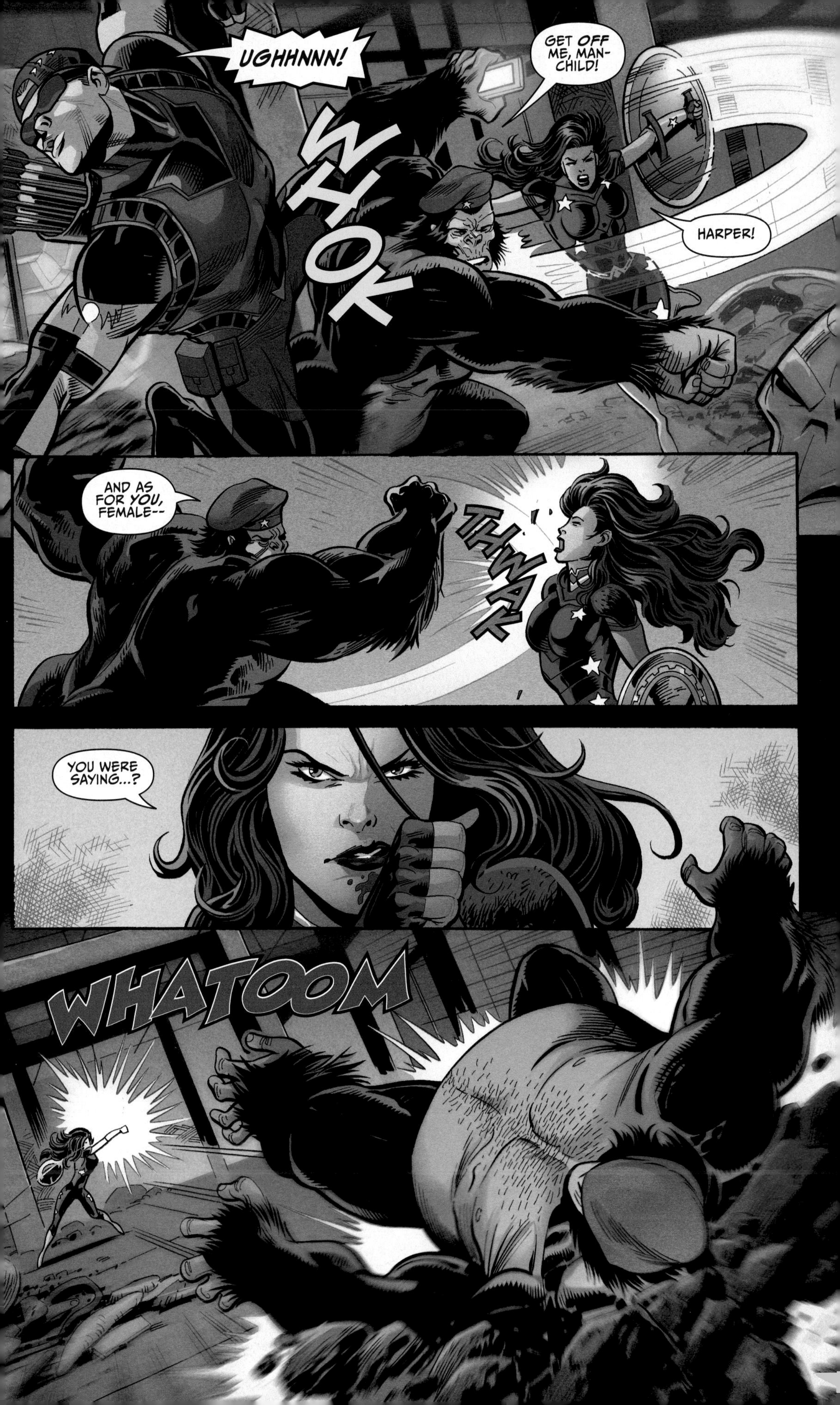
UGHHNNN!
GET OFF ME, MAN-CHILD!
WHOK
HARPER!
AND AS FOR YOU, FEMALE--
THWAK
YOU WERE SAYING...?
WHATOOM

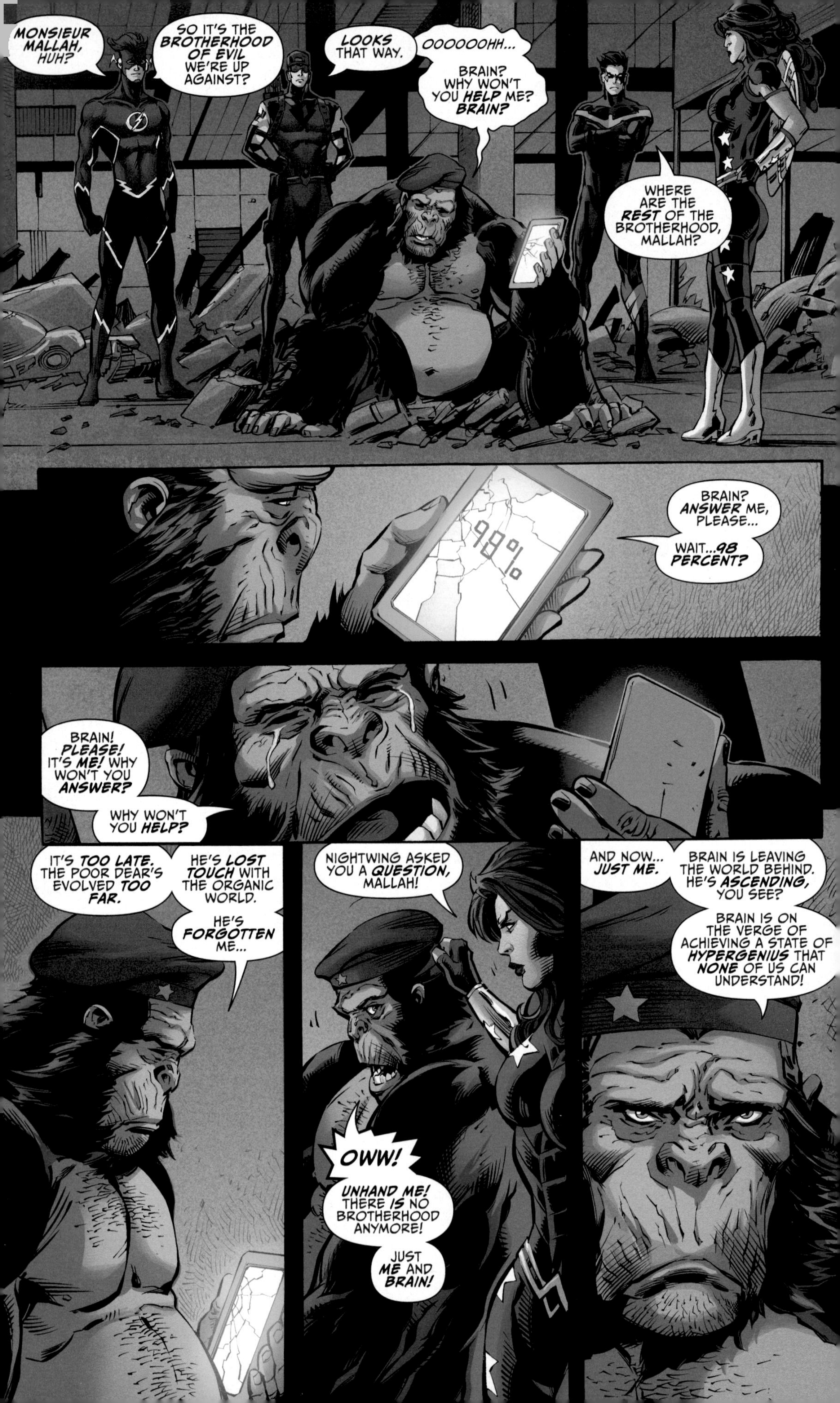
MONSIEUR MALLAH, HUH?
SO IT'S THE BROTHERHOOD OF EVIL WE'RE UP AGAINST?
LOOKS THAT WAY.
OOOOOOHH...
BRAIN? WHY WON'T YOU HELP ME? BRAIN?
WHERE ARE THE REST OF THE BROTHERHOOD, MALLAH?
98%
BRAIN? ANSWER ME, PLEASE...
WAIT...98 PERCENT?
BRAIN! PLEASE! IT'S ME! WHY WON'T YOU ANSWER?
WHY WON'T YOU HELP?
IT'S TOO LATE. THE POOR DEAR'S EVOLVED TOO FAR.
HE'S LOST TOUCH WITH THE ORGANIC WORLD.
HE'S FORGOTTEN ME...
NIGHTWING ASKED YOU A QUESTION, MALLAH!
OWW!
UNHAND ME! THERE IS NO BROTHERHOOD ANYMORE!
JUST ME AND BRAIN!
AND NOW... JUST ME.
BRAIN IS LEAVING THE WORLD BEHIND. HE'S ASCENDING, YOU SEE?
BRAIN IS ON THE VERGE OF ACHIEVING A STATE OF HYPERGENIUS THAT NONE OF US CAN UNDERSTAND!

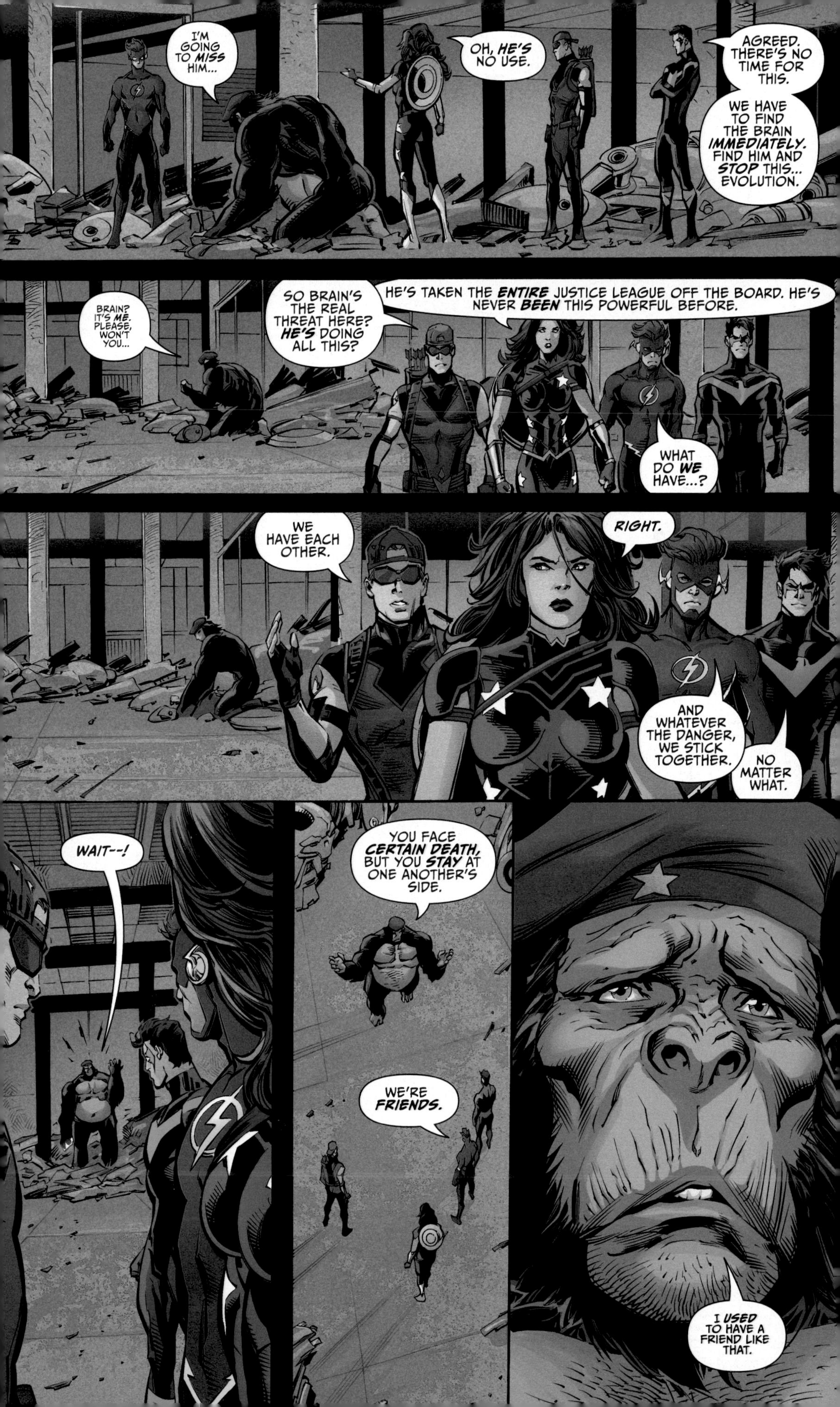

I'M GOING TO MISS HIM...
OH, HE'S NO USE.
AGREED. THERE'S NO TIME FOR THIS.
WE HAVE TO FIND THE BRAIN IMMEDIATELY. FIND HIM AND STOP THIS... EVOLUTION.
BRAIN? IT'S ME. PLEASE, WON'T YOU...
SO BRAIN'S THE REAL THREAT HERE? HE'S DOING ALL THIS?
HE'S TAKEN THE ENTIRE JUSTICE LEAGUE OFF THE BOARD. HE'S NEVER BEEN THIS POWERFUL BEFORE.
WHAT DO WE HAVE...?
WE HAVE EACH OTHER.
RIGHT.
AND WHATEVER THE DANGER, WE STICK TOGETHER.
NO MATTER WHAT.
WAIT--!
YOU FACE CERTAIN DEATH, BUT YOU STAY AT ONE ANOTHER'S SIDE.
WE'RE FRIENDS.
I USED TO HAVE A FRIEND LIKE THAT.

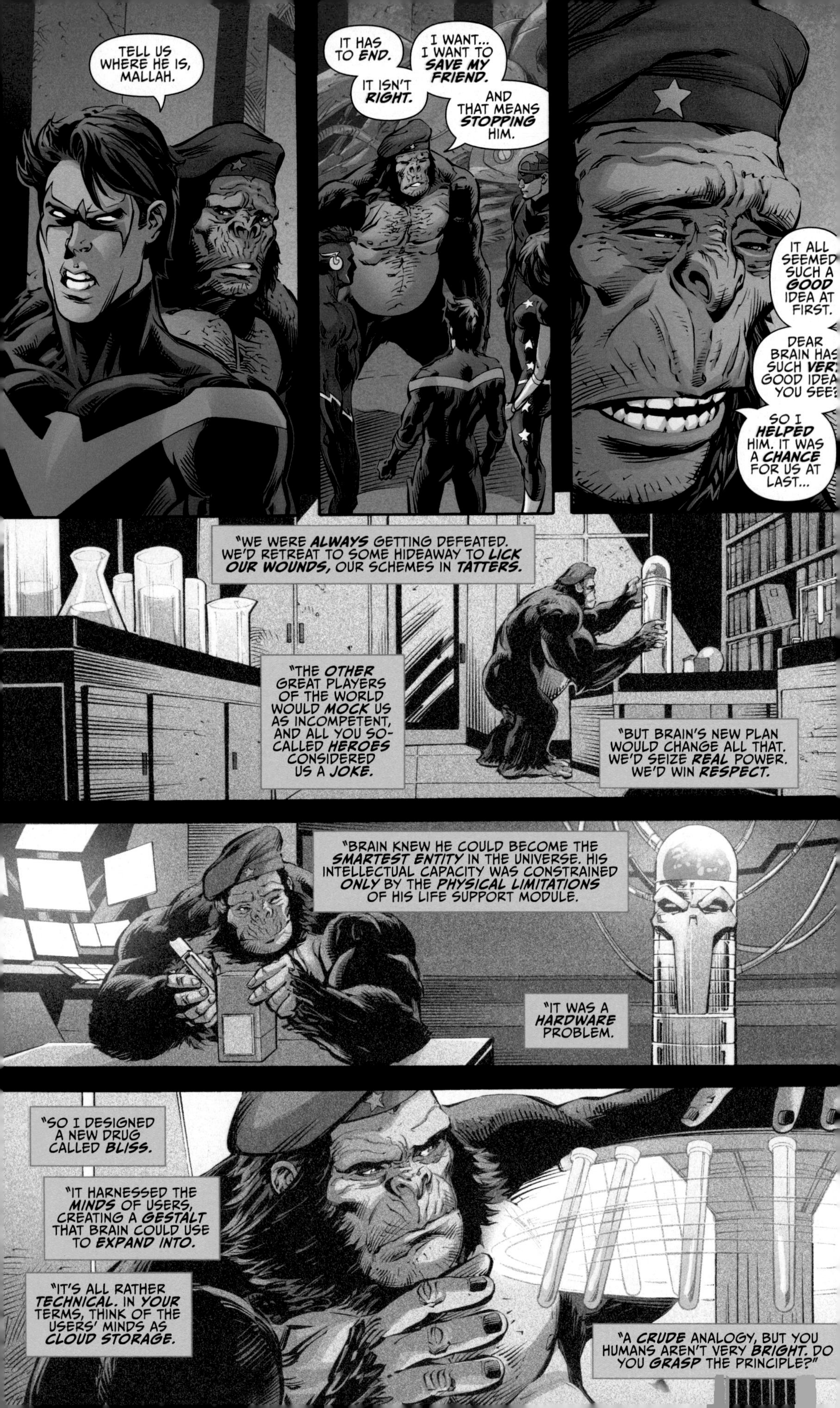

TELL US WHERE HE IS, MALLAH.
IT HAS TO END.
IT ISN'T RIGHT.
I WANT... I WANT TO SAVE MY FRIEND.
AND THAT MEANS STOPPING HIM.
IT ALL SEEMED SUCH A GOOD IDEA AT FIRST.
DEAR BRAIN HAS SUCH VERY GOOD IDEAS, YOU SEE?
SO I HELPED HIM. IT WAS A CHANCE FOR US AT LAST...
"WE WERE ALWAYS GETTING DEFEATED. WE'D RETREAT TO SOME HIDEAWAY TO LICK OUR WOUNDS, OUR SCHEMES IN TATTERS.
"THE OTHER GREAT PLAYERS OF THE WORLD WOULD MOCK US AS INCOMPETENT, AND ALL YOU SO-CALLED HEROES CONSIDERED US A JOKE.
"BUT BRAIN'S NEW PLAN WOULD CHANGE ALL THAT. WE'D SEIZE REAL POWER. WE'D WIN RESPECT.
"BRAIN KNEW HE COULD BECOME THE SMARTEST ENTITY IN THE UNIVERSE. HIS INTELLECTUAL CAPACITY WAS CONSTRAINED ONLY BY THE PHYSICAL LIMITATIONS OF HIS LIFE SUPPORT MODULE.
"IT WAS A HARDWARE PROBLEM.
"SO I DESIGNED A NEW DRUG CALLED BLISS.
"IT HARNESSED THE MINDS OF USERS, CREATING A GESTALT THAT BRAIN COULD USE TO EXPAND INTO.
"IT'S ALL RATHER TECHNICAL. IN YOUR TERMS, THINK OF THE USERS' MINDS AS CLOUD STORAGE.
"A CRUDE ANALOGY, BUT YOU HUMANS AREN'T VERY BRIGHT. DO YOU GRASP THE PRINCIPLE?"

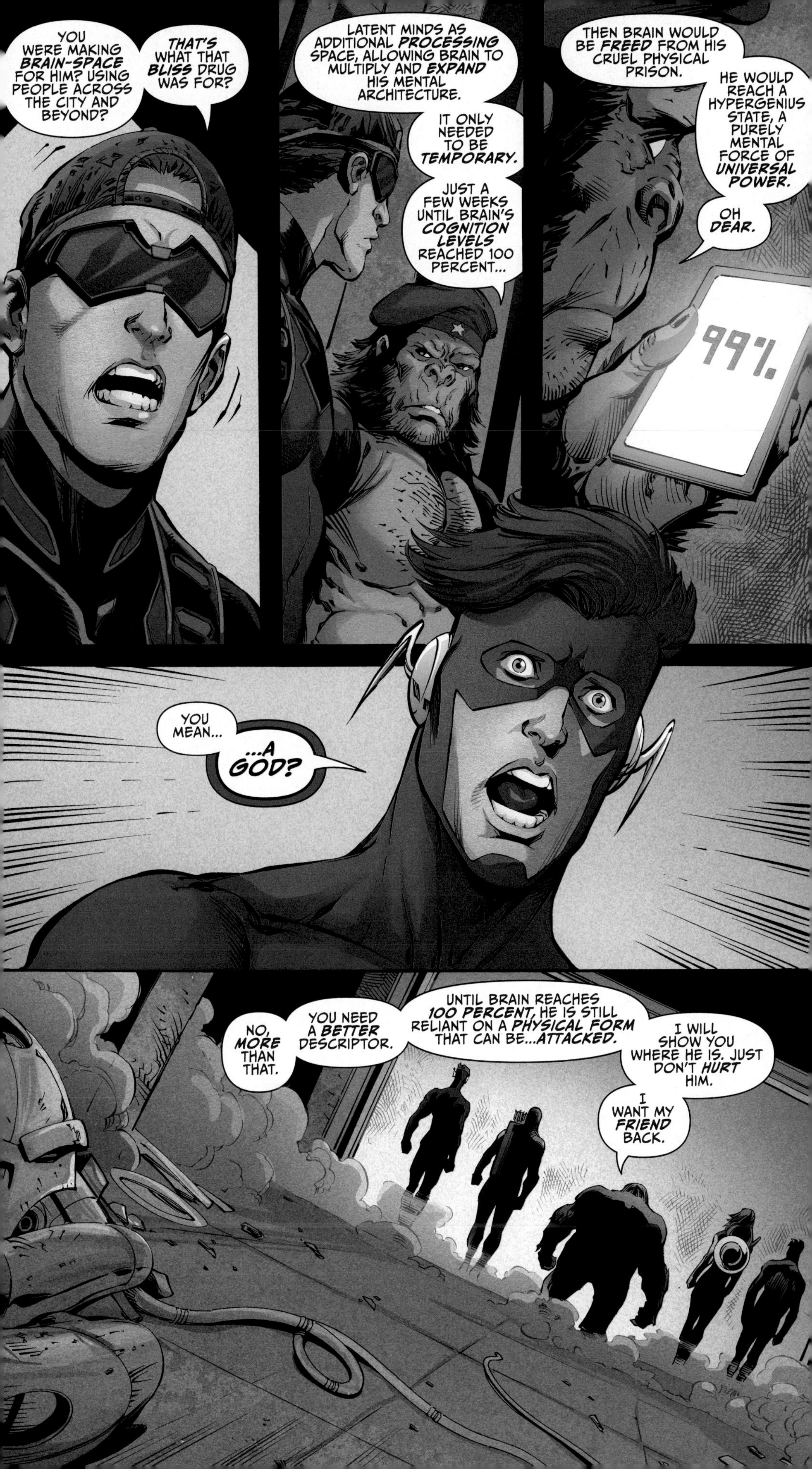

YOU WERE MAKING *BRAIN-SPACE* FOR HIM? USING PEOPLE ACROSS THE CITY AND BEYOND?
THAT'S WHAT THAT *BLISS* DRUG WAS FOR?
LATENT MINDS AS ADDITIONAL *PROCESSING* SPACE, ALLOWING BRAIN TO MULTIPLY AND *EXPAND* HIS MENTAL ARCHITECTURE.
IT ONLY NEEDED TO BE *TEMPORARY.*
JUST A FEW WEEKS UNTIL BRAIN'S *COGNITION LEVELS* REACHED 100 PERCENT...
THEN BRAIN WOULD BE *FREED* FROM HIS CRUEL PHYSICAL PRISON.
HE WOULD REACH A HYPERGENIUS STATE, A PURELY MENTAL FORCE OF *UNIVERSAL POWER.*
OH *DEAR.*
99%
YOU MEAN...
...A GOD?
NO, *MORE* THAN THAT.
YOU NEED A *BETTER* DESCRIPTOR.
UNTIL BRAIN REACHES *100 PERCENT,* HE IS STILL RELIANT ON A *PHYSICAL FORM* THAT CAN BE...*ATTACKED.*
I WILL SHOW YOU WHERE HE IS. JUST DON'T *HURT* HIM.
I WANT MY *FRIEND* BACK.

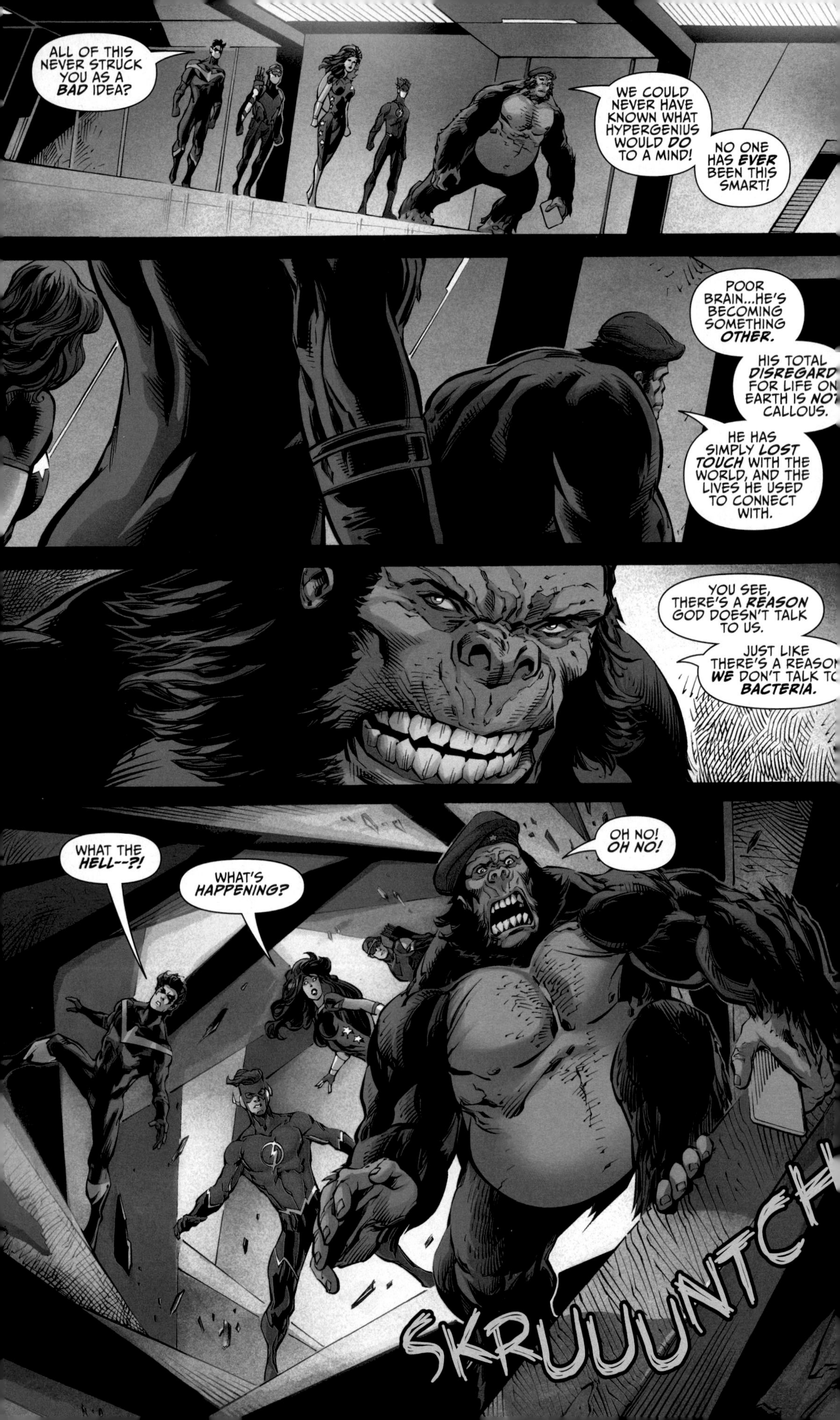
ALL OF THIS NEVER STRUCK YOU AS A BAD IDEA?
WE COULD NEVER HAVE KNOWN WHAT HYPERGENIUS WOULD DO TO A MIND!
NO ONE HAS EVER BEEN THIS SMART!
POOR BRAIN...HE'S BECOMING SOMETHING OTHER.
HIS TOTAL DISREGARD FOR LIFE ON EARTH IS NOT CALLOUS.
HE HAS SIMPLY LOST TOUCH WITH THE WORLD, AND THE LIVES HE USED TO CONNECT WITH.
YOU SEE, THERE'S A REASON GOD DOESN'T TALK TO US.
JUST LIKE THERE'S A REASON WE DON'T TALK TO BACTERIA.
WHAT THE HELL--?!
WHAT'S HAPPENING?
OH NO! OH NO!
SKRUUUNTCH

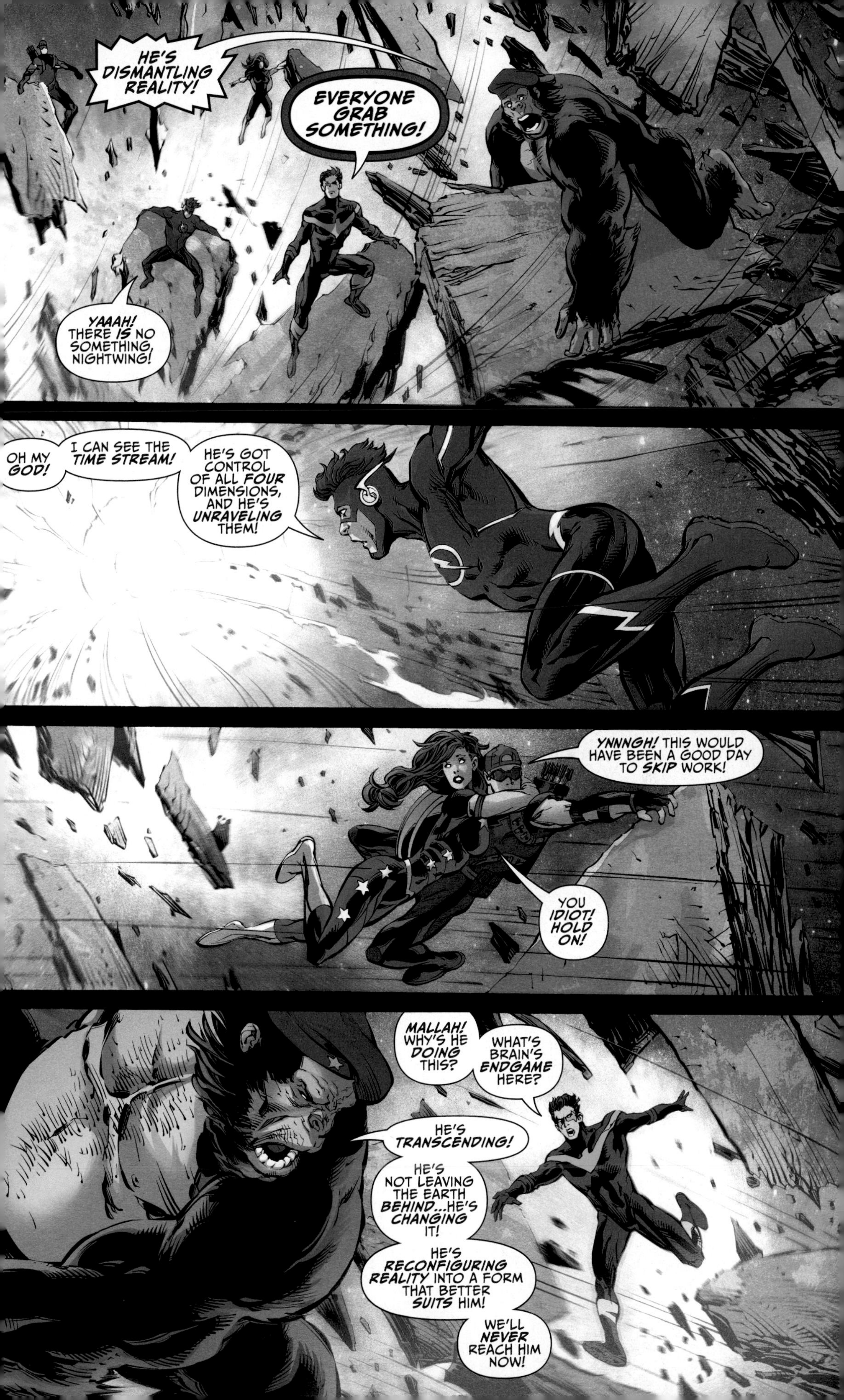
HE'S DISMANTLING REALITY!
EVERYONE GRAB SOMETHING!
YAAAH! THERE IS NO SOMETHING, NIGHTWING!
OH MY GOD!
I CAN SEE THE TIME STREAM!
HE'S GOT CONTROL OF ALL FOUR DIMENSIONS, AND HE'S UNRAVELING THEM!
YNNNGH! THIS WOULD HAVE BEEN A GOOD DAY TO SKIP WORK!
YOU IDIOT! HOLD ON!
MALLAH! WHY'S HE DOING THIS?
WHAT'S BRAIN'S ENDGAME HERE?
HE'S TRANSCENDING!
HE'S NOT LEAVING THE EARTH BEHIND...HE'S CHANGING IT!
HE'S RECONFIGURING REALITY INTO A FORM THAT BETTER SUITS HIM!
WE'LL NEVER REACH HIM NOW!

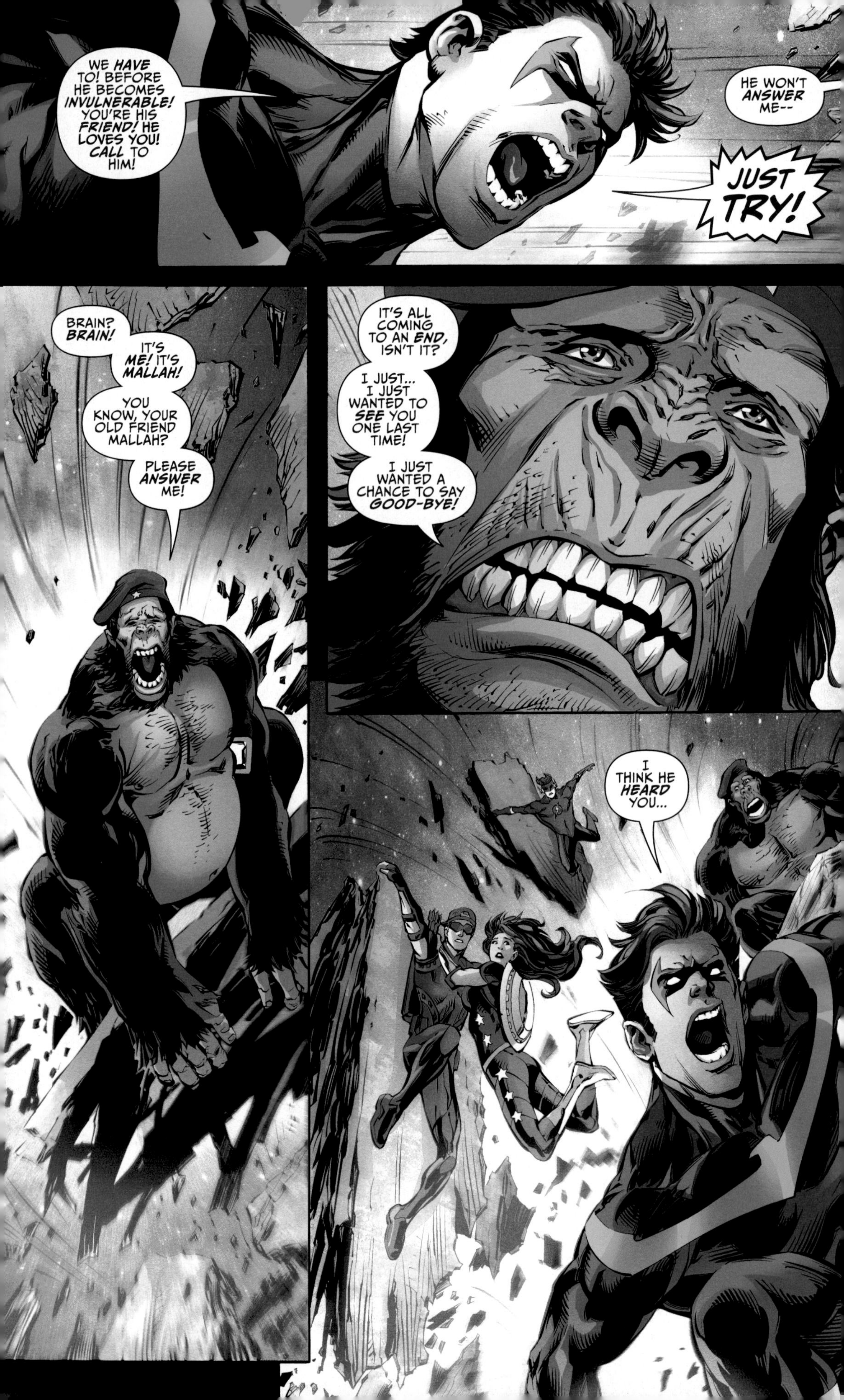
WE HAVE TO! BEFORE HE BECOMES INVULNERABLE! YOU'RE HIS FRIEND! HE LOVES YOU! CALL TO HIM!
HE WON'T ANSWER ME--
JUST TRY!
BRAIN? BRAIN!
IT'S ME! IT'S MALLAH!
YOU KNOW, YOUR OLD FRIEND MALLAH?
PLEASE ANSWER ME!
IT'S ALL COMING TO AN END, ISN'T IT?
I JUST... I JUST WANTED TO SEE YOU ONE LAST TIME!
I JUST WANTED A CHANCE TO SAY GOOD-BYE!
I THINK HE HEARD YOU...

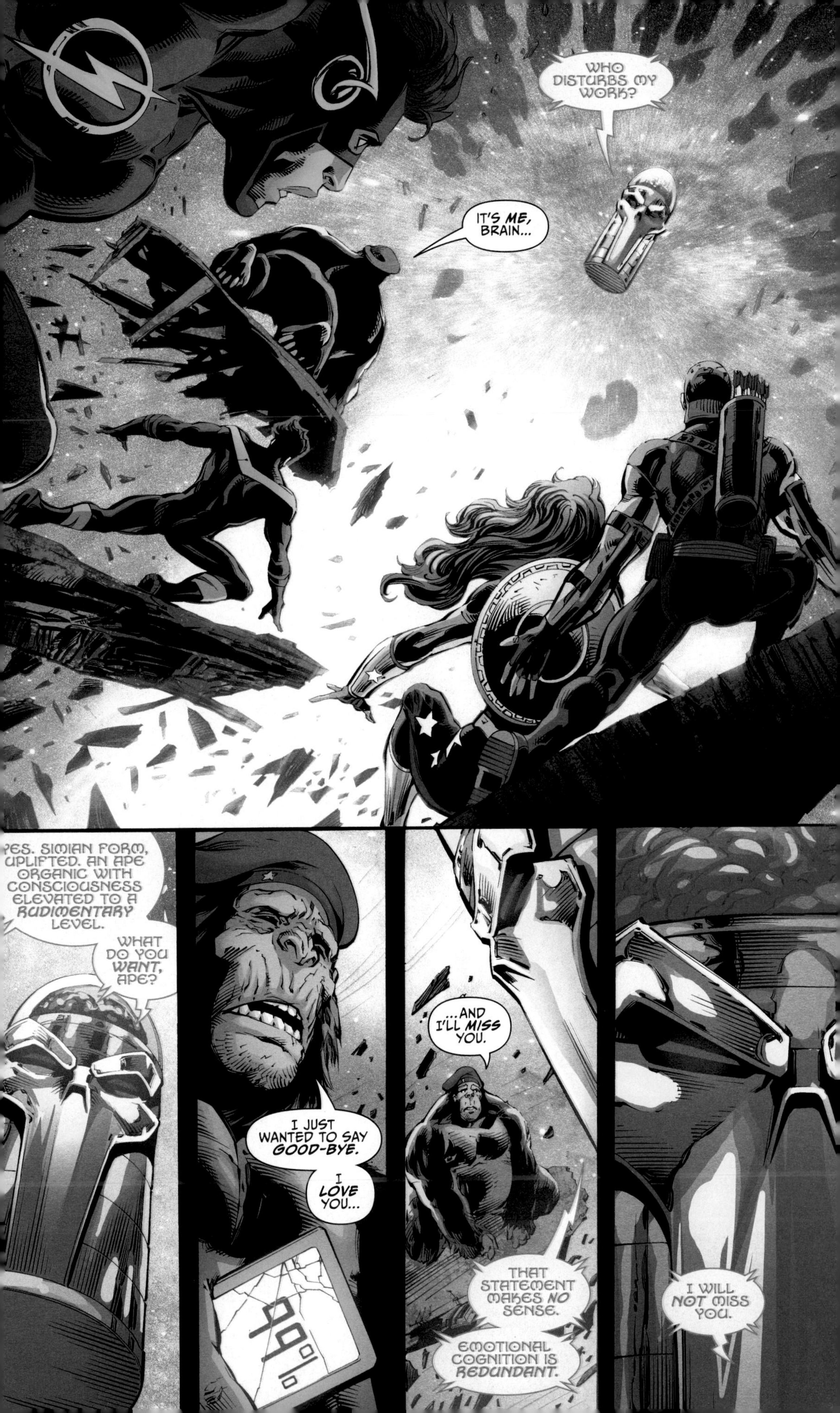
WHO DISTURBS MY WORK?
IT'S ME, BRAIN...
YES. SIMIAN FORM, UPLIFTED. AN APE ORGANIC WITH CONSCIOUSNESS ELEVATED TO A RUDIMENTARY LEVEL.
WHAT DO YOU WANT, APE?
I JUST WANTED TO SAY GOOD-BYE.
I LOVE YOU...
99%
...AND I'LL MISS YOU.
THAT STATEMENT MAKES NO SENSE.
EMOTIONAL COGNITION IS REDUNDANT.
I WILL NOT MISS YOU.

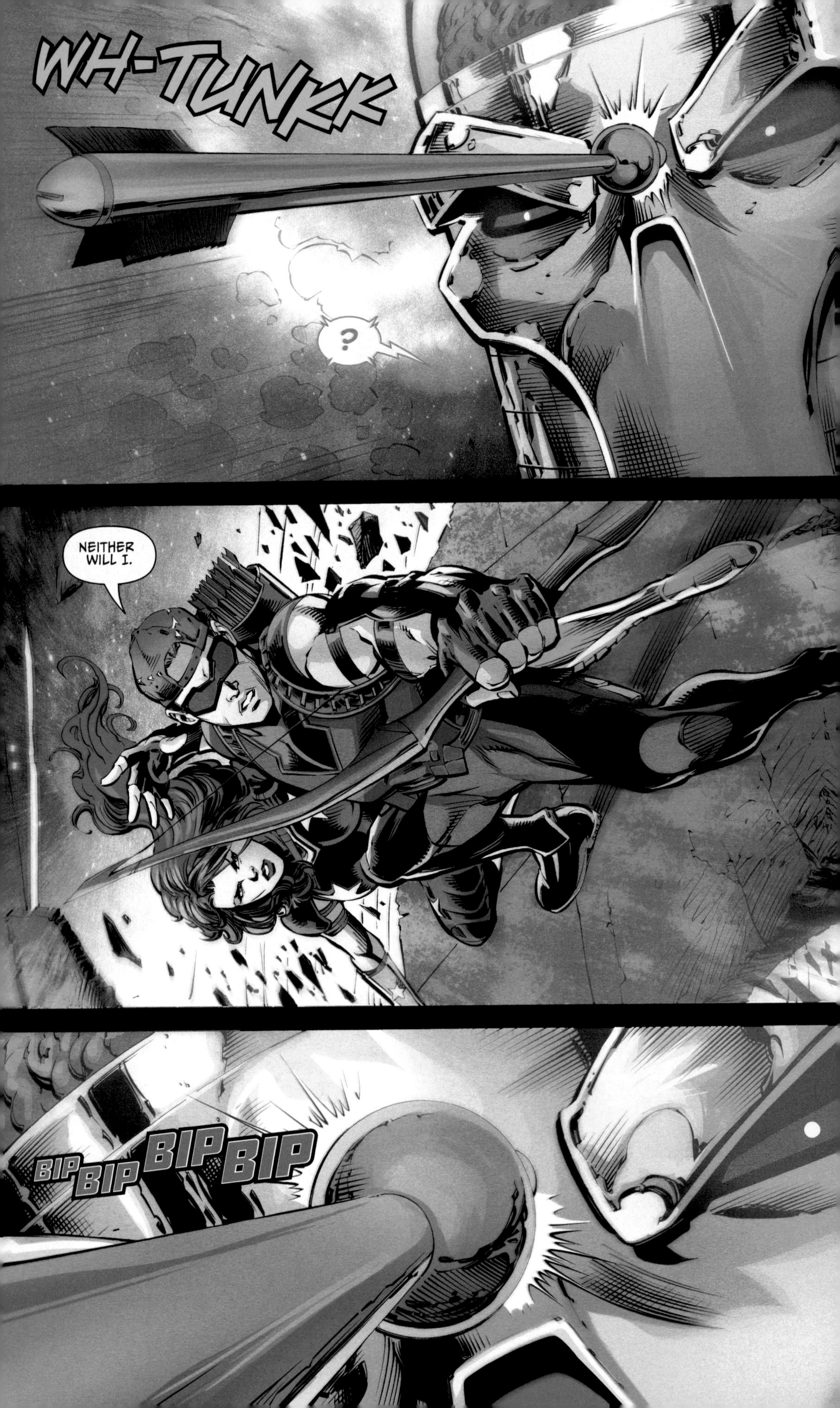
WH-TUNKK
?
NEITHER WILL I.
BIP BIP BIP BIP

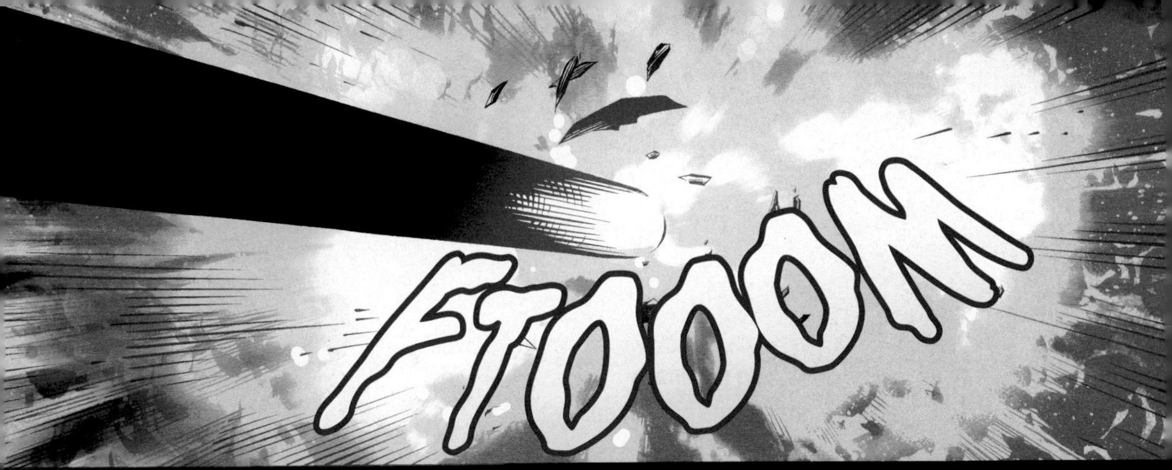
FTOOOM

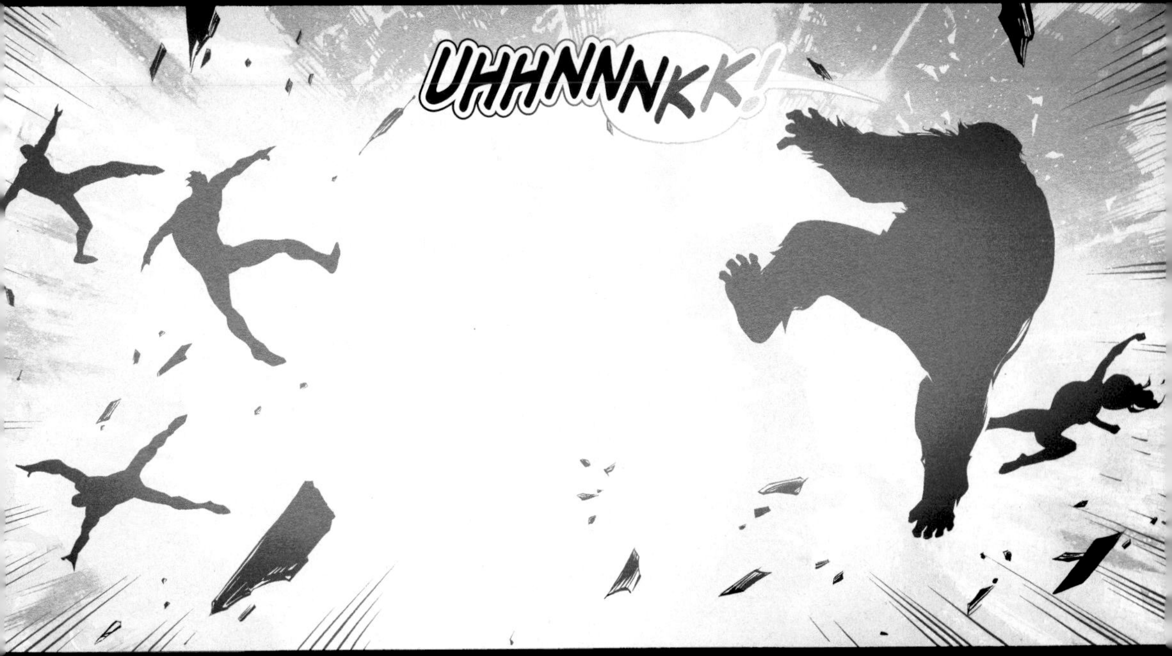
UHHNNNKK!

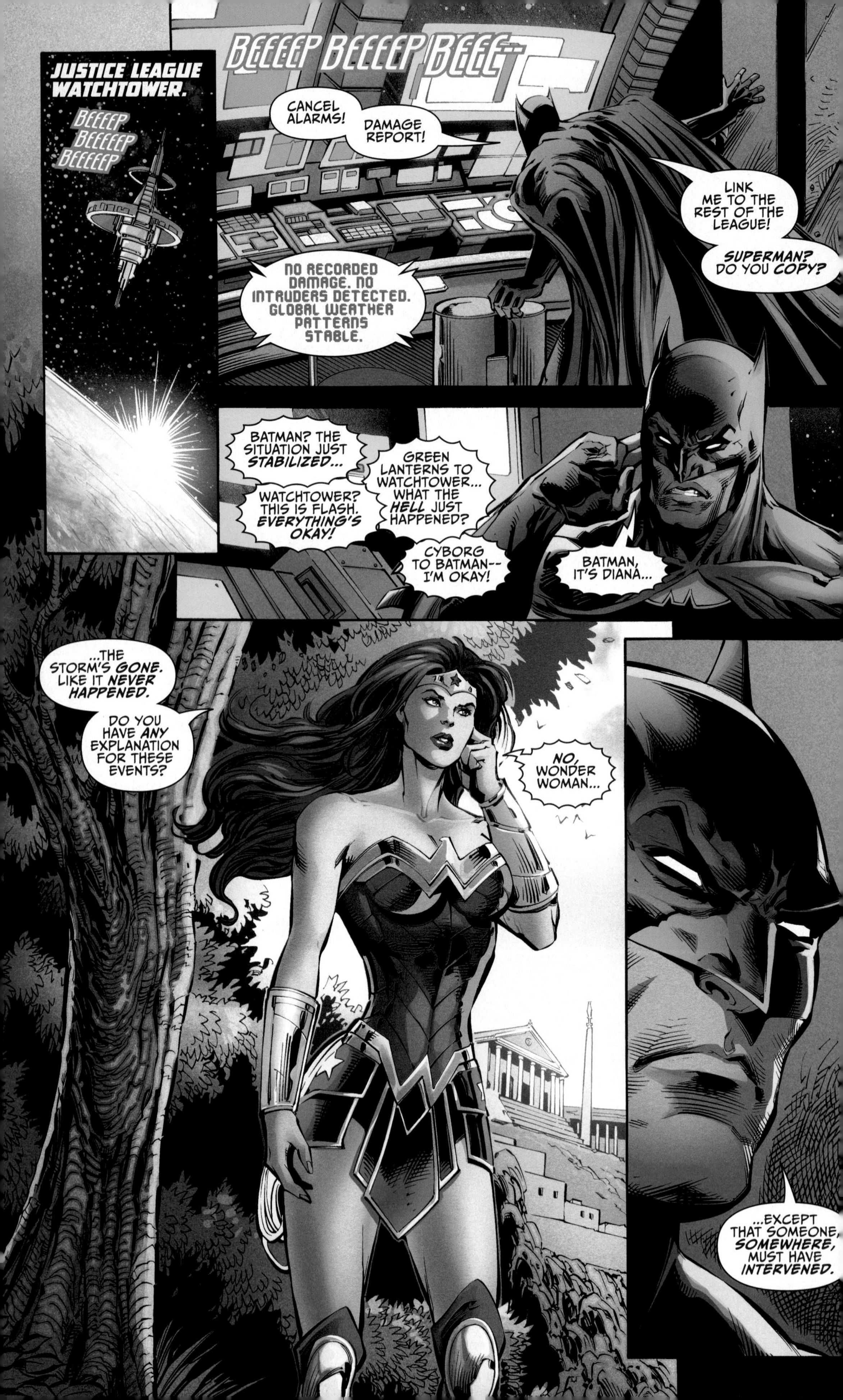

JUSTICE LEAGUE WATCHTOWER.
BEEEEP BEEEEEP BEEEEEP
BEEEEP BEEEEP BEEE--
CANCEL ALARMS!
DAMAGE REPORT!
NO RECORDED DAMAGE. NO INTRUDERS DETECTED. GLOBAL WEATHER PATTERNS STABLE.
LINK ME TO THE REST OF THE LEAGUE!
SUPERMAN? DO YOU COPY?
BATMAN? THE SITUATION JUST STABILIZED...
WATCHTOWER? THIS IS FLASH. EVERYTHING'S OKAY!
GREEN LANTERNS TO WATCHTOWER... WHAT THE HELL JUST HAPPENED?
CYBORG TO BATMAN-- I'M OKAY!
BATMAN, IT'S DIANA...
...THE STORM'S GONE. LIKE IT NEVER HAPPENED.
DO YOU HAVE ANY EXPLANATION FOR THESE EVENTS?
NO, WONDER WOMAN...
...EXCEPT THAT SOMEONE, SOMEWHERE, MUST HAVE INTERVENED.

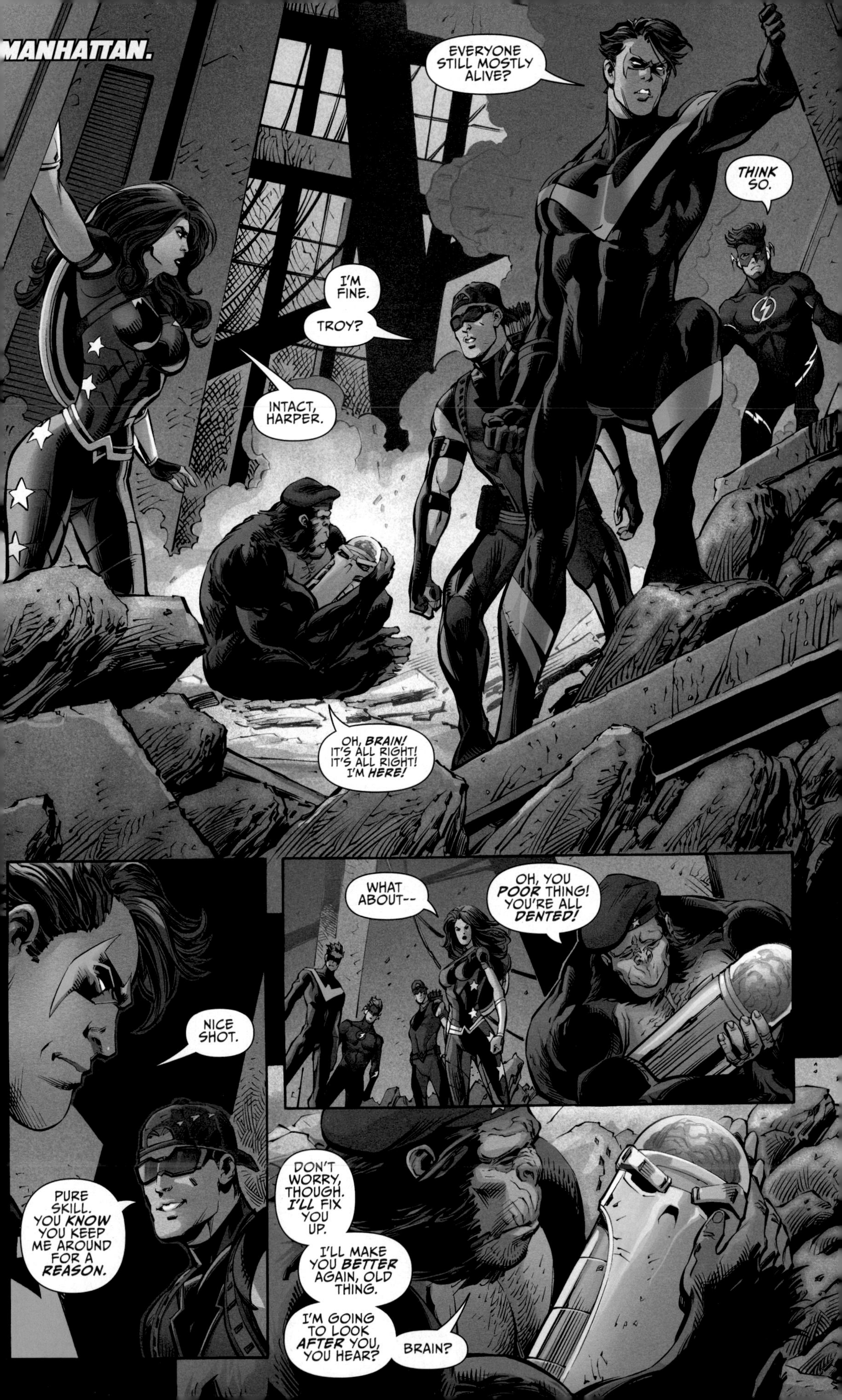
MANHATTAN.
EVERYONE STILL MOSTLY ALIVE?
THINK SO.
I'M FINE.
TROY?
INTACT, HARPER.
OH, BRAIN! IT'S ALL RIGHT! IT'S ALL RIGHT! I'M HERE!
NICE SHOT.
PURE SKILL. YOU KNOW YOU KEEP ME AROUND FOR A REASON.
WHAT ABOUT--
OH, YOU POOR THING! YOU'RE ALL DENTED!
DON'T WORRY, THOUGH. I'LL FIX YOU UP.
I'LL MAKE YOU BETTER AGAIN, OLD THING.
I'M GOING TO LOOK AFTER YOU, YOU HEAR?
BRAIN?

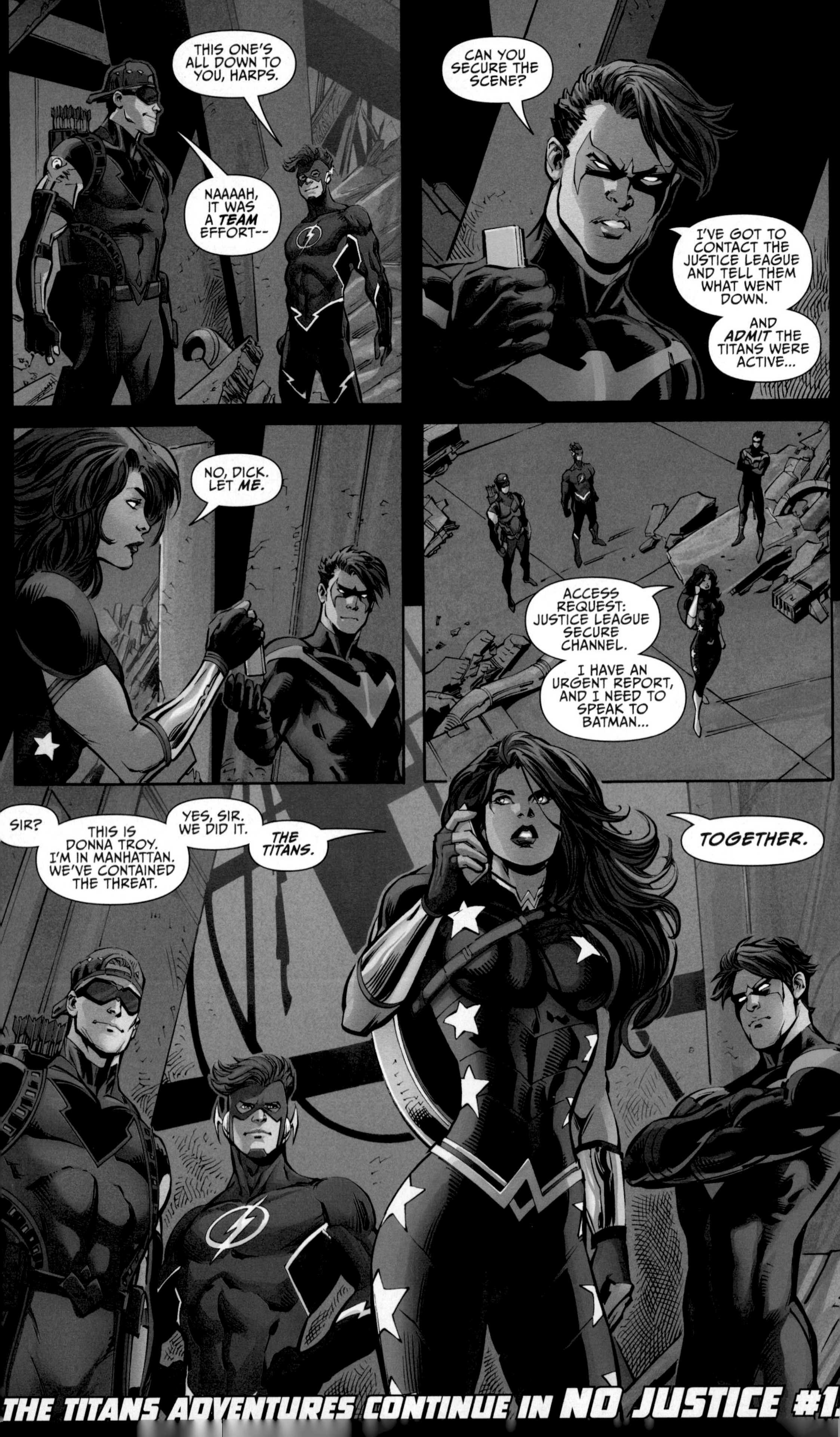

THIS ONE'S ALL DOWN TO YOU, HARPS.
NAAAAH, IT WAS A TEAM EFFORT--
CAN YOU SECURE THE SCENE?
I'VE GOT TO CONTACT THE JUSTICE LEAGUE AND TELL THEM WHAT WENT DOWN.
AND ADMIT THE TITANS WERE ACTIVE...
NO, DICK. LET ME.
ACCESS REQUEST: JUSTICE LEAGUE SECURE CHANNEL.
I HAVE AN URGENT REPORT, AND I NEED TO SPEAK TO BATMAN...
SIR?
THIS IS DONNA TROY. I'M IN MANHATTAN. WE'VE CONTAINED THE THREAT.
YES, SIR. WE DID IT.
THE TITANS.
TOGETHER.
THE TITANS ADVENTURES CONTINUE IN NO JUSTICE #1.

TITANS #22 variant cover by
NICK BRADSHAW and WIL QUINTANA

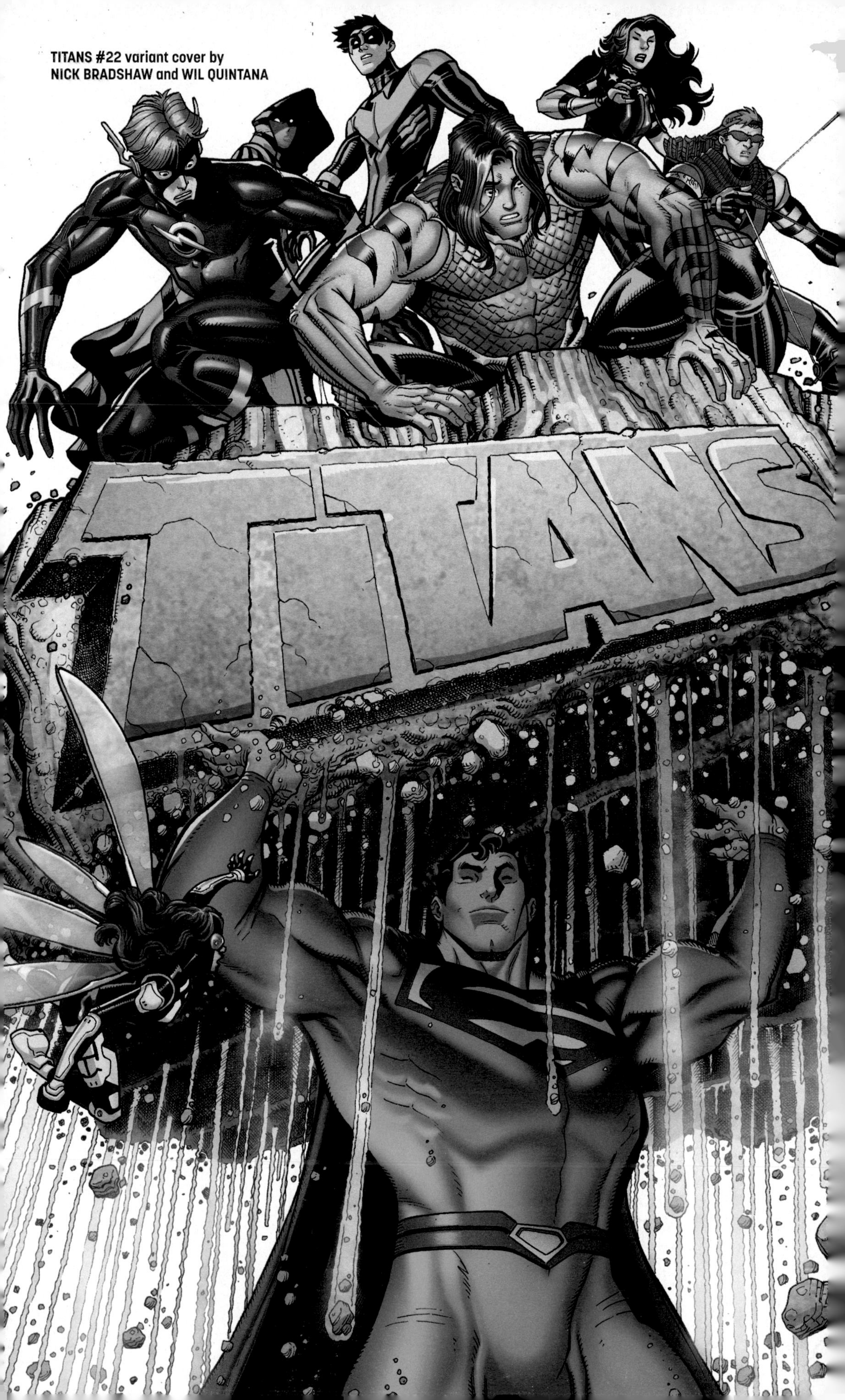
TITANS

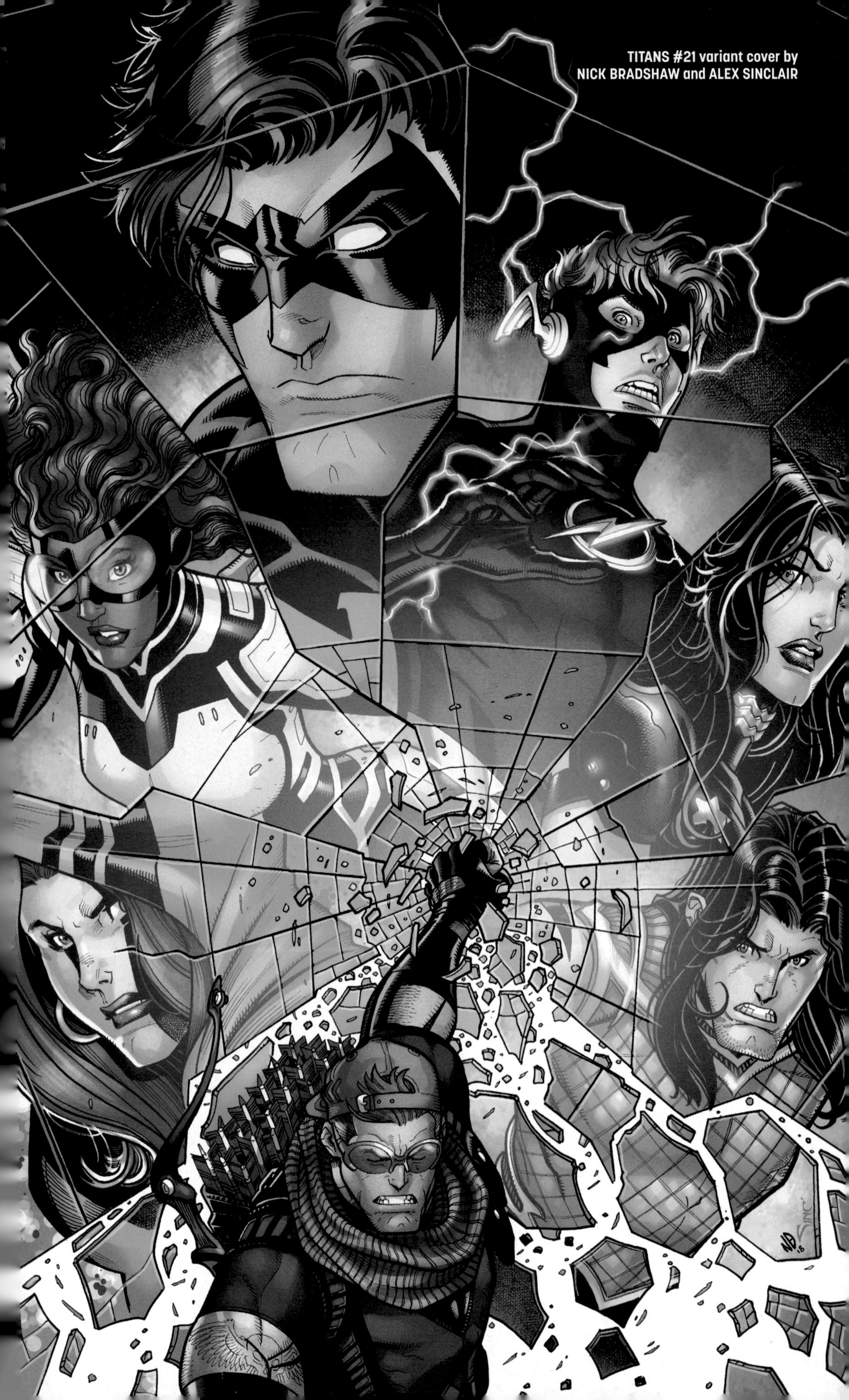

TITANS #21 variant cover by
NICK BRADSHAW and ALEX SINCLAIR

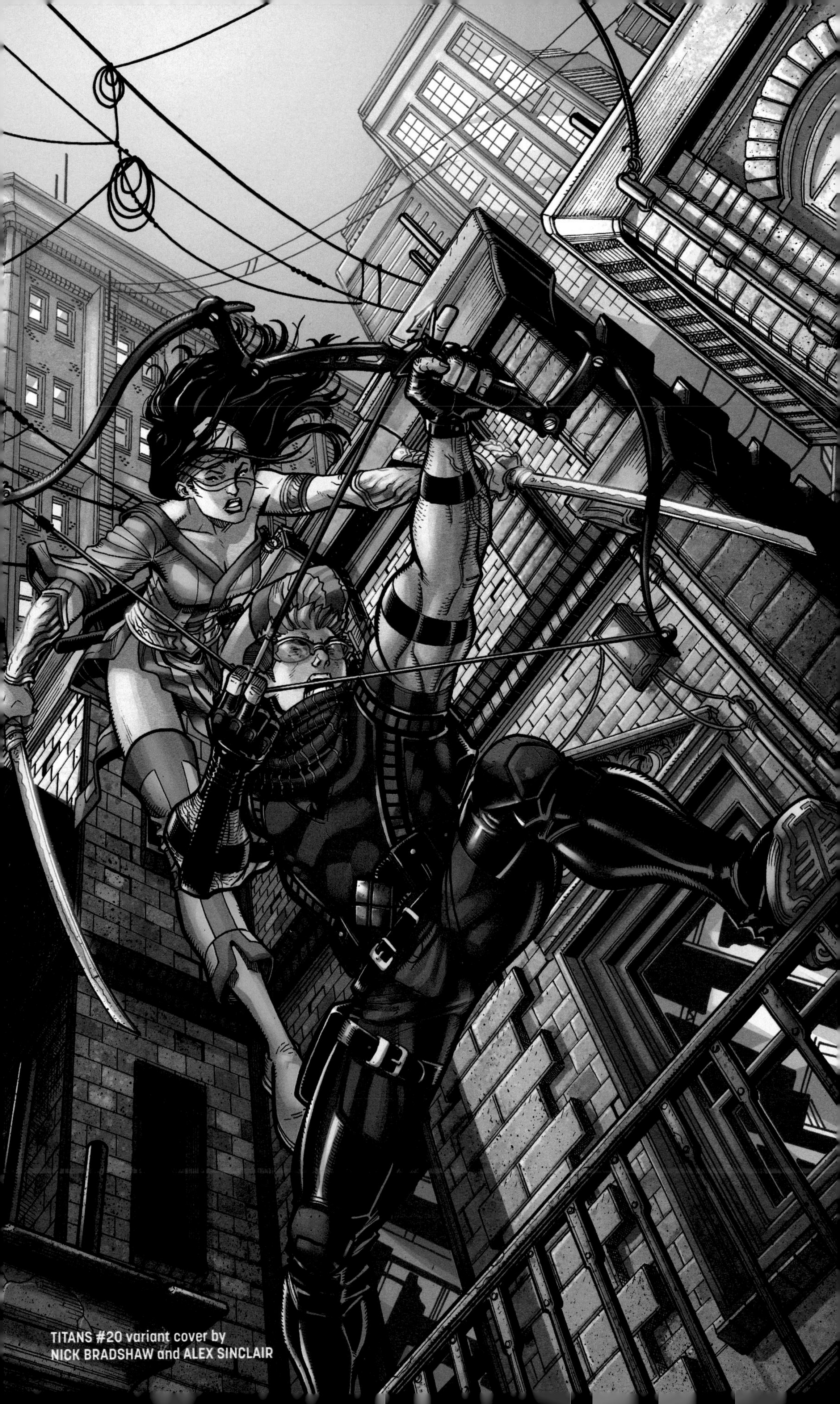

TITANS #20 variant cover by
NICK BRADSHAW and ALEX SINCLAIR

TITANS #19 variant cover by DAN MORA

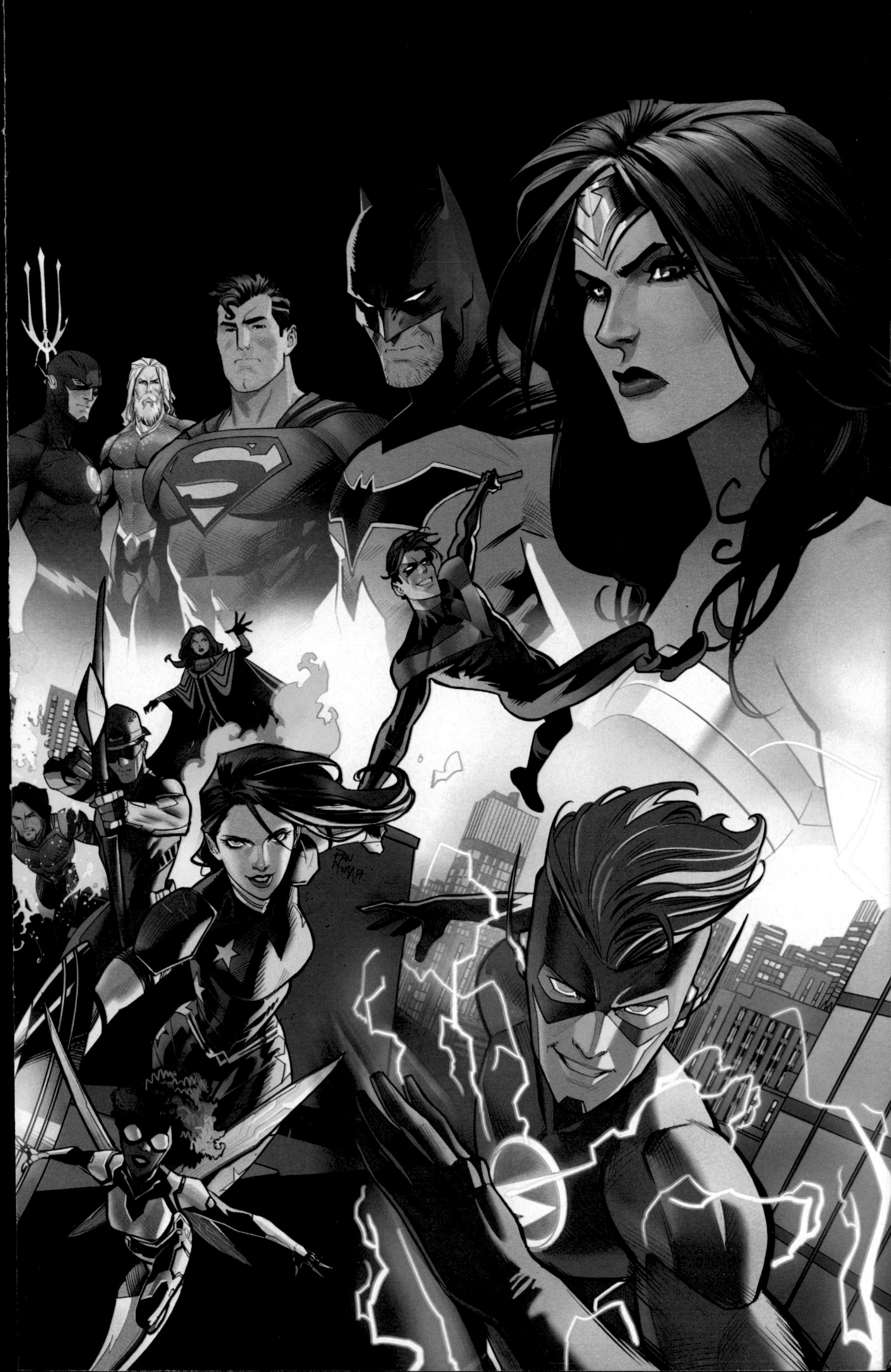